D0850987

classical dutch

by Jan Pinski

EVERYMAN CHESS

www.everymanchess.com

First published in 2002 by Gloucester Publishers plc (formerly Everyman Publishers plc), Northburgh House, 10 Northburgh Street, London EC1V 0AT

Copyright © 2002 Jan Pinski

The right of Jan Pinski to be identified as the author of this work has been asserted in accordance with the Copyrights, Designs and Patents Act 1988.

British Library Cataloguing-in-Publication Data
A catalogue record for this book is available from the British Library.

ISBN 978 1 85744 307 3

Distributed in North America by The Globe Pequot Press, P.O Box 480, 246 Goose Lane, Guilford, CT 06437-0480.

All other sales enquiries should be directed to Everyman Chess, Northburgh House, 10 Northburgh Street, London EC1V 0AT
tel: 020 7253 7887 fax: 020 7490 3708
email: info@everymanchess.com; website: www.everymanchess.com

EVERYMAN CHESS SERIES (formerly Cadogan Chess)
Chief advisor: Byron Jacobs
Commissioning editor: John Emms
Assistant editor: Richard Palliser

Typeset and edited by First Rank Publishing, Brighton.
Cover design by Horatio Monteverde.
Printed and bound in the US.

CONTENTS

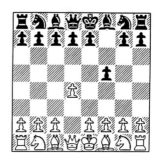

ACKNOWLEDGEMENTS

I would like to thank the following people for their help during the creation of this book. I would particularly like to thank International Master Jacob Aagaard and National Master Maciej Nurkiewicz for their assistance. I would also like to thank National Master Candidate Tomasz Olenderek, National Master Rafal Przedmojski and my editor, International Master Byron Jacobs, for their help.

This book is dedicated to the memory of my best friend and guide in the world of chess, Fide Master Wojciech Ehrenfeucht (1955-2002).

Jan Pinski,
Warsaw,
September 2002

INTRODUCTION

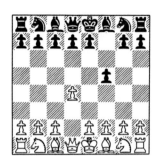

The Classical Dutch (or the Ilyin-Zhenevsky system as it is also called) is no longer enjoying the popularity it once did. Today I can only recall Nigel Short when I think of top Grandmasters who would consider using it in serious tournament games. The reasons are probably the availability of a high number of other possible defences and the reputation of this line as being better for White. After having gone deeply into all corners of the variation, I have come to the conclusion that Black can fight for equality as he can in all other kinds of openings. The way to get there, however, is very different.

The Classical Dutch covers the Dutch Defence (1 d4 f5) where the bishop is placed on e7 and the pawn on d6 (with the pawn on d5 we have the Stonewall Dutch, which would be the subject of a completely different book). The main position in the Ilyin-Zhenevsky system is given below.

see following diagram

This position is discussed in the first three chapters of the book. Chapter 3 considers 7...♕e8 and 7...♘e4, both of which give Black good chances for equality. Chapters 1 and 2 consider 7...a5, which is nowadays considered the main line and also gives Black a fair chance to reach a level game.

Though this is a big part of the book, there is much more to the Classical Dutch than just this position. In Chapter 8 I have included a good repertoire against all the tricky sidelines White has at his disposal on move two after 1 d4 f5, from the Gambit-style 2 g4?! to the positional 2 ♘c3. In Chapter 6 I have included positions where White develops the bishop via the f1-d3 diagonal (mainly after e2-e3) and one game where White plays g2-g3, ♗g2, e2-e3 and ♘ge2 (a famous World Championship game between Botvinnik and Bronstein, where Black could have won).

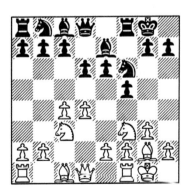

In Chapter 7 I consider the awkward development of the knight to h3 instead of f3, an idea that has only had a few successes. A more interesting idea for White is the early advance of the b-pawn, with the intention of grabbing maximum space on the queenside as fast as possible. This is very much similar to the Van Wely system of the Leningrad Dutch (1 d4 f5 2 ♘f3 ♘f6 3 c4 g6 4 g3 ♗g7 5 b4!?) and is considered in Chapter 4. From time to time White players have also decided on a more modest set-up with the knight on d2 instead of c3. I have shown how to deal with this kind of set-up in Chapter 5.

Before we turn to the different plans of the main lines in the Classical Dutch, I would like to show a very famous game that illustrates very well what the Ilyin-Zhenevsky system is capable of, even though in a strict sense it is a slightly different variation.

Bogoljubow-Alekhine

Hastings 1922

1 d4 f5 2 c4 ♘f6 3 g3 e6 4 ♗g2 ♗b4+!?

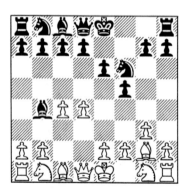

Here the game departs from the trodden path of the Classical Dutch, but it still has many structural similarities to the subject of our book.

5 ♗d2 ♗xd2+ 6 ♘xd2?!

This is not very harmonic. 6 ♕xd2 followed by ♘c3 is a more dynamic way to play the position, and also the way *Encyclopaedia of Chess Openings* (ECO) recommends that White should play. After 6...0-0 7 ♘c3 d6 8

♘f3 ♘e4 9 ♕c2 ♘xc3 10 ♕xc3 White supposedly has a small advantage.

6...♘c6 7 ♘gf3 0-0 8 0-0 d6 9 ♕b3

This manoeuvre is not impressive at all. After 9 ♕c2 White could still play for an advantage, even though it would probably be fruitless.

9...♔h8 10 ♕c3 e5!

This position has a lot in common with the Ilyin-Zhenevsky system – the only difference is the exchange of the dark-squared bishops.

11 e3

11 dxe5 dxe5 12 ♘xe5 ♘xe5 13 ♕xe5 does not work out due to the simple 13...♕xd2 and Black wins.

11...a5 12 b3 ♕e8 13 a3 ♕h5 14 h4

The e-pawn is still defended by tactics. After 14 dxe5 dxe5 15 ♘xe5 ♘xe5 16 ♕xe5 ♘g4 the queen and h2 are caught in a common fork.

14...♘g4 15 ♘g5 ♗d7 16 f3 ♘f6

Black is now threatening ...f5-f4, so White now has no choice but to play it himself.

17 f4 e4 18 ♖fd1 h6 19 ♘h3

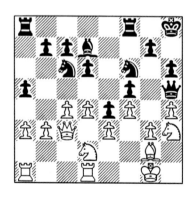

19...d5!

It is now hard to see how White will be able to create any kind of pressure on the kingside. Black has the advantage.

20 ♘f1 ♘e7 21 a4 ♘c6

After the weakening of the b4-square the knight returns. The final goal is, of course, the d3-square in order to attack the kingside once again.

22 ♖d2 ♘b4 23 ♗h1 ♕e8 24 ♖g2 dxc4 25 bxc4

White gives up a pawn on account of the positional deficit after 25 ♕xc4, when Black has the d5-square at his disposal and White cannot hope to survive the game.

25...♗xa4 26 ♘f2 ♗d7 27 ♘d2 b5!

Black takes over the d5-square anyway.

28 ♘d1

This is where the history of chess has one of its most famous combinations.

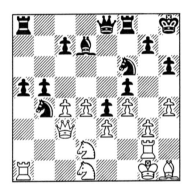

28...♘d3!!

The point of this move is revealed on move 31, but Black had to see much further to guarantee to himself that the combination was correct.

29 ♖xa5 b4 30 ♖xa8

30 ♕a1 ♖xa5 31 ♕xa5 ♕a8 32 ♕xa8 ♖xa8 is not much of a defence, as the rook now penetrates with deadly effect.

30...bxc3 31 ♖xe8 c2!

The point. Black will now get a new queen.

32 ♖xf8+ ♔h7 33 ♘f2 c1♕+ 34 ♘f1 ♘e1 35 ♖h2 ♕xc4 36 ♖b8 ♗b5 37 ♖xb5 ♕xb5 38 g4 ♘f3+ 39 ♗xf3 exf3 40 gxf5 ♕e2 41 d5 ♔g8 42 h5 ♔h7 43 e4 ♘xe4 44 ♘xe4 ♕xe4 45 d6 cxd6 46 f6 gxf6 47 ♖d2 ♕e2!

Finally another small combination which enables Black to enter a winning pawn endgame.

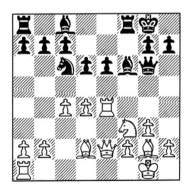

48 ♖xe2 fxe2 49 ♔f2 exf1♕+ 50 ♔xf1 ♔g7 51 ♔e2 ♔f7 52 ♔e3 ♔e6 53 ♔e4 d5+ 0-1

Of course the main problems for Black in this opening are to be found in Chapters 1-4 (see the diagram at the beginning of this Chapter). There are a few standard positions and plans that Black should know about. I have tried to give a brief overview here, so that you are aware of them when you play through the chapters.

The first one is very typical of what White wants.

Suba-Garcia Lopez
Seville 1994

White has been able to push with e2-e4 and now has pressure against the e6-pawn.

Black tries to gain counterplay in the standard way.

13...e5 14 dxe5 dxe5 15 ♗c3!

This move takes control over both d4 and e5.

15...♗f5 16 ♘h4!

This is a standard trick that is good to remember. After this White has the advantage due to his superior control over the dark squares and the strength of the bishop along the h1-a8 diagonal.

16...♗xh4 17 ♖xh4 ♖ae8 18 ♗d5+ ♔h8 19 ♕e3!

This is prophylaxis. It is hard to see how Black should proceed. He tries with a pawn sacrifice.

19...♘d4?

This is not good. After 19...b6 White would only have a small advantage.

20 ♗xd4 exd4 21 ♕xd4 c6 22 ♗f3 ♗b1!?

An attempt to keep a1-rook out of the game, but it's unsuccessful.

23 ♖g4 ♖e1+ 24 ♔g2 ♕f7 25 ♖f4 ♕e7

26 ♖xb1! ♖xb1 27 ♕e4 1-0

Forking the queen and the rook on b1.

White will generally have a small advantage if he opens up the centre with e2-e4, due to the weakness of the pawn on e6, so often emphasised by ♖f1-e1. Black will often prevent e2-e4 with ...♘f6-e4, or at least delay it sufficiently to develop counterplay.

Another standard positional trade connected to positions after the e-pawn has been exchanged for the f-pawn is the following.

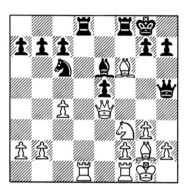

This position is taken from the game Arnson-Korchnoi, Leningrad 1951 (see Game 32). Here Black played **16...gxf6!** with a good game. This is a standard recapture, once White does not have the possibility to go behind the black pawns with ♗h6-g7 later, or disturb the black kingside with similar moves.

Another similar example is the following:

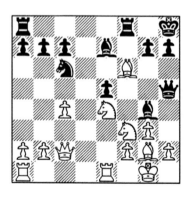

Oei-Lupu
Cappelle la Grande 1994

Here Black achieved a good game after **15...gxf6! 16 ♘ed2 ♘b4 17 ♕b3 ♖fd8 18 ♖e3 ♗c5 19 ♖c3 a5 20 ♘e4 ♗e7 21 ♖e3 a4 22 ♕c3 ♘c6 23 a3 ♕h6 24 ♖ee1 ♕g7 25 h3 ♗xf3 26 ♗xf3 f5 27**

♘d2 e4 28 ♘xe4 fxe4 29 ♕xg7+ ♔xg7 30 ♗xe4 ♗f6 31 ♗d5 ♘d4 32 ♗xb7 ♖ab8 33 ♗e4 ♖xb2 34 ♖ad1 ♖b3 35 f4 ♖xg3+ 36 ♔h2 ♖xa3 37 ♖g1+ ♔h6 38 ♗d5 ♖e8 39 ♖g2 ♖e2 0-1

Going back to the first diagram in this chapter, Black has two standard ways of developing counterplay. The more standard of these is based on ...♕d8-e8-h5 followed by a pawn storm on the centre. I will presume that this method is known to the readers and, if not, then it will be once you have made your way through this book.

The second is more positional and less known at club level.

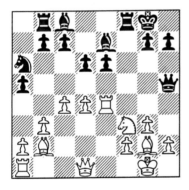

In this position Black has developed his knight to a6 instead of the standard c6. White has taken control over the centre, but still Black has a good position after **14...b5!**, as in Krivoshey-Salai, Slovakian League 1997 (see Game 7).

Another example of this strategy is presented here by a top German grandmaster.

Ribli-Lobron
Bundesliga 1996

1 ♘f3 d6 2 d4 f5 3 g3 ♘f6 4 ♗g2 e6 5 c4 ♗e7 6 0-0 0-0 7 ♘c3 a5 8 b3 ♕e8 9 ♗a3

Probably the bishop is better on b2.

9...♘a6!? 10 e3 c6 11 ♖c1 ♖b8

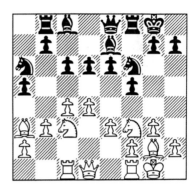

Black is fully prepared for the ...b7-b5 advance. After this White will have to choose between cxb5, which gives away control over d5, and allowing ...bxc4, which opens the b-file for Black's rook.

12 ♗b2 b5 13 cxb5 cxb5 14 ♘e1 ♗b7!

It is the control over d5 that is the most important thing in the position.

15 ♗xb7 ♖xb7 16 ♕e2 ♘c7 17 ♘d3 b4 18 ♘a4 g5 19 f3 g4 20 fxg4 ♘xg4 21 e4 ♗g5 22 ♘f4 ♘f6 23 exf5 ♗xf4 24 ♖xf4 ♘cd5 25 ♖f2 exf5 26 ♕xe8 ♖xe8 27 ♖xf5 ♖e2 28 ♖cf1 ♖c7 29 ♖5f2 ♖xf2 30 ♖xf2 ♔f7

This is a true image of positional triumph for Black. There is no scope for the a4-knight or the b2-bishop, and the extra pawn will not count in the long run.

31 h3 ♔g6 32 ♖e2 h5 33 ♖e6 ♖c2 34

♔f1 ♔f5 35 ♖e2 ♖c6 36 ♔f2 ♘e4+ 37 ♔f3 ♘g5+ 38 ♔g2 ♖c8 39 h4 ♘e4 40 ♔f3 ♘ef6 41 ♖g2 ♖c7 42 ♖e2 ♖c6 43 a3 ♖c7 44 axb4 axb4 45 ♖e1 ♖c2 46 ♖e2 ♖xe2 47 ♔xe2 ♔e4 48 ♗a1 ♘g4 49 ♘b2 ♘c3+ 50 ♔d2 ♘h2 51 ♘c4 ♘f3+ 52 ♔c1 ♘xd4 53 ♘xd6+ ♔d3 54 ♔b2 ♘d1+ 55 ♔c1 ♘c3 56 ♔b2 ♘de2 57 ♘f5 ♔d2 58 ♘d6 ♘xg3 59 ♘c4+ ♔d3 60 ♘e5+ ♔e4 61 ♘d7 ♘ge2 62 ♘f6+ ♔d3 63 ♘xh5 ♔d2 0-1

White trapped in zugzwang. His only logical idea is to move the knight from h5, and after that ...♘e2-f4-d3 with deliver mate.

CHAPTER ONE

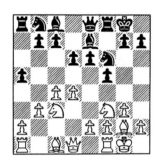

Main Line:
7 ♘c3 a5 8 b3 ♕e8

In the first two chapters we will investigate the positions arising after **1 d4 f5 2 c4 ♘f6 3 g3 e6 4 ♗g2 ♗e7 5 ♘f3 0-0 6 0-0 d6 7 ♘c3 a5**

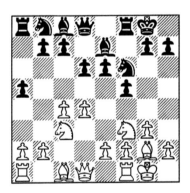

This is more or less the main line of the Dutch Classical and certainly one of the most critical lines in this book. White has tried a broad range of different possibilities against 7...a5, some of which are more dangerous than others. In this chapter we deal with the line **8 b3 ♕e8**, while in Chapter 2 we shall look at eighth move alternatives for White.

The most popular and also the most natural choice for White is 8 b3. This can be played with the idea of both ♗b2 and ♗a3. I have no doubt that the former is the healthier of the two, but I still have not been able

to prove any advantage for White in this line after 9 ♗b2 ♕h5 10 ♖e1 ♘e4 11 ♕c2 ♘xc3 12 ♗xc3 f4. This leads to unclear play, as can be seen in Game 3.

After 9 ♗b2, alternatives to 9...♕h5, including 9...♘a6, 9...♗d8 and 9...c6, will be discussed in Games 5-9, while 9 ♗a3 is studied in Games 10-13.

Game 1
Yusupov-Hickl
Cologne 1999

1 d4 e6 2 ♘f3 f5 3 g3 ♘f6 4 ♗g2 ♗e7 5 0-0 0-0 6 c4 d6 7 ♘c3 a5 8 b3 ♕e8

Black has also tried 8...♘a6?! but there is no sense in placing the knight on c7 in this position. 9 ♗b2 c6 10 e3 ♘c7 11 ♕c2 b5 12 ♘d2! d5 13 ♘f3! ♘d7 14 cxd5 cxd5 15 ♖fc1 ♗b7 16 ♘e2 ♗d6 17 ♘e5 ♕e7 18 ♘f4 a4? (18...♖fc8 19 ♘fd3 would just give White a very clear advantage.

see following diagram

---

19 ♕xc7!! with a winning position for White in Korchnoi-Bellin, Hastings 1975/76.
9 ♗b2

The bishop is probably better placed here than on a3.
9...♕h5 10 ♕c2 ♘c6 11 ♖ad1 ♗d7

Black needs to develop. After 11...♗d8 12 a3 (12 e3 e5 13 dxe5 dxe5 14 ♘d5 ♖e8 would be the kind of thing Black wishes for) 12...♖e8 13 e4 fxe4 14 ♘xe4 ♘xe4 15 ♕xe4 White has a standard advantage.

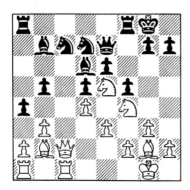

12 a3 ♖ae8?!

Black is playing without a plan. The alternatives are:

a) 12...e5? 13 dxe5 dxe5 14 ♘d5 ♖f7 15 ♗xe5! and White just wins.

b) However, after 12...♘d8 13 e4 fxe4 14 ♘xe4 ♖b8! (14...♗c6 15 ♘fd2 is a little better for White) 15 ♖fe1 ♘xe4 16 ♕xe4 b5! Black would have decent counterplay.

13 d5!

Black had prepared himself for 13 e4 and planned to meet it with 13...fxe4 14 ♘xe4 ♘xe4 15 ♕xe4 ♘d8! 16 ♕e3 ♗c6 with an acceptable position.

13...♘d8 14 ♘b5!?

This is an interesting positional sacrifice of an exchange. The only question is why? After the simple 14 ♘d4! c6 (14...e5? 15 ♘db5 exposes c7; after 15...f4 16 gxf4 ♗h3 17 f3 ♗xg2 18 ♔xg2 Black does not have a way to organise an attack) 15 dxe6 ♗xe6 16 ♘xe6 ♘xe6 17 e3 White is obviously better.

14...♗xb5 15 cxb5 ♘xd5

---

see following diagram

---

16 ♖xd5!

This was, of course, the idea. Otherwise White would just have lost a pawn.

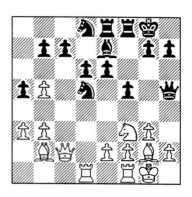

16...exd5 17 ♕xc7 f4!

Black is seeking counterplay.

18 ♘d4 ♔h8

After 18...fxg3 19 hxg3 ♗f6 20 ♕xd6 ♗xd4 21 ♗xd4 ♕xe2 22 ♗xd5+ ♔h8 23 ♕c7 ♖e7 24 ♕xa5 ♖fe8 Black is slightly worse.

19 ♗f3 ♕f7

19...♕e5 20 ♕xa5 fxg3 21 hxg3 ♗f6 22 ♕b6 ♕g5 also leaves White with slightly better chances.

20 ♕xa5 ♗f6 21 ♕d2 ♗e5

21...fxg3 22 hxg3 ♘e6 23 ♗xd5 ♗xd4 24 ♗xd4 gives White a tiny edge like in almost all lines.

22 a4

22...♕f6?!

This allows White to advance on the queenside, after which I do not see a plan that will save the game for Black. Following the stronger 22...b6! 23 b4 ♘e6 24 ♘xe6 (24 ♗xd5 fxg3 25 hxg3 ♗xg3! is an important detail to remember) 24...♕xe6 25 ♗xd5 ♕f6 26 ♗xe5 dxe5 27 a5 ♖d8 Black is struggling, but has fair chances of drawing.

23 a5! ♘e6 24 ♘xe6 ♖xe6 25 ♗xe5 dxe5 26 ♕xd5 ♖e7 27 b4 ♕g6 28 ♗e4 ♕g4 29 ♕d3 ♕e6

After 29...♖d7 30 ♕f3 ♕xf3 31 exf3 Black has a horrible endgame.

30 a6 ♖d7 31 ♕a3 ♕c4 32 ♗xb7 ♕xb5 33 ♗f3 ♖a7 34 ♖a1 ♖f6 35 ♕c3 g6 36 ♖a5 ♕b6 37 ♕xe5 fxg3 38 hxg3 ♖xa6 39 ♖b5 ♕e6 40 ♖b8+ ♔g7 41 ♖b7+ ♔h6 42 ♕c7 ♕g8 43 ♕c1+ g5 44 ♗e4 ♖f7 45 ♗d5 ♕h8 46 ♗xf7 1-0

Game 2
Flohr-Kotov
USSR Championship 1949

This game is very important for the understanding of the Ilyin-Zhenevsky system, as the pawn sacrifice Black plays is prototypical.

1 d4 e6 2 c4 f5 3 g3 ♘f6 4 ♗g2 ♗e7 5 ♘f3 d6 6 0-0 0-0 7 ♘c3 ♕e8 8 ♕c2 ♕h5

Black should be careful not to develop his queenside knight too soon with 8...♘c6?! 9 d5 ♘b4 10 ♕b3 ♘a6 11 dxe6 ♘c5 12 ♕c2 ♗xe6 13 b3. Now instead of 13...♕h5? 14 ♘d4 ♗c8 15 b4 with a clear advantage in Fain-Bogolubov, Nottingham 1936, Black should play 13...♘fe4 14 ♗b2 ♗f6 with a slightly inferior position.

9 b3 a5 10 ♗b2 ♘a6 11 ♖ae1

After 11 a3 Black can try to play originally with 11...♖b8 12 ♖ac1 c6 13 e4 e5!. This is a temporary pawn sacrifice that gives breathing space to the black pieces and puts pressure on the white centre. 14 dxe5 dxe5 15 ♘xe5 ♘c5 (the point; White now cannot capture on f5 as after the bishop recaptures, White will lose the b3-pawn) 16 b4 axb4 17 axb4 ♘cxe4 18 f3 ♘g5 19 ♘d3 ♗d6 20 ♘e2 ♘e6

with an unclear position in Danielian-Moser, Istanbul Olympiad 2000. The line 20...♘h3+!? 21 ♗xh3 ♕xh3 also looked worth a try.

11...c6 12 a3 ♗d8 13 e4

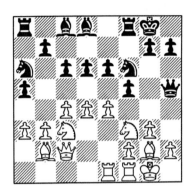

13...e5!?

A really cool pawn sacrifice. This is mainly possible due to the move 12 a3, weakening the b3-square.

14 dxe5 dxe5 15 ♘xe5 ♘c5!

The point. White now has a very inconvenient situation.

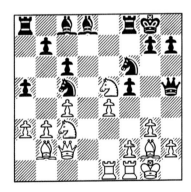

16 b4?!

This does not seem to do anything other than get rid of the weak b3-pawn. Better was 16 ♗f3! ♕h3 17 exf5 (17 ♗g2 ♕h5 is of course just a draw) 17...♗xf5 18 ♕d1! and White has some chances of obtaining an advantage with 18...♗c7 19 ♗g2.

16...♘cxe4 17 ♘xe4 fxe4 18 c5?

This gives Black control over the d5-square. 18 f4 ♗h3 is also good for Black, but this was the lesser evil.

18...♗e6 19 ♗xe4

19 ♕d1!? was perhaps better, but Black still appears to be better.

19...♘xe4 20 ♖xe4 ♗d5 21 ♖e2 axb4 22 axb4 ♗f6 23 f4 ♖a2 24 ♖ef2 ♖fa8 25 ♕d3 ♖8a4

25...♕h3!?, with the idea of advancing the h-pawn and to capture on g3 to weaken the kingside, was an alternative. After 26 g4 ♕xd3 27 ♘xd3 ♗xb2 28 ♖xb2 ♖xb2 29 ♘xb2 ♖a3 and Black stands better in this position.

26 g4 ♕h4 27 ♕f5 ♖a8 28 g5 ♕h5 29 h3 h6!

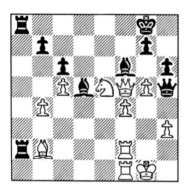

This is very precise play from Black. After the continuation 29...♗xe5? 30 fxe5 g6 White has an exceptionally beautiful mate with 31 ♕f8+!! ♖xf8 32 ♖xf8+ ♔g7 33 e6+ ♖xb2 34 ♖1f7 mate!

30 ♘d3

White also collapses after 30 ♕g4 in the face of the continuation 30...♕xg4+ 31 hxg4 hxg5.

30...♗xb2 31 ♘xb2 ♖2a3 32 ♔h2 ♖e3! 33 ♖g1

Or if instead 33 ♕g4 then after 33...♕xg4 34 hxg4 ♖aa3 35 ♖d2 ♖h3+ 36 ♔g1 ♖h1+ 37 ♔f2 ♖f3+ and White would have to resign.

33...♗e6 0-1

Game 3
Lalic-N.Pert,
British Championship 1999

My annotations for this game are partly based on those by Lalic in *Chess Informant 76*.

1 d4 e6 2 c4 f5 3 g3 ♘f6 4 ♗g2 ♗e7 5 ♘f3 d6 6 0-0 0-0 7 ♘c3 a5 8 b3 ♕e8 9 ♗b2 ♕h5 10 ♖e1 ♘e4

Black has some valid alternatives here:

a) 10...d5!? is of course only good for players who like to play the Stonewall. After 11 ♘e5 c6 12 e3 ♕h6 13 ♘a4 ♘bd7 14 c5?! (14 ♖c1 is better) 14...g5! Black developed an initiative in Farago-Naumkin, Budapest 1991.

b) 10...♘c6 looks sound. 11 d5 ♘d8 12 dxe6 (12 ♘d4?! e5 13 ♘db5 ♘e8 does not bring White any joy; this structure is better for Black and the white knights have difficulties finding good squares) 12...♘xe6 13 e4 fxe4 14 ♘xe4 ♘xe4 15 ♖xe4 ♗f6 16 ♗xf6 ♖xf6 17 ♘d4 ♕xd1+ 18 ♖xd1 ♘xd4 19 ♖exd4 and White had a small advantage due to his lead in development. Sliva S-Langier, Rancagua 1993.

11 ♕c2 ♘xc3 12 ♗xc3 f4

After 12...♕h6 13 e4 fxe4 14 ♕xe4 White is just better. The same goes for 12...♘c6 13 d5 ♘d8 14 ♘d4 as now 14...e5 15 ♘b5 is very uncomfortable.

13 e3 fxg3 14 fxg3 e5?!

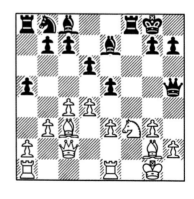

Black cannot play 14...♖xf3? due to 15

♕e2 ♖f5 16 g4 and White wins, but he should try 14...♘c6! 15 ♖f1 ♗f6 16 ♖f2 e5 when White does not seem to have any advantage at all. This is a standard rule in chess (which of course has its limitations). First develop, then open the position.

15 ♕e4!

After 15 ♖f1? ♗f5! 16 e4 ♗g4 17 ♕d3 ♘c6 Black's pieces have an easier life finding good squares.

15...♗d7

Black has no easy way to develop. After 15...♘d7 16 ♕d5+ ♔h8 17 dxe5 c6 18 ♕d4 he would have simply lost a pawn.

16 ♕d5+ ♔h8 17 ♕xb7 ♘c6

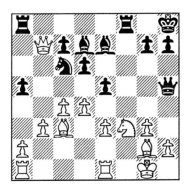

18 ♘xe5!

This is the beginning of a nice sequence giving White a winning advantage.

18...♖fb8

After 18...♖a7 19 ♕xc6! (19 ♘xd7 ♖xb7 20 ♘xf8 ♗xf8 21 ♗xc6 also looks excellent for White) 19...♗xc6 20 ♘xc6 ♕f7 21 ♘xa7 White has a close-to-winning advantage. 18...dxe5 19 ♗xc6 ♗xc6 20 ♕xc6 does not give Black any counterplay at all.

19 ♕xc7 ♖a7 20 ♕xd7

Well, she was never going to get out of there alive but, just like a gladiator, she has killed some beasts before going into the box.

20...♖xd7 21 ♘xd7 ♖c8 22 ♘b6 ♖b8 23 ♘d5

White is winning comfortably. All the pawns are just too much for Black to handle.

23...♗g5 24 e4 ♘b4 25 ♗xb4 axb4 26 ♖ad1 ♖a8 27 e5 dxe5 28 ♘f4 ♗xf4 29 ♗xa8 ♗e3+ 30 ♔g2 ♗xd4 31 ♗f3 1-0

Game 4
Markowski-Girinath
Calcutta 2001

---

1 g3 f5 2 ♘f3 ♘f6 3 ♗g2 d6 4 d4 e6 5 0-0 ♗e7 6 c4 0-0 7 ♘c3 a5 8 b3 ♕e8 9 ♗b2 ♕h5 10 e3

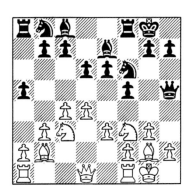

10...♕h6

Black should be careful here. After 10...♘e4?! 11 ♘xe4 fxe4 12 ♘d2 ♕xd1 13 ♖axd1 d5 14 f3 exf3 15 ♗xf3 White had a great lead in development and was therefore clearly better in Gligoric-Jamieson, Buenos Aires 1978. However, Black can try 10...♘a6!? and now:

a) 11 a3 ♖b8 (11...♗d7 is weaker; 12 ♘e1 ♕h6 13 ♘d3 gives some advantage to White, Timoshenko-Naumkin, Tashkent 1987) 12 ♘e1 ♕xd1 13 ♖xd1 c6 14 ♘d3 ♗d7, with the idea of ...b7-b5, gives Black counterplay.

b) 11 ♘e1 ♕xd1 12 ♖xd1 c6 13 ♘d3 ♗d7 14 a3 ♖fd8 15 b4 axb4 16 axb4 ♘c7 17 ♖a1 ♖xa1 18 ♗xa1 ♖a8 and White might have a very minor advantage, J.Ivanov-Sciortimo, Montecatini Terme 2002. But when you are Black, sometimes these kinds of positions will end up on your plate. You just have to make the most of them.

11 ♕e2

11 ♘e1 has also been tried: 11...c6 12 ♘d3 ♘bd7 13 e4 e5 14 exf5 exd4 15 ♗c1 ♕h5 16 ♘e2 c5 17 ♘ef4 ♕xd1 18 ♖xd1 ♘e5 19 ♘e6 ♗xe6 20 fxe6 and White was somewhat better, Bouton-Naumkin, Cappelle la Grande 1995.

11...g5!?

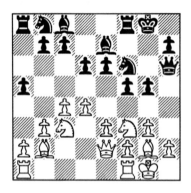

Normally one would develop, but after 11...♘c6 12 d5! exd5 13 cxd5 ♘b4 14 ♘d4 ♘a6 White was better in Sotnikov-Poluljachov, Russia 1995.

12 ♖fd1 ♘a6

12...♘e4 13 ♘d2 ♘xc3 14 ♗xc3 ♗f6 15 e4 looks better for White.

13 a3 ♖b8 14 ♘d2 c6

Black can also choose to play with his pieces. After 14...♗d7 15 e4 fxe4 16 ♘dxe4 ♘xe4 17 ♘xe4 b5! the position is unclear.

15 e4 e5 16 exf5

White can also choose 16 dxe5 dxe5 (16...♘g4 doesn't work due to 17 ♘f3 ♘xe5 18 ♘xe5 dxe5 19 exf5 and the exchange of pieces is to White's advantage. With the control over e4 he holds much the better chances.) 17 ♘f3 (Note that though 17 exf5 might be interesting, the position after 17...♗xf5 18 ♕xe5?? ♘g4! is only interesting for Black!) 17...♗c5! 18 ♘xe5 fxe4 with a complicated game ahead.

16...♗xf5 17 ♘ce4

After 17 dxe5 dxe5 18 ♘f3 e4 19 ♘e5 ♗c5! the position is unclear. Still, Black should not forget about his knight on a6. It

wants to join in the fight too.

17...exd4 18 ♗xd4

18 ♘xg5? looks like a very foolish combination, as the reply is a natural improvement of a badly placed piece: 18...♖be8 19 ♘ge4 ♘c5 20 ♗xd4 (otherwise Black will dominate the centre) 20...♘fxe4 21 ♘xe4 ♘xb3 22 ♖ab1 ♘xd4 23 ♖xd4 d5! 24 cxd5 ♗c5 and White is in great trouble – d4, e4 and f2 are all targets.

18...♖be8 19 ♖e1 ♘xe4

This is rather tame. Black also has some nice ideas with 19...♘g4!? 20 h3 ♘e5 when the knight is well placed. Now 21 c5?! d5 22 ♗xe5 dxe4 23 ♘xe4 ♗xe4 24 ♕xe4 ♗xc5 25 ♖a2 ♕e6 26 ♗f1 b5 27 ♗g2 ♘b8 leaves White struggling to find a good way to protect f2 and get out of the pin. After the improvement 21 g4! ♗g6 22 ♕e3 ♘d7 23 ♗b2 ♘ac5 we have an open game.

20 ♘xe4 ♗xe4 21 ♗xe4 ♗f6 22 ♗xf6 ♕xf6 23 ♕c2 ♖e7 24 ♗d3 ♖fe8 25 ♖f1!

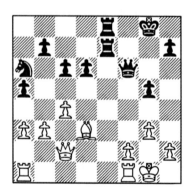

Black has no play on the open e-file now. After 25 ♗xh7+?? ♔h8 26 ♖xe7 ♕xa1+ White would lose. The same goes for 25 ♖xe7?? ♕xa1+.

25...♘c5 26 ♖ad1!

Counterplay against d6 keeps the balance.

26...♘e6 27 ♕d2 ♘c5 28 ♕c2

28 ♗b1?! ♘xb3 29 ♕xd6 ♕xd6 30 ♖xd6 ♘c5 would leave Black with a better knight.

28...♘e6 29 ♕d2 ♘c5 30 ♕c2 ½-½

Black has better placed pieces, but his weak

kingside has to be protected, so probably there is no advantage.

Game 5
Golubovic-Moser
Oberwart 2001

---

1 d4 f5 2 g3 ♘f6 3 ♗g2 e6 4 ♘f3 ♗e7 5 c4 d6 6 ♘c3 0-0 7 0-0 ♕e8 8 b3 a5 9 ♗b2 ♘a6 10 ♖e1

10 a3 is a relevant move too and is considered in Game 6. White can also consider the following lines:

a) 10 ♘e1 e5 11 dxe5 dxe5 12 e4 ♗c5! would give Black good counterplay.

b) 10 ♕c2 ♕g6 11 ♖ae1 ♗d7 12 a3 c6 13 ♘a4!? ♗e8 14 c5 ♕h5 15 cxd6 ♗xd6 16 ♘b6 ♖d8 17 ♘c4 gave White the advantage in Lutz-Weinzettl, Leibnitz 1990.

10...♕h5 11 e4 fxe4 12 ♘xe4 ♘xe4 13 ♖xe4

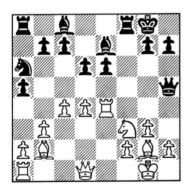

In this line White has a small but very clear advantage due to the weak pawn on e6. This superiority might not be overwhelming but it is practically eternal, as it is hard to imagine that Black would get rid of this weakness.

13...♗f6

There is no compensation after the following:

a) 13...e5? 14 dxe5 ♘c5 15 ♖e3 ♗g4 16 exd6 ♗xd6 17 ♕d4 ♖f6 18 ♘e5 ♗e6 and even better than 19 ♖ae1?! with a clear ad-

vantage as in Koepcke-Perry, correspondence 1997 is 19 ♗a3! with a winning position.

b) 13...♗d7 14 ♖e3 c6 15 ♕d2 would only be a little better for White after 15...♘c7, but after 15...b6?? 16 d5! e5 (or 16...cxd5 17 cxd5 e5 18 ♘xe5! dxe5 19 ♖xe5 ♕f7 [19...♗b4 20 ♕xb4] 20 d6 and White wins) 17 ♘xe5! dxe5 18 ♖xe5 ♕f7 19 dxc6 ♗b4 20 ♕e3 ♗e6 21 ♖xe6 ♗c5 22 ♗d4 Black had simply had enough and resigned in Kachiani-Moser, Istanbul Olympiad 2000.

14 ♕d2

This position has been played a few times and other good moves have been tried:

a) 14 h4!? ♗d7 15 ♘g5 ♕xd1+ 16 ♖xd1 ♗xg5 17 hxg5 ♖ad8 18 ♗c3 and perhaps White has more than just a small advantage here, Markos-Moser, Liepzig 2002.

b) 14 ♕e2!? c5 15 ♖d1 ♗d7 16 ♘e5! ♕xe2 17 ♖xe2 ♗c8 18 ♘f3 was somewhat better for White in Damianovic-Gundersen, Eupen 1999.

c) 14 ♖e2 ♖b8 15 ♕d2 ♗d7 16 ♘e1 ♘b4 17 ♘d3 was just a tiny bit better for White in Grunberg-Lechtynski, Karlovy Vary 1973.

14...♗d7 15 ♖ae1 ♖ae8

Or 15...♗c6 and now:

a) 16 g4?! is insufficient due to 16...♕g6 17 ♖xe6 ♕xg4 18 d5 ♗d7 19 ♖6e4 ♕g6 20 ♗xf6 ♕xf6 21 ♕d4 ♕xd4 22 ♘xd4 ♘c5 23 ♖e7 ♖fe8 24 ♖xe8+ ♖xe8 25 ♖xe8+ ♗xe8 26 f4! and only with this move does White keep the black advantage to a minimum. The advantage is of course structural and will give Black some good options in the endgame.

b) 16 ♖4e3 ♖ae8 17 h3 b6 18 a3 and White is better.

16 ♘e5??

A terrible blunder. After 16 ♖4e3! ♗c6 17 a3!, with the idea b3-b4, White has the advantage.

16...dxe5 17 dxe5 ♗e7 18 ♕xd7 ♘c5 19 ♕xc7 ♘xe4 20 ♗xe4??

White still has not found the problem with his operation. 20 ♖xe4 ♖d8! (20...♕d1+ 21 ♗f1 gets Black nowhere) 21 ♗c3 ♖d1+ 22 ♖e1 ♖xe1+ 23 ♗xe1 ♕e2 24 ♕xa5 b6 25 ♕d2 ♖xf2 gives Black a strong position. Now he has the big trick.

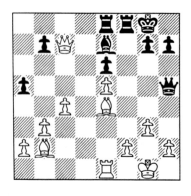

20...♗b4?!

Black should play 20...♖xf2!! 21 ♔xf2 ♕xh2+ 22 ♗g2 (or 22 ♔e3 ♗g5+ and Black

wins) 22...♖f8+ 23 ♔e3 ♕xg3+ and the White king is not getting away. Remember this standard trick – it is very useful.

21 ♖b1

White cannot escape. After 21 ♖f1 ♕e2 22 a3 ♗e7 Black wins one of the bishops.

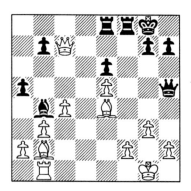

21...♖xf2!

Better late then never.

22 ♔xf2 ♕xh2+ 23 ♔e3 ♕d2+

All roads leads to Rome...

24 ♔f3 ♖f8+ 25 ♔g4 ♕e2+ 26 ♔h3 ♕xe4 27 ♖g1 ♕f5+ 28 g4 ♕f3+ 29 ♔h2 ♗d2 0-1

Game 6
Farago-Lucaroni
Marostica 1997

---

1 d4 f5 2 g3 ♘f6 3 ♗g2 e6 4 c4 ♗e7 5 ♘f3 0-0 6 0-0 d6 7 ♘c3 ♕e8 8 b3 a5 9 ♗b2 ♘a6 10 a3 ♗d7

10...c6, followed by ...♖b8, is in my opinion the strongest continuation for Black, for example 11 ♖c1 (or 11 ♕c2 b5 12 e3 ♗b7 13 ♘g5 b4 14 ♘e2 ♕d7 with an unclear position) 11...♖b8! (11...♗d7 12 e3 ♗d8 13 ♖e1 e5 was okay for Black in Furman-Simagin, USSR 1947, but White could have played more dangerously) 12 ♘d2 (12 ♕d3 b5 does not change anything) 12...e5 13 c5?! (13 e3 is better) 13...exd4 14 cxd6 ♗xd6 15 ♘c4 was played in V.Sokolov-Matulovic, Yugoslavia 1967. Now 15...♗c7 16 ♕xd4 b5! 17 ♘d2

♕e6 would have given Black a more comfortable position.

11 ♘e1 c6 12 ♘d3 ♗d8

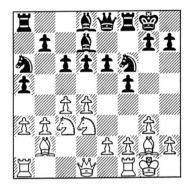

After 12...♘c7 13 e4 fxe4 14 ♘xe4 ♘xe4 15 ♗xe4 White has a standard advantage in Sosonko-Duckstein, Zürich 1984.

13 e4 e5 14 dxe5 dxe5 15 ♕e2

Also possible was 15 exf5 ♗xf5 16 ♖e1 ♗c7 (16...e4? 17 ♘xe4 ♘xe4 18 ♗xe4 ♗xe4 19 ♕g4 obviously does not work out) 17 ♕e2 ♗xd3! 18 ♕xd3 ♖d8 19 ♕c2 ♕h5 when Black has good counterplay.

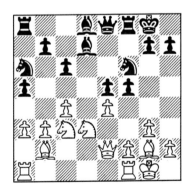

15...♗b6

Here the alternatives should be investigated:

a) 15...f4?! looks risky. The knight on a6 is too far away from the centre of the action. 16 gxf4 exf4 17 e5 ♘g4 18 h3 ♘h6 19 ♖fe1 f3!? 20 ♗xf3 ♗xh3 21 ♗h5 ♕e7 22 ♘e4 and White has control.

b) But 15...♗c7! 16 ♖fe1 (16 exf5 ♗xf5 should be okay for Black) 16...f4! gives Black good play. After 17 gxf4 exf4 18 e5?! (18 h3! would be better here) 18...♘g4 Black has considerable chances.

16 ♘a4

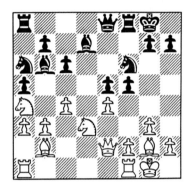

Here White has some alternatives:

a) 16 exf5 ♗xf5 17 ♘xe5 ♘c5 18 ♖ae1 ♖d8 gives Black excellent play against b3, d3 and f2.

b) 16 ♘xe5!? is interesting. Play can continue 16...♕xe5 (the only move; 16...♘c5 17 ♘xd7 ♘fxd7 18 b4 ♘xe4 19 ♘xe4 fxe4 20 c5 is brilliant for White, and 16...fxe4 17 ♘xd7 ♕xd7 18 ♖ad1 ♕f5 19 ♘xe4 is also very good) 17 ♘d5 ♗d4 18 ♗xd4 ♕xd4 19 ♖ad1 ♕e5 20 ♘xf6+ ♖xf6 21 ♖xd7 ♘c5 (21...fxe4? 22 ♗xe4 would lose time because of the threat of ♗xh7+) 22 f4 ♕e6 23 ♖d4 ♘xb3 24 ♖dd1 ♕e7 25 e5 ♖e6 26 ♕d3 ♕xa3 27 ♕xf5 with a complete mess. White needs to win on the kingside soon, as Black will simply advance his a-pawn until it promotes.

16...♗d4!?

This is apparently necessary because of 16...♗a7 17 ♘xe5 fxe4 18 ♘xd7 ♕xd7 19 ♗xf6 ♖xf6 20 ♗xe4 ♖af8 21 c5! and White seemingly has the advantage. However, after 21...♘xc5 22 ♘xc5 ♗xc5 23 ♕c4+ ♕e6 Black has found at least one way to keep the balance. So probably 16...♗a7 was a better choice.

17 ♗xd4 exd4 18 e5 ♘e4

18...♘g4?! 19 h3 ♘h6 20 ♖fe1 looks good for White; the same goes for 18...♖d8 19 ♕d2!, pointing at a5.

19 f3 ♘g5 20 ♘b6 ♖d8 21 ♕d2

Here it was also possible to play 21 ♖fe1 ♘e6 22 f4 with an advantage.

21...♘e6 22 ♕xa5!?

This allows counterplay. Possible was 22 f4 and the advantage is not in doubt.

22...f4!

The only chance to fight back!

23 ♘xd7

23 g4 ♕e7 24 ♘xd7 ♖xd7 25 b4 ♖a8 26 ♕a4 is also advantageous for White.

23...♖xd7 24 ♗h3 fxg3 25 hxg3 ♘ac7 26 ♕d2 ♕g6 27 ♔h2?

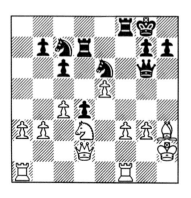

This steps into a minor combination. Better was 27 ♔g2 ♖df7 28 f4! with an overwhelming advantage.

27...♘g5 28 f4

This is also not accurate. After 28 ♗xd7! ♘xf3+ 29 ♖xf3 ♖xf3 30 ♖d1 ♖e3!? (ambitious; 30...♕xg3+ 31 ♔h1 ♕h4+ 32 ♕h2 ♕e4 33 ♕g2 ♕h4+ leads to a draw) 31 ♘e1 ♕xg3+ 32 ♔h1 d3 33 ♘xd3 ♕h4+ 34 ♕h2 ♕e4+ 35 ♕g2 White is still okay.

28...♘xh3 29 ♔xh3

White has some problems with his king.

29...♘e6 30 ♖ae1

30 ♔h2 h5! and the attack is on the way.

30...♖df7 31 ♔g2?

31 ♔h2! was still the cautious approach,

with Black's best reply being 31...h5!.

31...h5! 32 ♖f3

After 32 ♔h2 comes 32...h4 33 ♖g1 ♘g5!! (tactics are required; 33...♕h7 34 g4 ♘xf4 35 e6 ♕xd3 36 exf7+ ♖xf7 37 ♕xd3 ♘xd3 38 ♖e8+ ♔h7 39 ♖d1 is good for White) 34 ♕e2! (34 fxg5 ♖f3! is cut-throat business) 34...hxg3+ 35 ♖xg3 ♕h6+ 36 ♔g2 ♘e6 37 ♕d2 ♘xf4+ 38 ♘xf4 ♖xf4 39 e6 ♕f6 with a clear advantage. Now the tables are turned for the last time.

32...♘g5??

Just an oversight. After 32...h4! 33 ♕f2 ♘g5 34 e6 ♘xe6 Black has a strong attack.

33 e6!

Now White just wins.

33...♘xe6 34 ♘e5 ♕f5 35 ♘xf7 ♖xf7 36 ♕d3 ♕g4 37 ♖e4 h4 38 f5 1-0

Game 7

Krivoshey-Salai

Slovakian League 1997

1 ♘f3 f5 2 g3 ♘f6 3 ♗g2 e6 4 0-0 ♗e7 5 c4 0-0 6 ♘c3 d6 7 d4 ♕e8 8 b3 a5 9 ♗b2 ♘a6 10 e3 ♖b8!?

Black has two main ideas with this move. He wants to protect the b7-pawn and he is also preparing the advance ...b7-b5 for later. The alternatives are less recommendable:

a) 10...c6?! 11 ♕e2 ♘c7 (11...♗d7 12 e4 fxe4 13 ♘xe4 is a standard advantage for White) 12 ♘a4 b5 13 ♘b6 ♖b8 14 ♘xc8

♕xc8 15 cxb5 cxb5 16 d5! was better for White in Helmers-Duckstein, Lucerne 1979.

b) 10...♗d8?! 11 a3 c6 12 b4 e5 13 b5 ♘b8 14 ♘d2 gave White a strong initiative in Miles-Roos, Baden-Baden 1981. Almost all the black pieces are on the back rank.

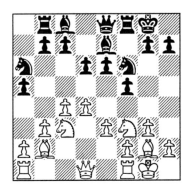

11 ♖e1

White has also tried:

a) 11 ♘e1 c6 12 a4 ♘b4 13 ♘d3 ♘xd3 14 ♕xd3 ♕h5 15 ♕d1 ♕h6 16 ♕e2 e5 17 f3 ♖e8 18 ♖ae1 ♗d8 19 ♕c2 ♗c7 and Black had good counterplay in the game Bolbochan-Pelikan, Buenos Aires 1978.

b) 11 a3 ♗d7 12 ♕e2 c6 13 e4 fxe4 14 ♘xe4 ♘xe4 15 ♕xe4 b5 and Black's position was reasonable, Kulikov-Otman, Moscow 1994. On 16 cxb5 there follows 16...♖xb5 with an attack on b3 and the manoeuvre ...♘a6-c7-d5 in mind.

11...♕h5

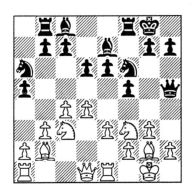

12 e4

White needs to act. After 12 a3 c6! 13 ♘d2 ♕xd1 14 ♖axd1 ♗d7 15 e4 fxe4 16 ♘cxe4 b5! Black is well in the game.

12...♘xe4 13 ♘xe4 fxe4 14 ♖xe4 b5! 15 ♗c3

It is natural to avoid getting a weakness in the b-file. 15 cxb5 ♖xb5 16 ♘d2 (on 16 ♕e2 Black can try 16...♘b4!? 17 a3 ♘a6 when the weakness on b3 is uncomfortable for White) 16...♕xd1+ 17 ♖xd1 ♘b4 and Black has a good game.

15...bxc4 16 bxc4 ♗d7?!

Too slow. Better was 16...c5! 17 ♖e1 ♗f6 18 ♖c1 ♘b4 with a perfect position for Black.

17 ♕e2?!

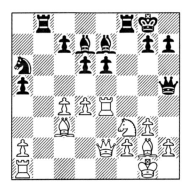

White is equally slow. After 17 ♘e1! ♕xd1 18 ♖xd1 a4 19 ♗h3 Black has problems.

17...♗f6

17...a4 18 ♖e1 ♗f6 19 ♘d2 ♕xe2 20 ♖4xe2 c5 was a good alternative.

18 ♖e1

The pawn grabbing with 18 g4 would be risky: 18...♕g6 19 ♗xa5 c5 20 ♖d1 cxd4 21 ♘xd4 ♘c5 and Black has good compensation.

18...c5 19 ♗a1

The exchange sacrifice with 19 ♖xe6?! ♗xe6 20 ♕xe6+ ♔h8 21 ♕xd6 cxd4 22 ♘xd4 ♖bd8! gives Black a better game.

19...cxd4 20 ♘xd4

The alternative 20 ♗xd4 ♘c5 is also fine for Black.

20...♕xe2 21 ♖4xe2 ♘c5 22 ♖d2

White is defending. After 22 ♘b3 ♘xb3 23 axb3 ♖xb3 24 ♖d2 ♗e7 25 c5 a4 26 cxd6 ♗d8 the a-pawn would give Black a better endgame.

22...♖b4 23 ♘b3 ♗xa1 24 ♖xa1 ♖xb3 25 axb3 ♘xb3 26 ♖xd6 ♘xa1 27 ♖xd7 ♖c8 28 ♗h3 ♖c6 29 ♖b7 ½-½

29 f4 ♘b3 30 ♔f2 ♔f8 31 ♖a7 ♘d4 would also draw.

Game 8
Itkis-Shtyrenkov
Alushta 2001

---

1 d4 e6 2 ♘f3 f5 3 g3 ♘f6 4 ♗g2 ♗e7 5 0-0 0-0 6 c4 d6 7 ♘c3 a5 8 b3 ♕e8 9 ♗b2 ♗d8

This idea does not impress.

10 e3 e5 11 dxe5 dxe5 12 e4 ♘c6 13 exf5 ♗xf5 14 ♖e1 ♘d7

Black also does not equalise after 14...♗g4?! 15 h3 ♗h5 (15...♗xf3 16 ♕xf3 is just a picnic for White) 16 g4 ♗f7 17 ♘xe5 ♘xe5 18 f4 with a strong initiative for White.

15 ♘d5 ♗g4 16 h3 ♗h5 17 ♗a3

Also good is 17 ♘f4 ♗f7 18 ♘d3 with a clear advantage.

17...♖f7 18 g4?!

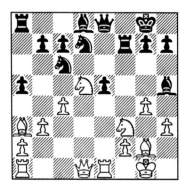

But this is not good. Here White should have played 18 ♘f4! ♗xf3 19 ♗xf3 ♘f6 20

♗b2 ♖e7 21 ♘d5 when the advantage is beyond question.

18...♗g6 19 ♕d2 a4 20 b4

This is also not a very nice move to play, but when things start to go wrong, they usually do so in style.

20...e4 21 ♗b2?!

This is also a bit slow. White has two better options at his disposal.

a) 21 h4!? ♕f8 22 ♘g5 ♗xg5 23 ♕xg5 ♖xf2 (23...♘de5?! 24 h5 ♖xf2 25 ♖f1 would give White a large advantage) 24 ♖f1 ♖xf1+ 25 ♖xf1 ♕d8 26 b5 ♗xg5 27 hxg5 ♘ce5 28 ♘e7+ ♔h8 29 ♘xg6+ hxg6 (29...♗xg6?! 30 ♗xe4 and the knight on g6 is out of play) 30 ♗xe4 ♘xc4 31 ♗b4 and White has compensation for the pawn, so the game is still undecided.

b) But really strong looks 21 ♘f4!? ♗f6 22 ♖ad1 ♖d8 23 ♘xg6! (23 ♕c1!? still promises White a sizeable advantage) 23...♘de5 (23...hxg6 24 ♕c2 is just good for White; he simply rules on the light squares) 24 ♕xd8 ♘xf3+ (24...♘xd8? 25 ♘fxe5 and Black cannot defend his pieces) 25 ♗xf3 ♘xd8 26 ♖xe4 ♗e7 27 ♘e5 ♖f6 28 ♖e3 and now:

b1) 28...♔h8 29 ♖de1 c6 30 ♘xc6 ♘xc6 31 ♗xc6 ♕xc6 32 ♖xe7 ♕f3 (32...h6? 33 ♗b2 ♖g6 34 ♖1e4 gives White a technically winning position as Black has no counterplay) 33 ♖e8+ ♖f8 34 ♖xf8+ ♕xf8 35 b5 ♕c8 36 ♖e4 with good chances of winning the endgame.

b2) 28...c6 29 b5 with a promising position as White wins after both 29...♗xa3? 30 ♘xc6 ♕xe3 31 ♖xd8+ and 29...♖e6 30 ♗xe7 ♖xe7 31 bxc6 bxc6 32 ♖ed3.

21...♕f8 22 ♘g5 ♗xg5 23 ♕xg5 ♘xb4

Black again should stay clear of the tactics after 23...♖xf2? 24 ♖f1 ♖xf1+ 25 ♖xf1 ♕d6 (25...♕d8 26 ♕f4 ♘f8 27 ♘xc7 ♖c8 28 ♗xe4! also wins for White) 26 c5 ♕g3 27 ♘e7+ ♘xe7 28 ♕xe7 ♕e3+ 29 ♔h1 ♘f6 30 ♖xf6! gxf6 31 ♕xf6 when Black will soon find himself mated.

24 ♘xc7 ♖c8?

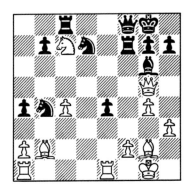

Now it was high time to capture on f2, something that can be very difficult to determine when things have been bad for so many moves. After 24...♖xf2! there a quite a few branches.

a) 25 ♗xg7? ♕d6! (25...♔xg7?? 26 ♘e6+ and White wins, but 25...♖xg2+!? 26 ♔xg2 ♕f3+ gives a perpetual) 26 ♘xa8 ♕g3 27 ♕d8+ ♘f8 28 ♕xf8+ ♖xf8 29 ♗xf8 ♘c2 30 ♖f1 ♕e3+ 31 ♔h1 ♘xa1 and Black wins.

b) 25 ♖f1? ♖xf1+ 26 ♖xf1 ♕d8 27 ♕xd8+ ♖xd8 is better for Black.

c) 25 ♘xa8 ♖xb2 (with the threat of ♕f2+) 26 ♖f1 ♕xa8 is also good for Black.

d) 25 ♗d4! ♖xg2+ 26 ♔xg2 ♕f3+ 27 ♔h2 ♖c8 28 ♘d5 ♖xc4 with a very complicated game ahead.

25 ♘e6 ♕e7 26 ♗xe4 ♗xe4

26...♕xe6?? 27 ♗d5 and White wins.

27 ♖xe4 ♘f8 28 ♖ae1?

This walks directly into a strong knight move. After 28 ♗a3 h6 (28...♖c6? 29 ♗xb4 ♕xb4 30 ♘d8! is very strong for White) 29 ♕xe7 ♖xe7 30 ♖b1 ♖xe6 31 ♖xe6 ♘xe6 32 ♖xb4 White has good chances to prove an advantage in the endgame with his extra pawn.

28...♘d3! 29 ♕xe7 ♖xe7 30 ♘xf8 ♖xe4 31 ♖xe4 ♘xb2 32 ♘d7 ♘xc4 ½-½

Here the players agreed a draw, which is a little strange as Black can easily play on to win the game with no risk at all for 100 moves.

1 d4 e6 2 ♘f3 f5 3 g3 ♘f6 4 ♗g2 ♗e7 5 0-0 0-0 6 c4 d6 7 ♘c3 a5 8 b3 ♕e8 9 ♗b2 c6

In my opinion White has the better game after this move.

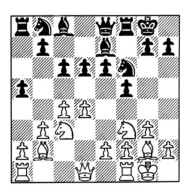

10 ♖e1

Also possible are the following:

a) 10 a3 ♗d8 11 c5 (11 e3 e5 is probably not too bad for Black) 11...dxc5 12 dxc5 ♗c7 and Black has control over the centre.

b) 10 ♕c2 ♘a6 11 e4 ♘b4 12 ♕e2 ♘xe4 13 ♘xe4 fxe4 14 ♕xe4 e5 (14...♕h5 15 a3 is also better for White) 15 ♘h4 was played in Vukic-Farago, Harrachov 1967. Now 15...♗xh4 16 ♕xh4 ♗f5 17 dxe5 ♘d3 18 ♗c3 dxe5 19 ♗e4 ♕g6 20 f3 ♗xe4 21 ♕xe4 ♕xe4 22 fxe4 leads to an edge for White.

10...d5

Now the game has changed into a 'stonewall' structure. After 10...b5 11 cxb5 cxb5 12 d5! e5 (12...b4 13 ♘a4 ♘xd5 14 ♘d4 ♕f7 15 ♗xd5 exd5 16 ♘b6 ♖a7 17 ♘xc8 ♖xc8 18 ♕d3 is clearly better for White according to Rudolf Maric) 13 ♘xe5 b4 14 ♘a4 dxe5 15 d6 ♖a7 16 ♖c1! 16...♗a6 17 dxe7 ♕xe7 18 ♕c2 and White has a strong initiative and the two bishops.

11 e3 b6

Black needs to restrain himself. After 11...b5?! 12 ♘e5 ♘e4 13 ♘e2 ♗f6 14 f3 ♘d6 15 cxb5 cxb5 16 ♖c1 b4 17 ♘f4 ♗a6 18 ♕d2 White was clearly better in Chuchelov-Spice, Eupen 1997.

12 ♘e5 ♗a6 13 ♖c1!?

This is a natural move, but even stronger was 13 ♘a4! ♕d8 14 c5 with an advantage.

13...♖a7 14 ♘e2?!

White still some advantage after 14 ♘a4 ♘fd7 15 ♘d3 ♕f7 though it is nothing spectacular.

14...g5 15 ♖c2

White could also play 15 cxd5 exd5 16 a3! with an unclear game, but should not go into 16 ♕c2 ♗b4 17 ♖ed1 ♘g4 18 ♘d3 ♕h5, when Black is mobilising an attack.

15...♗b4

This loses time. Better was 15...♘fd7! 16 cxd5 cxd5 17 ♘xd7 ♕xd7 with an unclear position.

16 ♗c3!

This prepares c4-c5, creating a weakness in Black's a-pawn. After 16 ♖f1 ♗d6 17 f4 the game is unclear.

16...♗d6 17 c5!?

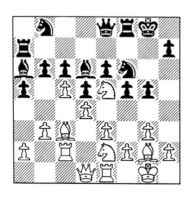

Opening up the long diagonal for the bishop in order to dominate the weak squares around the black king. 17 f4 ♕h5 18 ♘c1 g4 19 c5 bxc5 20 dxc5 ♗c7 21 ♕d4 is a big mess where White seems to have a slight advantage too.

17...bxc5 18 dxc5 ♗c7

18...♗xc5 19 ♗d4 ♗xd4 20 ♘xd4 ♖c7 21 ♕d2! would win back the pawn at the same time as all the pieces have been liberated.

19 ♕d4 ♗d8 20 g4

20 ♖d2 with a small advantage was simpler.

20...♗xe2 21 ♖exe2 ♖g7 22 h3 ♗c7 23 f4 h5!

Black needs to seek counterplay before she is buried alive.

24 ♗f3?

White completely overlooks her only move. It's not 24 gxh5 ♕xh5 25 ♕a4 gxf4 26 exf4 ♘e4 when Black is fine, but rather 24 h4! gxh4 25 g5 and White has a small but clear advantage.

24...♘bd7 25 ♘xd7

Also after 25 ♘xc6 fxg4 26 hxg4 ♕a8! 27 ♘e5 ♘xe5 28 fxe5 ♘d7 White is beginning to face serious problems.

25...♕xd7 26 ♖g2?

This is passive, but Black also has a wonderful position after 26 gxh5 gxf4+ 27 ♖g2 e5!.

26...fxg4 27 hxg4 h4?

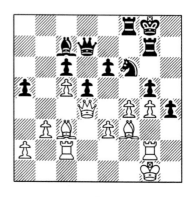

This move is hard to understand. The correct winning line was 27...hxg4 28 ♗xg4 gxf4 29 ♖cf2 ♖xg4 30 ♖xg4+ ♘xg4 31 ♕h8+ ♔f7 32 ♕h5+ ♔e7 33 ♕xg4 ♕e8 and it is the white king that is in trouble, not the black one.

28 a3?

28 ♖cf2 gives White some chances.

28...♕e7

Also interesting was 28...♘e8!? with the idea of 29 ♕d2 ♖h7 30 ♗xa5 ♗xa5 31 ♕xa5 gxf4 32 ♕c3 fxe3 33 ♕xe3 e5 and Black is much better.

29 b4

There is also no adequate defence after 29 ♕a4 h3 30 ♖ge2 gxf4 31 ♕xc6 fxe3 32 ♖xe3 ♘xg4!.

29...e5! 30 fxe5 ♘d7 31 ♕d1 axb4 32 axb4 ♘xe5 33 ♖cf2 ♖gf7 34 ♗e2 h3 35 ♖xf7 0-1

White resigned as 35...♕xf7 36 ♖h2 ♘f3+ 37 ♗xf3 ♗xh2+ 38 ♔xh2 ♕xf3 39 ♕xf3 ♖xf3 is a winning endgame for Black.

Game 10
Rajkovic-Poluljahov
Namestovo 1993

---

1 d4 f5 2 c4 e6 3 ♘f3 ♘f6 4 g3 ♗e7 5 ♗g2 0-0 6 0-0 d6 7 ♘c3 a5 8 b3 ♕e8 9 ♗a3 ♘a6

The set-up with ...♘c6 and ...♕h5 is investigated in Game 13.

10 ♖e1 c6 11 ♘a4 ♘d7 12 ♗b2

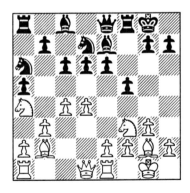

12 d5!?, as in Game 11, is probably better. After the alternative 12 e4 b5!? we have:

a) 13 exf5!? is very brave, but 13...bxa4 14 fxe6 ♘f6 15 bxa4 ♖b8 16 ♘h4 g6! (16...♘c7 17 ♘f5 should not be allowed) 17 d5 cxd5 18 cxd5 ♘b4 shows that it's also not very good.

b) 13 cxb5 cxb5 14 e5! (White has already committed himself to this with 12 e4) 14...bxa4 15 exd6 ♗f6 16 ♘g5 ♘b6 17 ♗xa8 ♗xg5 and the position is a wild mess.

12...b5 13 cxb5 cxb5 14 ♘c3 b4 15 ♘a4 ♗b7 16 ♖c1 ♕b8! 17 ♕d2 ♗d5

17...♘c7!? to control d5 rather than occupying it was worth considering.

18 ♘g5 ♗xg2

18...♕b7 19 ♗xd5 ♕xd5 20 ♘h3! would give the white knight a pleasant gain of tempo on arrival at f4.

19 ♔xg2 ♗xg5 20 ♕xg5 ♘f6 21 f4?!

This is played without a plan. Better was 21 f3 ♕b7 22 ♗a1 ♘d5 23 ♘b2 f4 (23...♘c3 24 ♘c4 would give White the advantage) 24 ♘c4 with an unclear position.

21...♕b7+ 22 ♔g1 ♖ad8 23 ♕f3 ♘d5

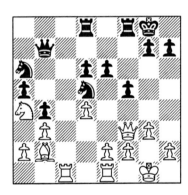

White has not succeeded in bringing the knight on a4 into the game and therefore stands slightly worse.

24 e3

24 ♗a1?! f4! shows that White has wasted his chance for free play, and should start to be more careful.

24...♘b8 25 ♕g2!

White organises e3-e4, which gives him counterplay against the e6-pawn.

25...♘d7 26 e4 fxe4 27 ♖xe4 ♖f6 28 ♖ce1 ♘f8 29 ♖4e2 ♕f7 30 ♗c1 ♖c8 31 ♕e4 ♘g6?!

It is not clear what the knight is doing here. After 31...♕h5 Black is just a little bit better. The a4-knight is still not playing.

32 ♗g5 ♖f5 33 ♗d2 ♖e8?!

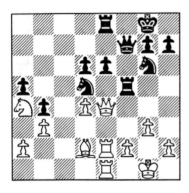

Too passive. After 33...e5! 34 ♖c1 ♖f8 35 ♖f1 ♖f3 Black would still have some initiative.

34 ♘b2 ♘c3 35 ♗xc3 bxc3 36 ♘a4 ♖f3 37 ♔g2 ♖f8 38 ♖f1 e5 39 dxe5

White should still be careful. After 39 ♘b6?! exd4 40 ♕xd4 ♕b7! 41 ♕d5+ ♕xd5 42 ♘xd5 ♖d3 Black has some advantage.

39...♘xe5 40 ♘b6 ♕h5

White was planning ♘c4.

41 ♕d5+

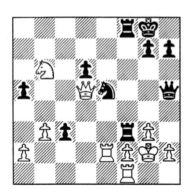

41...♕f7

41...♔h8 42 ♕xd6 ♘g6 43 ♘d7 ♖xg3+ 44 hxg3 ♘f4+ 45 gxf4 ♕g4+ leads to a draw by perpetual check as after 45 ♕xf4 ♖xf4, the queen protects e8.

42 ♕xf7+ ♖3xf7 43 ♘d5 ♖c8 44 ♖c2 ♖c5 45 ♖d1 ♘g4 46 ♘f4!

White is defending well. Black was threatening the trick of 46...♖xf2+! winning a vital pawn.

46...g5 47 h3 ♘xf2 48 ♔xf2 gxf4 49 g4 d5 50 ♖d3 ♖fc7 51 ♔f3 ♔f7 52 ♖d4 ♔e6 53 ♖xf4 ♖b5 54 ♔e3 ♖b4 55 ♖f5 a4 56 bxa4 ♖xa4 57 ♔d3 ♖a3 58 ♖f8 ♔e5 59 ♖e8+ ♔f4 60 ♖d8 ♔e5 ½-½

Game 11
Hlian-Poluljahov
Azov 1995

1 d4 f5 2 ♘f3 ♘f6 3 g3 e6 4 ♗g2 ♗e7 5 0-0 0-0 6 c4 d6 7 b3 ♕e8 8 ♗a3 a5 9 ♘c3 ♘a6!?

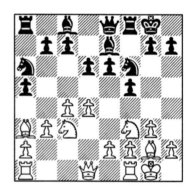

10 ♖e1

Two strong Hungarian Grandmasters have treated this position differently.

a) 10 e3 c6! 11 ♖c1 ♖b8 12 ♗b2 b5 is the main idea in the black set-up. The knight might not look good at a6, but it will soon find a pleasant future. In the meantime White has to deal with the treat of ...bxc4. Probably best is 13 ♘d2 and not 13 cxb5 cxb5 after which Black has won control over the light squares in the centre. 14 ♘e1 ♗b7 15 ♗xb7 ♖xb7 16 ♕e2 ♘c7 17 ♘d3 b4 gave Black a good game in Ribli-Lobron, Bundesliga 1996.

b) 10 ♖c1 and now:

b1) 10...♗d7 11 e3 ♘b4 12 ♗b2 ♕h5 13 a3 ♘a6 14 ♘d2 gave White the advantage in Portisch-Corden, Hastings 1969/70. Black

---

obviously did not have any idea of why he was putting the knight on a6.

b2) 10...♖b8! 11 ♗b2 c6 12 ♕d3 b5! and Black has good counterplay.

Neither e2-e3 nor ♖c1 does anything to control the ...b7-b5 idea.

10...c6 11 ♘a4

11 e4? would be premature due to 11...fxe4 12 ♘d2 (12 ♘xe4 ♘xe4 13 ♖xe4 d5! and Black wins material) 12...d5 13 ♗xe7 ♕xe7 and Black is just a pawn up. Danner-Naumkin, Budapest 1995.

11...♘d7

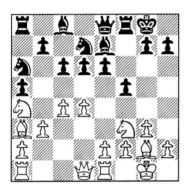

12 d5!?

The idea behind this is a pawn sacrifice. White is gaining the d4-square for his knight and preventing the b5 idea in return. 12 ♗b2 ♖b8! and ...b7-b5 hurts White a lot more.

12...cxd5?!

Black should consider declining the sacrifice with 12...exd5! 13 cxd5 c5 and the position remains unclear, but most likely not worse for Black.

13 ♘d4!

13 cxd5 e5 would be a positional mistake, allowing Black to get a preferable structure.

13...♖f6

Black has no obvious choices. After 13...e5? 14 ♗xd5+ ♔h8 15 ♘b5 his position is hideous, and after 13...♘f6? 14 ♘b6 ♖b8 15 cxd5 e5 16 ♘xc8 ♕xc8 17 ♘e6 it is nothing but awful. Also 13...♘dc5?! 14 cxd5 (14 ♘b6?! ♖b8 15 ♘xc8 ♖xc8 16 cxd5 e5 17

♘e6 ♖f6 would not be so bad for Black) 14...e5 15 ♘e6! ♘xe6 16 dxe6 ♕d8 17 ♖c1 would give White good chances to develop an initiative.

14 ♖c1!?

After 14 ♘b5 ♘dc5! 15 ♗xc5 dxc5 16 ♘b6 ♖b8 17 ♘a7 ♗d7 18 cxd5 e5 the position would have been unclear.

14...♖b8

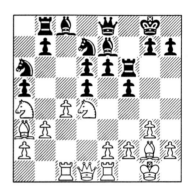

This time Black has a real alternative. Not 14...dxc4?! 15 ♘b5! which is uncomfortable, but 14...♘dc5!? is interesting:

a) 15 cxd5 ♘xa4! (15...e5 would be bad due to 16 ♘xc5! ♘xc5 17 ♗xc5 dxc5 18 ♘e6 with a lovely position for White) 16 bxa4 e5 would give Black a fine position.

b) 15 ♘b6 15...♖b8 16 cxd5 e5 17 ♘xc8 (17 ♘e6 ♘xe6 18 ♘xc8 ♘ec5! would be fine for Black) 17...♖xc8 18 ♘e6 b6 would give an unclear game. The knight looks well placed on e6, but does not really do so much on its own.

15 ♕d2 dxc4 16 bxc4

White has sacrificed a pawn, but his pieces have gained a lot of activity in return. The position is still very unclear.

16...♘dc5

Also possible is 16...♘ac5 17 ♕xa5 ♕h5 18 ♘xc5 dxc5 19 ♖cd1 with a mess!

17 ♘b6 a4 18 ♖ed1 ♗d7?!

This is not very ambitious. Black should also look at 18...♘e4?! 19 ♗xe4 fxe4 20 ♘b5 ♖h6 21 ♗xd6 ♕h5

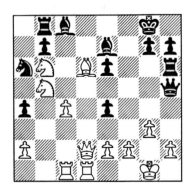

and now:

a) 22 g4!? ♕xg4+ 23 ♗g3 e5 24 ♘xc8 ♖xc8 25 ♕d5+ and here Black can play both 25...♖e6 and 25...♔f8 with a very unclear position as a result. Both kings are exposed and both players have both good and bad pieces.

b) 22 ♕xh6 ♕xh6 23 ♗xe7 e5! 24 ♗d6 ♗g4 25 ♗xb8 ♘xb8 26 ♖d8+ ♔f7 27 ♖b1 ♘c6 is also not clear.

c) 22 h4! ♗xh4 23 gxh4 ♕xh4 24 ♕xh6 (the only move) 24...♕xh6 25 ♗xb8 ♘xb8 26 ♘xc8 ♕g5+ 27 ♔f1 ♕h4 28 e3 ♘c6 and White looks to be in pretty good shape.

However, after 18...♖h6 19 ♘b5 e5 (19...♕h5? would be too soon due to 20 ♘xd6! 20...♕xh2+ 21 ♔f1 ♗d7 22 ♘xf5! 22...exf5 23 ♘xd7 ♖d8 24 ♕d5+ and White wins) 20 ♘xc8 ♖xc8 21 ♗xb7 ♘xb7 22 ♕d5+ ♔h8 23 ♕xb7 ♘c5 Black has a quite attractive position, even though the chances remain pretty balanced.

19 ♖b1! ♕d8

Or 19...♗c6!? 20 ♘xc6 bxc6 21 ♕c2 (21 ♕a5? ♕d8! would leave the knight in permanent trouble) 21...d5! (Black finds his compensation in the centre; 21...f4?! 22 ♘xa4 would not be sufficient) 22 ♘xa4 ♖xb1 23 ♖xb1 ♘e4 24 ♗xe7 ♕xe7 25 ♖b6 ♕a7! (aiming at f2!) 26 e3 ♘ac5 and the game remains unclear.

20 ♘xd7! ♕xd7 21 ♗xc5 ♘xc5

21...dxc5? 22 ♘xf5 would be a terrible blunder.

22 ♘c6 ♖c8 23 ♘xe7+ ♕xe7 24 ♕xd6 ♖f7 ½-½

The endgame looks pretty level. Bishop and rook is better than knight and rook, but the knight is well placed on c5.

Game 12
Kotov-Sokolsky
Moscow 1947

---

1 d4 e6 2 ♘f3 f5 3 g3 ♘f6 4 ♗g2 ♗e7 5 0-0 0-0 6 c4 d6 7 b3 ♕e8 8 ♗a3 a5

Also possible is 8...e5 9 dxe5 dxe5 10 ♗b2 e4 11 ♘d4 c6 12 ♘c3 ♕g6 13 ♕c2 with a level game.

9 ♘c3 ♘a6 10 ♗b2

White has not received any benefits from the loss of time he has suffered.

10...♕h5 11 a3 c6 12 ♘a2?!

This move would not have been made by a top player of our day. 12 e3, with the idea of ♘c3-e2, looks more prudent.

12...♘e4 13 ♘d2

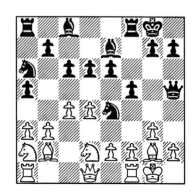

13...e5!

White's pieces are not very well placed, which gives Black the freedom of opening the position with this pawn sacrifice.

14 ♘xe4 fxe4 15 ♗xe4 ♗g4 16 f3 ♗h3 17 ♖f2 exd4 18 ♗xd4?!

Again this does not bring harmony to the position. After 18 ♕xd4 ♗f6 19 ♕d2 the position would have remained unclear.

18...♘c5 19 ♘c3 ♘xe4 20 ♘xe4 d5!

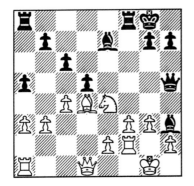

Black is not giving White any breathing space to organise a defence.

21 g4 ♕f7 22 cxd5 ♕xd5 23 ♗b6 ♕e6?

Black is counting on the ...♗h4 idea, which turns out to be worthless. Better was 23...♗xg4 24 ♕xd5+ cxd5 25 fxg4 dxe4 26 ♖xf8+ ♔xf8 with a level endgame.

24 ♕d3! ♗h4

24...a4! was probably better. It is always hard to decide when things go wrong in a downward trend. Black is playing his plan, but it turns out to be no good.

25 ♕c4 ♕xc4 26 bxc4 h5

Black needs to free his bishop.

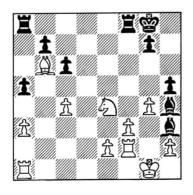

27 gxh5!!

A brilliant concept – White gives up the exchange. If instead 27 ♘g3 then 27...hxg4 28 f4 ♖ae8 and Black has a strong position.

27...♗xf2+ 28 ♔xf2 ♗e6

28...♖ae8 29 ♘d6 ♖e6 30 c5 ♖e5 would

perhaps have offered a bit more confusion, even though Black is in trouble once he loses the b7- and a5-pawns.

29 ♖g1 ♗xc4

This is not the way to defend. Now White wins easily.

30 h6 g6 31 ♖xg6+ ♔h7 32 ♖d6 ♖f5

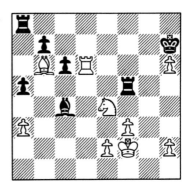

33 h4!

Forcing ♘g5 after which the game is finished.

33...♖g8 34 ♗e3!

Taking full control over g5.

34...♖g6 35 ♖d7+!

35 ♘g5+ ♖fxg5 36 ♖d7+ ♖g7 37 ♖xg7+ ♖xg7 38 hxg7 ♔xg7 also wins for White, but this is faster.

35...♖f7 36 ♖d8 ♖xh6 37 ♗xh6 ♔xh6 38 ♘d6 ♖f4 39 ♔g3 1-0

Black is right out of luck.

> **Game 13**
> **Paunovic-Naumkin**
> *Namestovo 1987*

1 d4 e6 2 ♘f3 f5 3 g3 ♘f6 4 ♗g2 ♗e7 5 0-0 0-0 6 c4 d6 7 ♘c3 a5 8 b3 ♕e8 9 ♗a3 ♕h5 10 ♕c2 ♘c6

This is a standard position in the Classical Dutch.

11 ♖ad1!

White should first develop and only then think about advancing in the centre. After 11 d5 ♘b4! 12 ♗xb4 axb4 13 ♘b5 ♗d8 14 dxe6 ♗xe6 15 ♘bd4 ♗c8 16 c5, as in Mikenas-Rostein, Riga 1962, Black can get a strong position with 16...d5!, when his control over the dark squares promises him an advantage.

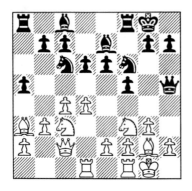

11...♗d7?!

Here Black should try 11...♘b4! 12 ♕b1 ♘g4 13 ♗c1 ♘f6 14 a3 ♘c6 15 ♘b5 (15 d5? would be a mistake on account of 15...♘d4!) 15...♗d8 16 d5 ♘ce5 with an unclear game, Csom-Glek, Moscow 1989.

12 d5

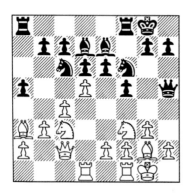

12...♘b4!?

Black cannot play this passively – his structure is not built for it. After 12...♘d8!? 13 ♘e5! ♘g4 14 ♘xg4 fxg4 15 dxe6 ♗xe6 16 ♘d5 ♗xd5 17 ♗xd5+ ♔h8 18 f3 White would have the advantage, but still this is better than the game.

13 ♗xb4 axb4

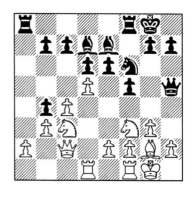

14 dxe6!

This is the problem in this line for Black. White gains the d5-square for his knight or all the light squares.

14...bxc3?

After this White has a clear advantage. It was better to try 14...♗xe6!? 15 ♘d5! ♗xd5 (15...♗d8 16 ♘f4 ♕e8 17 ♘xe6 ♕xe6 18 ♘d4 gives White a material advantage to supplement the positional one) 16 cxd5 ♘e4 17 ♖d4!? ♗f6 18 ♖xb4 and White apparently has the advantage. The game should now continue 18...♘c3 19 a4 ♖fe8 (19...b5 20 ♘d4 ♗xd4 21 ♗f3! gives White a clear advantage) 20 ♖xb7 ♘xe2+ 21 ♔h1 f4 22 g4! (22 ♕xc7? fxg3 23 ♕xd6 ♖ad8! would give Black excellent counterplay) 22...♕xg4 23 ♕xc7 and White has better prospects, but all of this is not easy to see.

15 exd7 ♘xd7 16 ♘d4 c6 17 a4 f4 18 ♕xc3 fxg3 19 ♕xg3

19 fxg3! would leave White a clear pawn up with Black having no serious compensation.

19...♖f6 20 ♕h3 ♕e8 21 ♘f5 ♗f8

21...♘c5 22 e4 ♗f8 23 ♖fe1 would transpose to the game.

22 e4 ♘c5 23 ♖fe1 ♕e5 24 ♕e3 ♘e6 25 ♔h1?

I do not know what happened to White in this phase of the game. He has a clear advantage and only needs to play a few precise moves to really prove it, but now it is slip-

ping away. Better was 25 ♘xd6! ♖h6
(25...♗xd6 26 ♖xd6 ♖xf2 27 ♕xf2 ♕xd6 28
e5 would give White a clear plus) 26 ♘f5
♕xh2+ 27 ♔f1 ♖g6 28 ♕h3 ♕e5 29 ♕h5
and White is certainly better.

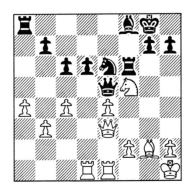

25...g6 26 ♘xd6?

Now this does not work out as the knight
has no good retreat square. 26 ♘g3 ♘f4
would give Black good compensation, but
things are about to change!

26...♘c5!

Now the knight is trapped.

27 f4

27 b4 ♗xd6! also doesn't work.

**27...♖xf4 28 ♕d4 ♕xd4 29 ♖xd4 ♘xb3
30 ♖dd1 ♗xd6 31 ♖xd6 ♘c5**

The knight is perfectly placed here and
cannot be removed in any way. Black is simply winning.

32 a5 ♖xa5 33 ♖d8+ ♔g7 34 e5 ♖a2 35

h3 ♖ff2 36 ♖dd1 ♖xg2 37 e6 ♖ge2 38
e7 ♔f7 0-1

Game 14
Orlinkov-Kobalija
Moscow 1994

**1 d4 f5 2 g3 ♘f6 3 ♗g2 e6 4 ♘f3 ♗e7
5 0-0 0-0 6 c4 d6 7 b3 a5 8 ♘c3 ♕e8 9
♕c2**

White is starting a hybrid between two
plans here. Instead he should choose between b2-b3 and ♗g5.

**9...♕h5 10 e4 e5 11 dxe5 dxe5 12 ♗g5
fxe4 13 ♘xe4 ♘c6 14 ♘xf6+**

After 14 ♗xf6 gxf6! Black is already better. White has really no compensation for the
weaknesses on the dark squares. 14...♗xf6 15
♖fe1, however, is good for White.

14...♗xf6 15 ♗xf6 ♖xf6

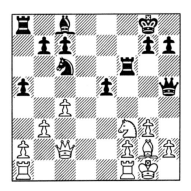

16 ♕e4?

Here White misplaces the queen. Instead
he should have tried 16 ♘h4! and now Black
has a choice:

a) 16...♘d4!? 17 ♕e4 ♕e2 and here 18
♖ae1 keeps the balance.

b) 16...g5!? 17 ♗d5+ ♔h8 18 ♗xc6 ♖xc6
19 ♘f5 ♕f3 20 ♘e3 is unclear.

c) 16...a4 17 ♗xc6 ♖xc6 18 ♕e4 ♗e6
with good play for Black.

16...♗g4!

A key aspect of utilising a lead in development is to try to increase it.

17 ♘d2 ♖d8!

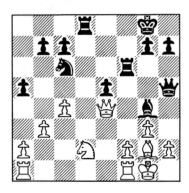

All the black pieces are playing!

18 ♕e3 ♘d4!

Bringing the knight into the attack with the creation of further threats. 18...♖h6? 19 h4 ♘d4 20 ♗xb7! ♘c2 21 ♕g5 would give White counterplay.

19 ♘e4

White is under a cloud after 19 f3 ♖h6 20 h4 (20 fxg4 ♕xh2+ 21 ♔f2 ♖f6+ is goodnight for White) 20...♗f5 21 ♘e4 (or 21 ♖ac1 ♖g6! 22 g4 ♕xh4 23 gxf5 ♖xg2+ 24 ♔xg2 ♘xf5 25 ♕f2 ♕g5+ 26 ♔h1 ♖xd2 and Black wins) 21...♘c2 22 ♕g5 ♕xg5 23 hxg5 ♖g6 24 ♖ad1 ♖f8 25 ♖f2 ♗xe4 26 fxe4 ♖xf2 27 ♔xf2 ♘d4 – Black has excellent winning chances in the endgame.

19 ♗d5+?! loses directly to 19...♖xd5! 20 cxd5 ♗f3! 21 h4 ♕g4 22 ♘xf3 ♘xf3+ 23 ♔g2 ♘xh4+ 24 ♔g1 ♕h3 25 gxh4 ♖g6+ 26

♕g5 ♖xg5+ 27 hxg5 ♕g4+ 28 ♔h2 ♕h5+ 29 ♔g3 ♕xg5+ and the queen is stronger than the uncoordinated rooks.

19...♖f5

Wrong would be 19...♘e2+?! 20 ♔h1 ♖h6 21 h4 ♕xh4+?! 22 gxh4 ♖xh4+ 23 ♗h3 ♖xh3+ (23...♗xh3?? 24 ♕g5! and suddenly White wins) 24 ♕xh3 ♗xh3 25 ♖fd1 and White has some chances of saving the endgame, even though it is clearly better for Black.

20 ♖ab1

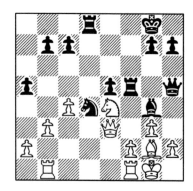

20...♘f3+!

The simplest way. After 20...♘e2+? 21 ♔h1 ♕xh2+ 22 ♔xh2 ♖h5+ 23 ♗h3 ♗xh3 24 ♕g5! ♖xg5 25 ♔xh3 White can still fight.

21 ♗xf3 ♗xf3

The move ...♕xh2+ is threatened.

22 h4 ♖d4! 23 ♘g5 ♖xh4! 24 ♕xf3 ♖xf3 0-1

Summary

In this Chapter we have looked at 7...a5 8 b3 ♕e8. For now Black looks to be in good shape, but the positions are very messy and nothing can be taken for granted just because it is now written down in a book. This is probably the place where white players will try to come with improvements in the future, and with good reason. This still looks like the most natural way to organise the pieces.

1 d4 f5 2 c4 ♘f6 3 g3 e6 4 ♗g2 ♗e7 5 ♘f3 0-0 6 0-0 d6 7 ♘c3 a5 8 b3 ♕e8 (D) 9 ♗b2

      9 ♕c2 – *Game 14*

      9 ♗a3

            9...♕h5 – *Game 13*

            9...♘a6

                  10 ♗b2 – *Game 12*

                  10 ♖e1 c6 11 ♘a4 ♘d7

                        12 d5 – *Game 11*

                        12 ♗b2 – *Game 10*

9...♕h5

      9...♗d8 – *Game 8*

      9...c6 – *Game 9*

      9...♘a6

            10 ♖e1– *Game 5*

            10 a3 (D) – *Game 6*

            10 e3 – *Game 7*

10 ♕c2

      10 ♖e1 – *Game 3*; 10 e3 – *Game 4*

10...♘c6

      10...♘a6 – *Game 2*

11 ♖ad1 ♗d7 (D) – *Game 1*

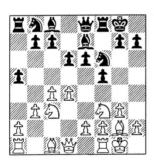
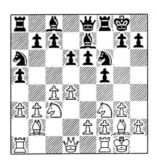

    8...♕e8   *10 a3*   *11...♗d7*

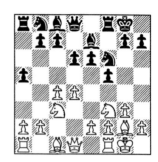

CHAPTER TWO

Main Line: 7 ♘c3 a5 – 8th Move Alternatives

1 d4 f5 2 c4 e6 3 ♘f3 ♘f6 4 g3 ♗e7 5 ♗g2 0-0 6 0-0 d6 7 ♘c3 a5

In this chapter we will be looking at eighth move alternatives for White against 7...a5. First of all there is 8 ♕c2!? (Games 15-16), which is responsible for a quick break in the centre with e2-e4. This line gives a slight advantage for White as far as I have been able to deduce, but Black has plenty of play. One of the critical positions is where Black sacrifices a pawn for full activity. I feel that the pawn is perhaps more important than the activity, but it is a very narrow choice, and I might be wrong.

8 ♖e1 (Games 19-22) is not really dangerous as after the idea 8...♘e4, White has neither 9 ♘xe4 nor 9 ♕c2 ♘xc3 10 ♕xc3 followed by b2-b4, as he has after 7...♘e4 in Chapter 3. The move 8 ♗g5 leads to a quite interesting game after both 8...♕e8 (Game 17) and 8...♘c6 (Game 18), but in both cases without any great chances for an advantage for White.

> ### Game 15
> ### Kallai-Poluljahov
> *Budapest 1992*

1 d4 e6 2 c4 f5 3 ♘f3 ♘f6 4 g3 ♗e7 5 ♗g2 0-0 6 0-0 d6 7 ♘c3 a5 8 ♕c2 ♘c6

9 e4 ♘b4 10 ♕e2 fxe4 11 ♘xe4 ♘xe4 12 ♕xe4 e5 13 g4

The more natural 13 dxe5 is considered in the next game.

13...h5!

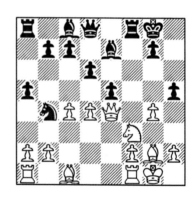

Fire versus fire! Black is not afraid.

14 h3?!

This has not worked out in practice. Also possible are the following:

a) 14 a3!? hxg4 15 axb4 gxf3 16 ♗xf3 c6 17 dxe5 ♗f5 18 ♕e3 dxe5 19 ♖d1 ♕c7 20 bxa5 ♖xa5 21 ♖xa5 ♕xa5 with a level playing ground.

b) 14 dxe5 ♗xg4 (14...hxg4 15 exd6 ♕xd6 16 ♘g5 ♗f5 17 ♕xb7 c6 looks good for Black too) 15 ♖d1 (15 ♕xb7? ♖b8 16 ♕e4 ♗f5 17 ♕d4 ♘c2 18 ♕d5+ ♔h8 19 exd6

♕xd6 is more or less a catastrophe for White) 15...♕e8 16 a3 ♘c6 and Black's position is preferable.

c) 14 gxh5? ♗f5 is in Black's favour.

14...hxg4 15 hxg4 c6?

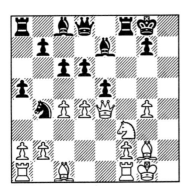

Black is playing too slowly, and if there is one thing you should try to avoid in the Classical Dutch, it's to lose the momentum once you've got it. Here the best move was 15...♕d7! 16 g5 (uncomfortable, but probably necessary is 16 ♗h3 exd4 17 ♘xd4 ♗f6 with a strong position for Black) and now:

a) 16...♕f5? 17 ♘h4! ♕xe4 18 ♗xe4 exd4 19 a3 ♘c6 (19...d5 20 ♗g2! does not improve anything) 20 ♗d5+ ♔h7 21 g6+ ♔h8 22 ♔g2 and White will enter the h-file with evil intentions.

b) 16...♕g4! 17 ♕xg4 ♗xg4 18 ♘h4 ♗e2 19 ♖e1 ♗xc4 20 ♘g6 ♘c2 21 ♘xe7+ ♔f7 and Black is on his way to a very good result.

16 a3?

Now White in turn misses his chance. After 16 dxe5! d5 (16...dxe5 17 ♘xe5 ♗d6 18 ♖d1 ♕f6 19 ♘f3 ♗c7 20 ♗e3 does not offer full compensation for the pawn either) 17 ♕g6 ♕e8 18 ♕xe8 ♖xe8 19 cxd5 cxd5 20 ♘d4! ♗c5 21 a3 ♗xd4 22 axb4 ♗xg4 23 ♗xd5+ White is in great shape.

16...d5 17 cxd5 cxd5 18 ♕xe5 ♘d3 19 ♕h5 ♘f4

19...♖a6?! 20 ♘e1! would expose the weakness of the d5-pawn.

20 ♗xf4 ♖xf4 21 ♘e5 ♖a6 22 ♘g6?

White could still have held a strong position after 22 ♖ac1! ♖h6 23 ♘g6! ♖xh5 24 ♖xc8 ♖xg4 25 ♘xe7+ ♔f7 26 ♖xd8 ♔xe7 27 ♖b8 ♖hg5 28 ♖xb7+ ♔d6 29 ♖d1 ♖xg2+ 30 ♔f1 ♖g1+ 31 ♔e2 ♖xd1 32 ♔xd1 ♖g4 33 ♔e2 ♖xd4 34 ♖xg7 a4 35 f3. Black has practical difficulties in defending this endgame.

22...♖xg6 23 ♕xg6 ♖xg4 24 ♕d3 ♗d6 25 ♖ac1

25 ♖fe1?! ♕h4 26 ♖e8+ ♔f7 27 ♖e5 ♗xe5 28 dxe5 ♗e6 is unclear, or maybe even slightly better for Black, but 25 ♖fc1!? ♗d7 26 ♔f1 ♕g5 27 ♕h3 ♗b5+ 28 ♔g1 ♗d7 29 ♖e1 ♕g6 would keep matters just 'unclear'.

25...♖xg2+! 26 ♔xg2 ♕g5+ 27 ♔h1??

A terrible blunder by the Hungarian IM, who is now a GM. 27 ♕g3! ♗xg3 28 ♖xc8+ ♔h7 29 fxg3 ♕d2+ 30 ♖f2 ♕xd4 with a likely draw was necessary, even though Black will probably insist on testing his opponent for some moves.

27...♗f5! 28 ♖c8+

28 ♕e3 ♕h4+ 29 ♔g2 ♕g4+ 30 ♔h1 ♗e4+ 31 f3 ♕h3+ would lead to mate.

28...♔h7 0-1

Game 16
Pavlovic-Naumkin
Wildbad 1991

1 d4 e6 2 c4 f5 3 g3 ♘f6 4 ♗g2 ♗e7 5 ♘f3 0-0 6 0-0 d6 7 ♘c3 a5 8 ♕d3 ♘c6 9 e4 ♘b4 10 ♕e2 fxe4 11 ♘xe4 ♘xe4

12 ♕xe4 e5 13 dxe5 ♗f5 14 ♕xb7 ♖b8 15 ♕a7 ♗d3

15...♖a8 16 ♕d4 ♘c2 does not work due to 17 ♕d5+ ♔h8 18 ♘d4! and Black is in trouble.

16 ♖e1

16 exd6 ♗xd6? (or 16...cxd6? 17 ♖d1 ♗f6 18 a3!) 17 ♗g5 ♕d7 (17...♘e8 18 ♖fe1 ♕h5 19 b3!) 18 ♖fc1 ♕f5 looks like a critical line for the pawn sacrifice. After 19 ♗e3, which looks strongest, Black has 19...♘c6 20 ♘d4 ♘xa7 21 ♘xf5 ♖xf5 22 ♗xa7 ♖xb2 with a very active position for the pawn, but maybe this is not quite enough. A logical place for further study!

16...♘c2 17 exd6 ♗xd6

17...♘xe1? 18 ♘xe1! and White wins.

18 ♗g5 ♕d7?!

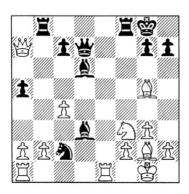

A dubious move. Better was 18...♕c8!, threatening ♖a8. 19 ♕xa5 ♕f5 20 ♕xf5 ♖xf5 21 b3 ♖bf8! (21...♘xa1 22 ♖xa1 ♖bf8 23 ♘e1 ♗xc4 24 bxc4 ♖xg5 25 ♗d5+ ♔h8 26 a4 ♖e5 27 ♔f1 gives White good chances to bag a full point in the endgame) 22 ♖ad1 ♘xe1 23 ♘xe1 ♗e2 24 ♖d5 ♗c5 25 ♖xc5 ♖xc5 26 ♗e7 ♖a5 gives Black an active position, and it seems like the rook is stronger than the knight and two pawns. Notice that after 27 ♗xf8 ♔xf8 28 a4 ♗d1! all the queenside is exposed.

19 c5 ♘xe1

Not possible is 19...♖a8 20 ♕b7! (20 ♘e5 ♗xe5 21 ♗xa8 ♗d4 22 ♗f4 ♘xa1 23 ♖xa1

♗xf2+ is less clear) 20...♗xc5 21 ♘e5 ♗xf2+ 22 ♔h1 and White has a winning position.

20 ♖xe1 ♖a8 21 ♕b7 ♗xc5 22 ♘e5??

A terrible blunder. After 22 ♕b3+! 22...♔h8 23 ♖d1 ♗xf2+ 24 ♔xf2 ♕f5 25 ♕xd3 ♕xg5 26 ♔g1 White is simply winning.

22...♗xf2+ 23 ♔h1 ♕f5?

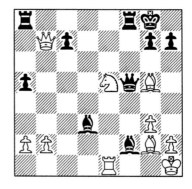

Black also misses the chance. After 23...♖ae8! 24 ♕d5+ ♗f7! White needs to play 25 ♖e2! (as 25 ♘xd7 ♖xe1+ 26 ♗f1 ♗e4+ decides) 25...♕xd5 26 ♗xd5 ♗xe2 27 ♗xf7+ ♔f8 28 ♗xe8 ♔xe8, when Black remains slightly better in the endgame.

24 ♕d5+?

White misses what would have been a magnificent prize-winning combination. 24 ♗h3!! ♕xh3 (24...♕xg5 25 ♕d5+ ♔h8 26 ♘f7+ and mate follows) 25 ♕d5+ ♔h8 26 ♘f7+ with mate in a few moves.

24...♔h8 25 ♘xd3?

White would still be better after 25 g4! c6 26 ♕xc6 ♕c8 (26...♖ac8? 27 gxf5 ♖xc6 28 ♗xc6 ♗xe1 29 ♘xd3 ♖xf5 30 ♗e3 and White wins) 27 ♕xa8 ♕xa8 28 ♗xa8.

25...♗xe1 26 ♕xf5 ♖xf5 27 ♗xa8 ♖xg5!

Black needs the time. After 27...♗xg3?! 28 hxg3 ♖xg5 29 ♔g2 White is even better, as the playing pieces are more important than the pawn.

28 ♘xe1 ♖e5 29 ♘f3

29 ♘d3 ♖e3 30 ♘f4 g5 31 ♘d5 ♖e2 looks promising for Black too.

29...♖e2 30 a4 ♖xb2 31 ♗c6 ♖c2 32 ♘e5 ♖c5!

Precise play. After 32...♔g8? 33 ♘c4! White picks up the a-pawn due to ♗d5+.

33 ♘f7+ ♔g8 34 ♘d8 ♖c2 35 ♗d5+ ♔f8

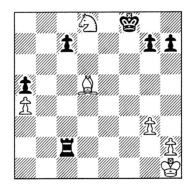

36 ♘e6+??

36 ♘b7 ♔e7 37 ♔g1 is probably just a drawn endgame, even though it is not decided yet.

36...♔e7 37 ♘xg7

37 ♘d4 ♖d2 38 ♘c6+ ♔d6 39 ♗f3 ♖f2 40 ♘d4 ♖a2 41 ♘b5+ ♔e5 42 ♘xc7 ♖xa4 would give excellent winning chances too.

37...♔f6 38 ♘e6 c6 39 ♗b3 ♖c3 40 ♘d8 ♔e7 41 ♘xc6+ ♖xc6 42 ♔g2 ♖b6 43 ♗d5 ♔d6 44 ♗f7 ♖b2+ 45 ♔h3 ♖e2 46 ♗c4 ♖e4 47 ♗b5 ♖b4 48 ♗e8 ♖b8 49 ♗f7 ♔e5 50 g4?

A tougher defence was 50 ♗h5 ♖b4 51 ♗e8 ♔d5 though Black will probably win this too.

50...♔f6 51 ♗d5 ♖b4 52 ♗c6 ♔g5 0-1

Game 17
Zaitsev-Naumkin
Moscow 1989

For annotating this game I have based my notes on those by GM Igor Zaitsev published in *Chess Informant 48*.

1 d4 e6 2 c4 f5 3 ♘f3 ♘f6 4 g3 ♗e7 5 ♗g2 0-0 6 0-0 d6 7 ♘c3 a5 8 ♗g5!?

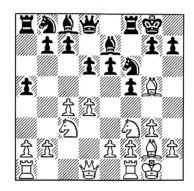

White's idea is to fight for the control of the centre.

8...♕e8 9 ♖c1 ♕h5

The deeper nuances behind 8 ♗g5 are illustrated in the following line: 9...♕g6 10 e4! 10...fxe4 11 ♘xe4 ♕xe4 12 ♘h4!. Normally the queen is trapped in such situations, but here Black has the g4-square. Still, White is not too unhappy. 12...♕g4 13 ♕xg4 ♘xg4 14 ♗xe7 ♖f7 (14...♖e8 15 ♗g5 is a little better for White)

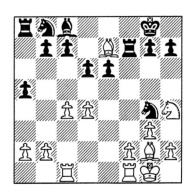

and now:

a) 15 c5 is very creative, but doesn't really work: 15...♖xe7 16 cxd6 ♖f7! (16...♖e8? 17 dxc7 ♘c6 18 ♖xc6! bxc6 19 ♗xc6 would give White a clear advantage) 17 d5 c6 18 ♖fe1 e5 19 f4 e4 20 ♖xe4 ♘f6 and the consequences of White's play are unclear.

b) 15 ♗g5! with a small advantage.

10 ♖e1 ♘c6 11 ♗xf6 ♗xf6 12 e4

White has succeeded in carrying out his plan, but at the price of giving up the two bishops.

12...e5 13 dxe5 dxe5 14 ♘d5 ♗d8?

This is rather passive. The move 14...fxe4!? is something for the fans of 'the wizard from Riga', Mikhail Tal.

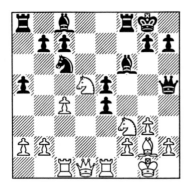

a) 15 ♖xe4 (this puts the fire out) 15...♗f5 16 ♘xf6+ gxf6 (16...♖xf6 17 ♖h4 ♕e8 18 ♕d5+ ♗e6 19 ♕b5 looks better for White) 17 ♕d5+ ♔h8 18 ♖ee1 with unclear play.

b) 15 ♘xc7 (the most testing move) 15...♖d8 16 ♕e2 exf3 17 ♗xf3 ♕g5 18 ♘xa8 ♘d4 19 ♕d1 (19 ♕e4 ♗f5 20 ♕xb7 ♖d7 21 ♗d5+ ♔h8 22 f4 ♕h5 23 ♕b6 ♘e2+ 24 ♖xe2 ♕xe2 gives an unclear position too) 19...e4! 20 ♗xe4 ♗g4 21 h4 ♕h5 with wild complications.

15 exf5 ♕xf5

The only possible recapture. After 15...♗xf5? 16 ♘xe5 ♕h6 17 ♘xc6 bxc6 18 ♘e3 White has a clear edge, and if 15...♖xf5 16 g4! ♕xg4 17 ♘e3 he wins material.

16 ♕e2 ♗d7

After 16...♕f7 17 ♘xe5 ♘xe5 18 ♕xe5 ♕xf2+ 19 ♔h1 ♕f5 20 ♕xf5 ♗xf5 21 ♘e7+ ♗xe7 22 ♖xe7 White also has an overwhelming position.

17 ♖cd1

Here White is somewhat slow. After 17 ♘xe5! ♘xe5 18 ♕xe5 ♕xf2+ 19 ♔h1 ♖f5 20 ♕c3 c6 21 ♘e7+ ♗xe7 22 ♖xe7 ♖f7 23 ♖ce1 he clearly has a strong initiative.

17...♗e8!?

Black is going for active counterplay.

18 ♘xe5 ♗h5 19 f3?!

Here White has 19 g4! ♘xe5 20 gxh5 ♘g4 21 ♖d4 with advantage, as after 21...♕xf2+ 22 ♕xf2 ♘xf2 23 ♖f1 c5 24 ♖f4 ♖xf4 25 ♘xf4 ♘g4 26 ♗xb7 the black position cannot be saved.

19...♖e8 20 g4 ♕xe5 21 ♕xe5 ♘xe5 22 gxh5 ♔f8 23 ♖e4?!

More exact was 23 f4 ♘d7 24 ♖xe8+ ♔xe8 25 ♖e1+ ♔f8 26 f5 ♘c5 27 ♘f4 and White has full control over the situation.

23...c6 24 ♘f4

Or 24 f4!? cxd5 25 ♖xe5 dxc4 26 ♗xb7 ♖b8 27 ♖b5 ♖e2 28 ♖c1 ♖e7 29 ♖f5+ ♖f7 30 ♖xf7+ ♔xf7 31 ♗d5+ ♔f6 32 ♖c2 ♔f5 33 ♗xc4 ♗f6 with a small advantage for White.

24...♔f7 25 ♔f1 ♗f6 26 b3 ♖ed8?!

26...a4 27 b4 b6! 28 ♘d3 ♘xd3 29 ♖xe8 ♖xe8 30 ♖xd3 ♖d8 and, after the exchange of rooks, the position is just a dead draw.

27 ♖xd8 ♖xd8 28 ♔e2 a4

Or 28...b5 29 ♗h3!.

29 bxa4 ♖a8

After 29...♘d7?! 30 ♘d3 ♘b6 31 ♘c5 ♗c3 32 f4 ♖d2+ 33 ♔f3 ♖xa2 34 ♘xb7 ♘xa4 35 ♘d8+ ♔f8 36 ♘xc6 White has a clear advantage.

30 c5!

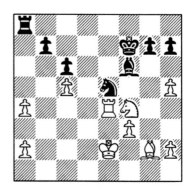

Fixing some weaknesses for the light-squared bishop to attack.

30...♘d7 31 ♘d3 ♗c3

Black is in a downward trend and should have done something in order to get out of it. The complicated 31...♗e7! 32 ♗h3 ♘xc5 loses a piece to 33 ♖xe7+ (33 ♖f4+ ♔e8 34 ♘xc5 ♗xc5 35 ♖c4 with a little pressure is also possible). But after 33...♔xe7 34 ♘xc5 b6 35 ♘d7 ♖xa4 36 ♘xb6 ♖xa2+ 37 ♔d3 ♖xh2 Black will escape with a draw.

32 ♗h3 ♘f6 33 ♖c4 ♖e8+ 34 ♔f2 ♗a5 35 ♗g4

White has good control here.

35...♗d2 36 ♖c2 ♗e3+ 37 ♔f1 ♘d5 38 ♖b2 ♗d4

38...♗e7 39 ♗c8! is good for White and 38...♖b8 39 a5! would expose Black to a very annoying a-pawn.

39 ♖xb7+ ♔f6 40 ♗d7 ♖e3 41 ♗xc6

The queenside has finally collapsed and White will cruise to victory.

41...♖xf3+ 42 ♔e2 ♖e3+ 43 ♔d2 ♘c3 44 ♔c2 ♘g5 45 ♖d7 ♘f6 46 ♗b5 ♖e2+ 47 ♔b3 ♘e4 48 ♖d5+ ♔h4 49 c6 ♗e7 50 ♖d4 ♔g5 51 ♖xe4 1-0

Game 18
Tolstikh-Veresagin
Volgograd 1994

---

1 ♘f3 e6 2 c4 f5 3 g3 ♘f6 4 ♗g2 ♗e7 5 0-0 0-0 6 ♘c3 d6 7 d4 a5 8 ♗g5 ♘c6

There is no equality after 8...♘e4. Following 9 ♗xe7 ♕xe7 10 ♘xe4 fxe4 11 ♘d2 d5 12 e3 ♘c6 13 f3 exf3 14 ♖xf3 ♖xf3 15 ♕xf3 dxc4 (an unhappy concession, but it is hard to see how Black could avoid it) 16 ♘xc4 White is somewhat better, Piket-Lobron, Wijk aan Zee 1993.

9 ♗xf6 ♗xf6 10 e4 e5

After 10...fxe4 11 ♘xe4 a4 12 ♖e1 a3 13 b3 White is a little better due to the weakness of the pawn on e6.

11 dxe5 ♘xe5

This seems forced as 11...dxe5 12 ♕d5+ ♕xd5 13 ♘xd5 fxe4 14 ♘d2 ♗d8 15 ♘xe4 gives White a typical advantage.

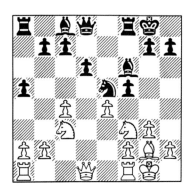

12 exf5 ♗xf5 13 ♘d4

Here White could have decided to grab a pawn with 13 ♘xe5 ♗xe5 14 ♗xb7 ♖b8 15 ♗d5+ ♔h8 16 ♕d2 ♕f6 17 ♖ac1. However, after a move like 17...a4!? it seems that Black has found good counterplay with the dark-squared bishop and the pressure against b2.

13...♗g4 14 ♕b3?

This is not nearly as good as 14 f3 ♗d7 15 f4 ♘c6 16 ♗d5+, even though Black is fine after 16...♔h8 17 ♘xc6 bxc6 18 ♗e4 ♗xc3 19 bxc3 ♕f6.

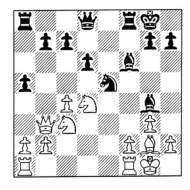

14...c5!

Preventing c4-c5, gaining control over central squares and gaining time too. The slight weakness of the d5-square is no great loss...

15 ♘c2

15 ♗d5+ ♔h8 16 ♘db5 ♘f3+ 17 ♗xf3 ♗xf3 looks very good for Black.

15...♘f3+

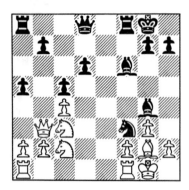

16 ♔h1?!

It is a bitter pill to swallow, but White was forced to play 16 ♗xf3 ♗xf3 after which Black quite obviously has the advantage.

16...♘d2 17 ♕xb7 ♘xf1 18 ♖xf1 ♗xc3 19 bxc3

19 ♕xa8 ♕xa8 20 ♗xa8 ♖xa8 21 bxc3 ♗e2 22 ♖e1 ♗xc4 would present White with a very difficult endgame indeed.

19...♕f6

White does not have enough for the exchange.

20 ♕d5+ ♔h8 21 ♕d2 ♗f3 22 ♘e3

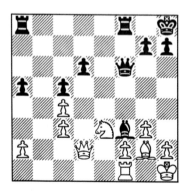

22...♖ab8

22...♖ae8!? 23 ♗xf3 ♕xf3+ 24 ♔g1 ♖f6 was another possibility, with a clear advantage for Black.

23 ♗xf3 ♕xf3+ 24 ♔g1 a4?!

24...♖be8 25 a3 ♖e6 with a clear advan-

tage was better. A black rook on the 6th rank protects d6 and threatens the white king.

25 a3?

The last chance was 25 ♕xd6 ♖b2 26 a3, when Black would have had some problems winning this position.

25...♖b6 26 ♘d5 ♖b3

Now White has no counterplay and Black will simply go and collect some pawns.

27 ♘f4 ♖fb8 28 ♕e1 ♕xc3 29 ♕e6 ♕d4 30 ♕d7 ♖xa3 31 ♘e6 ♕f6 32 ♖e1 ♖a1

Cynical but effective!

33 ♖xa1 ♕xa1+ 34 ♔g2 ♕f6 35 ♕a7 ♖e8 36 ♘f4 ♕e7 37 ♕xa4 ♕e4+ 38 ♔g1 ♖a8 39 ♕d1 0-1

White resigned before Black got around to playing 39...♖b8!.

Game 19
Gallagher-Williams
Port Erin 2001

---

1 d4 f5 2 g3 ♘f6 3 ♗g2 e6 4 ♘f3 ♗e7 5 0-0 0-0 6 c4 d6 7 ♘c3 a5 8 ♖e1

Another way to fight for the centre.

8...♘e4

The natural way to deal with this.

9 ♕c2

White has other options in this position:

a) 9 ♗f4!? ♗f6 (9...g5!? 10 ♗c1 ♗f6 with unclear play would be a novel plan) 10 ♕c2 ♘xc3 11 bxc3 ♘c6 (11...♘d7 12 e4 fxe4 13 ♕xe4 would give White the usual small structural advantage) 12 ♖ad1 ♘e7 13 h4 ♘g6 14 ♗c1 d5?! (this gives Black problems) 15 cxd5 exd5 16 c4 c6 17 cxd5 cxd5 18 ♘e5 and White has a strong initiative, Oll-Beim, Diern 1996. Better for Black is 14...♕e8! (but not 14...a4 15 e4 fxe4 16 ♕xe4 and White is better) 15 e4 fxe4 16 ♕xe4 ♕f7 and Black is better placed to meet the central pressure. This position needs practical tests.

b) 9 ♘xe4 fxe4 10 ♘d2 d5 11 f3 exf3 12 ♘xf3 c5 gave Black good counterplay in Notaros-R.Marcic, Novi Sad 1974.

9...♘xc3 10 ♕xc3

The alternative 10 bxc3 ♗f6 11 e4 fxe4 12 ♕xe4 ♘c6 13 ♗a3 e5 14 d5 ♘e7 15 c5 b5 16 cxb6 cxb6 17 c4 ♗f5 18 ♕e3 was played in Suba-Pamers, Suances 1997. Now 18...♗g6!, with the idea 19 ♘d2 ♘f5, would have given Black good counterplay.

10...♘c6

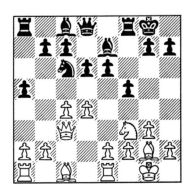

Black obtained a decent position after 10...♗f6 11 ♕c2 (11 b3?! ♘c6 12 ♗b2 e5 13 dxe5 dxe5 14 ♖ad1 ♕e7 15 e4 fxe4 16 ♖xe4 ♗f5 was better for Black in Ayas Fernandez-Pomes Marcet, Barcelona 1996) 11...♘c6 12 ♖d1 ♕e7 13 d5 ♘b4 14 ♕d2 exd5 15 cxd5 ♗d7. The position is equally balanced, though far from boring, San Segundo-Pomes Marcet, San Sebastian 1995.

11 e4

After 11 d5 ♗f6 12 ♕d2 ♘e7 13 ♘d4 e5 14 ♘b5 ♗d7 15 ♕c2 h5! 16 ♗d2 h4 Black was in the midst of organising a terrible at-

tack against the white king, Pigusov-Atalik, 1997.

11...e5 12 exf5 ♗xf5 13 ♗e3

Or 13 dxe5 dxe5 14 c5 ♗f6 (not very healthy is 14...e4 15 ♘d2 ♕d4 16 ♘xe4 ♕xc3 17 bxc3 ♗xe4 18 ♗xe4 ♗xc5 19 ♗e3 ♗xe3 20 ♖xe3, when White has a dangerous initiative) 15 ♕b3+ (White takes the risk and wins the pawn; 15 ♗e3 ♔h8 16 ♖ad1 ♕e7 does not disturb Black) 15...♔h8 16 ♕xb7 ♘b4! 17 ♘xe5 ♘c2 18 ♗f4 ♖b8 19 ♖ad1 ♕e7 20 ♕a7 (20 ♕c6 ♘xe1 21 ♖xe1 ♖xb2 gives a rather messy game too) 20...♘xe1 21 ♖xe1 ♖xb2 and the position is unclear.

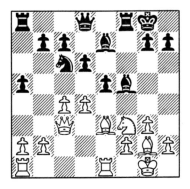

13...♗e4 14 ♘d2?!

This leaves Black with full control over the centre. After 14 ♗d2!? Black plays 14...♗xf3 15 ♗xf3 ♗f6! with an even position, but not 15...♘xd4 16 ♗xb7 ♖b8 17 ♗d5+, which looks better for White.

14...♗xg2 15 ♔xg2 d5!

White must have underestimated this in some way.

16 a3

It is starting to look bad for White. After 16 ♕b3 exd4! (16...♘xd4 17 ♗xd4 exd4 18 cxd5 ♗b4 is less clear) 17 cxd5 a4 18 ♕c4 dxe3 19 dxc6+ ♔h8 20 ♘e4 exf2 21 ♘xf2 bxc6 White has an exposed king and some other worries.

16...♗f6

The white centre is collapsing and Black is clearly better.

17 ♘f3 exd4 18 ♘xd4 ♕d7 19 ♖ad1 ♘e5 20 c5

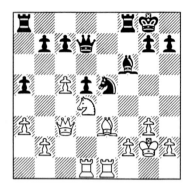

It is painful for any player to make these kind of inactive moves. So Gallagher, known for his attacking style, must have felt pretty bad here.

20...♘f3!!

Obviously the knight is immune, but it's also very annoying.

21 ♖f1 ♕g4 22 ♕d3 ♗xd4

Now the knight cannot be removed from f3.

23 ♗xd4 ♘h4+

Preventing h2-h3. After 23...♖a6?! 24 h3 ♕h5 25 ♗e3! White has bought himself some time to solve his problems.

24 ♔h1 ♘f3 25 ♔g2

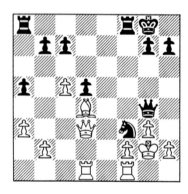

25...c6

Well, some things you have to live with. By the way, 25...h5?! 26 h3 ♕d7 27 ♗e3

♖ad8 28 ♗f4 ♘h4+ 29 ♔h2 does not give Black any advantage.

26 h3 ♕e6 27 ♗e3 g5?!

This is too slow. Black missed his chance with the strong 27...♘e5! 28 ♕b3 a4 29 ♕xb7 ♖ab8 30 ♕a6 ♖xb2 with a very strong attack, for example 31 ♗d4? ♘f3! 32 ♕a7 (or 32 ♗xb2? ♕e4 and Black wins) 32...♘xd4 33 ♖xd4 ♕e3 and the white kingside collapses.

28 ♗d4?

Psychologically, White must already have given up. He could still defend with 28 ♗f4! ♘h4+ 29 gxh4 gxf4 30 ♖g1 and the exposure of the black king causes a headache.

28...♖ae8 29 b4 axb4 30 axb4 ♕d7 31 ♗a1 ♕e6 32 ♖c1 d4 33 ♖fd1 ♖f7!

Preparing an attack on f2.

34 ♕c4 ♕e4!

With deadly threats.

35 ♔f1 ♘d2+! 0-1

The queen or the king. It's not hard to decide.

> ### Game 20
> ## Van Wely-Comas Fabrego
> *Pamplona 1998*

1 d4 e6 2 c4 f5 3 g3 ♘f6 4 ♗g2 ♗e7 5 ♘f3 d6 6 0-0 0-0 7 ♘c3 a5 8 ♖e1 ♘e4 9 ♕c2 ♘c6?!

This is less recommendable than 9...♘xc3. White simply grabs the pawns and gains a clear advantage.

10 ♘xe4 ♘b4 11 ♕b1 fxe4 12 ♕xe4 e5

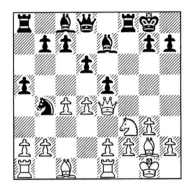

This was of course Black's creative idea, but White is still hungry!

13 dxe5 ♗f5 14 ♕xb7 ♖b8 15 ♕a7 ♘c2

15...♖a8 16 ♕d4! does not gain anything, as after 16...♘c2 17 ♕d5+ ♚h8 18 ♘d4! White has a clear advantage.

16 ♗d2!

This is really strong play. Any computer prefers 16 ♘d4?! ♘xe1 17 ♘c6 ♕e8 18 ♕xc7 ♘xg2 19 ♘xe7+ ♚h8 20 ♚xg2, but now Black can gain good counterplay after 20...♗e4+ 21 f3 ♕h5! – the threats are becoming serious.

16...dxe5 17 ♗c3 e4

Black is also in deep trouble after 17...♖a8 18 ♕b7 ♖b8 19 ♕d5+ ♕xd5 20 cxd5 ♘xe1 21 ♖xe1 e4 22 ♘d4 ♗b4 23 ♘xf5 ♗xc3 24 bxc3 ♖xf5 25 ♗xe4 ♖e5 26 ♗d3, when White has a clear advantage, though admittedly Black has a little counterplay.

18 ♖ad1 ♕c8 19 ♘d4 ♖a8

After the alternative 19...♘xe1 White has a convenient choice between the replies 20 ♖xe1 with a clear advantage and the more adventurous 20 ♘c6!? with some aggressive possibilities.

20 ♘c6 ♗d6 21 ♖xd6 ♖xa7 22 ♘e7+ ♚h8 23 ♘xc8 ♗xc8 1-0

Here Black resigned – why? Well, after 24 ♖c1 cxd6 25 ♖xc2 ♗b7 26 ♖d2 ♖a6 27 ♖d4 ♚g8 28 ♗xe4 ♗xe4 29 ♖xe4 the position is

simply not playable. Against a great player like Van Wely, you are wasting your time defending a lost endgame like this.

Game 21
Rajkovic-R.Maric
Bad Wörishofen 1989

1 d4 e6 2 g3 f5 3 ♗g2 ♘f6 4 ♘f3 ♗e7 5 0-0 0-0 6 c4 d6 7 ♘c3 a5 8 ♖e1 ♘e4

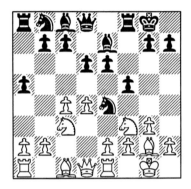

9 ♕c2 ♘c6 10 ♗e3?!

For 10 ♘xe4! see the previous game.

10...♘xc3 11 ♕xc3

After 11 bxc3?! e5 12 ♗c1 e4 White has no good square for his knight and Black is slightly better.

11...♗f6 12 ♖ad1

12 c5 would be best met with a fight to occupy d5: 12...♘b4! (12...♕e8 13 cxd6 cxd6 14 ♖ac1 gives White the advantage) 13 ♖ec1 ♖e8 14 cxd6 cxd6 15 ♕d2 b5 16 ♗g5 ♗b7 17 ♗xf6 ♕xf6 and Black is in no way worse.

12...♕e8

This is where the queen belongs. After 12...♕e7?! 13 ♕b3 a4 14 ♕a3 White is on his way to playing c4-c5 and has an edge.

13 ♗g5

13 c5 ♘b4 14 cxd6 cxd6 15 a3 ♘d5 looks very good for Black.

13...e5 14 ♗xf6

14 dxe5 dxe5 15 ♗xf6 ♖xf6 16 e4 f4 17 ♖d5 with unclear play was a viable option.

14...♖xf6 15 d5?!

Positionally, this is a bad decision. After 15 dxe5 White could still transpose to the previous note.

15...♘b8 16 b3 ♘d7 17 a3 ♘c5

The knight took his time to reach the centre, but White had nothing useful to do in the meantime. Now White has to be careful not to be overrun by the black initiative.

18 b4?

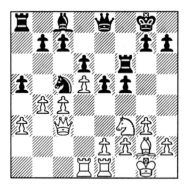

Necessary was 18 ♘d2 ♕h5 (18...f4 19 b4 axb4 20 axb4 ♘a4 is another possibility) 19 b4 ♘a4 20 ♕c2 axb4 21 axb4 f4 with unclear play.

18...♘e4

Compared to a4, this is a fantastic square for the knight.

19 ♕b2 f4 20 ♖f1

White tries to defend, but really it is too late. Black wins after 20 ♘xe5? fxg3 21 fxg3 ♘f2!.

20...♕h5 21 ♘xe5

White is desperate. The following lines show why:

a) 21 gxf4 ♖g6 22 ♔h1 ♖xg2 23 ♔xg2 ♗h3+ 24 ♔h1 ♕g4! and the only way to avoid mate is to give up the knight and then an exchange, after which the game is over.

b) If White does nothing with a move like 21 ♖a1, there comes 21...♗h3 22 ♗xh3 ♕xh3 23 ♕c2 fxg3 with the idea of 24 fxg3 ♘xg3! with a devastating attack. And after 24 ♕xe4 ♖f4!, the minimum White loses is his queen!

21...♖h6! 22 ♘f3 ♗g4 23 ♘h4?

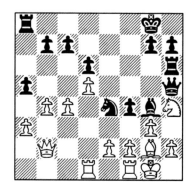

White simply collapses. 23 ♖fe1! would have offered more resistance.

23...♗xe2 24 ♗xe4 ♗xd1 25 f3 fxg3 26 hxg3 g5 27 ♘g2 ♖e8 28 ♕d2 ♗b3 29 ♕d3 ♕h2+ 30 ♔f2 ♖h3 31 ♗xh7+ ♖xh7 32 ♕xb3 ♖e2+ 0-1

Game 22
Anand-Lobron
Frankfurt 1997

1 d4 f5 2 g3 ♘f6 3 ♗g2 e6 4 c4 ♗e7 5 ♘c3 0-0 6 ♘f3 d6 7 0-0 a5 8 ♖e1 ♘e4 9 ♘d2

White uses all his force to fight for the e2-e4 advance.

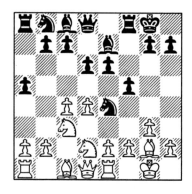

9...♘xc3

After 9...♘xd2 10 ♕xd2 e5 11 dxe5 dxe5 12 ♕d5+ ♕xd5 13 cxd5 ♘a6 14 ♗d2 Black

---

might be doing okay, for example:

a) 14...♗c5!? does not look natural as the bishop is taking the knight's square, but after 15 ♖ac1 ♗d7 16 d6 (otherwise ...♖ae8 and ...b5 are coming) 16...cxd6 17 ♗xb7 ♖a7 18 ♗g2 ♘c7 Black has good counterplay. The line 15 ♘b5 ♗d7 16 ♘a3 a4 17 ♘c4 ♖ae8 should also not cause Black any problems.

b) 14...♖b8 15 ♘b5 ♗d7 16 ♘a3 b6 17 ♘c4 ♗d6 18 ♖ac1 and White had some advantage in Ftacnik-Lobron, Germany 1996.

10 bxc3 e5 11 e4 f4

Black was fine after 11...♘c6 12 exf5 ♗xf5 13 ♘f1 ♗f6 14 ♘e3 ♗d7 15 ♖b1 ♖b8 16 ♗b2 ♔h8 17 ♕d2 ♗g5 18 h4 ♗h6 in Greenfeld-Bellin, Montecatini Terme 1997.

12 ♖b1

This is very natural. Worse is 12 ♘f3?! fxg3 13 fxg3 ♘c6 14 ♗e3 ♗g4 15 h3 ♗xf3 16 ♗xf3 ♗g5 and Black already was slightly preferable, Ravic-Naumkin, Jyvaskyla 1993. It is interesting to see how Black played in the rest of the game: 17 ♗f2? (this loses to clever tactics; necessary was 17 ♔g2) 17...♕f6 18 ♔g2 ♗d2! 19 ♕xd2 ♕xf3+ 20 ♔g1 ♕h5 (White is terminally ill on the light squares) 21 d5 ♘e7 22 ♔g2 ♖f3 23 ♖e3 ♖af8 24 ♖f1 ♘g6! (after this White loses by force) 25 ♕e2

25...♘f4+! 26 gxf4 ♕xh3+ 27 ♔g1 ♕g4+ 0-1 After the rook check on h3 White will have to part with his queen and his good sense of humour.

12...♘c6 13 ♘f3 fxg3

Black should be careful to avoid the following line: 13...♖b8? (with the idea of developing the c8-bishop) 14 dxe5 dxe5 15 ♕d5+ ♔h8 16 ♘xe5 ♕xd5 17 exd5 ♘xe5 18 ♖xe5 and there is of course no compensation for the pawn.

14 hxg3 ♗g4

Here I prefer 14...♖f7!?. With this move, Black creates the f8-square for his queen and stops the tricks with possible checks on d5 as in the note to Black's 13th move. Play may continue 15 c5 a4 16 ♗a3 (16 d5 ♘b8 17 ♕e2 is also possible, but should Black really fear this? Where is White's point of attack?) 16...♕f8! 17 d5 ♘d8 with an unclear game.

14...♔h8, on the other hand, looks insufficient due to 15 c5 ♗f6 16 cxd6 cxd6 17 ♗a3 and d6 is weak.

15 ♖xb7 ♕c8

15...exd4 16 cxd4 ♗xf3 17 ♗xf3 ♘xd4 18 ♕xd4 ♖xf3 19 ♕d5+ ♔h8 20 ♗e3 would give White a small but lasting advantage.

16 ♖b2 ♕e8?!

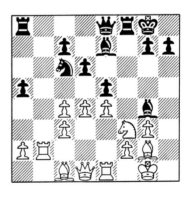

Black wants to develop his queen to h5, but this plan does not have a great sting. Better looks to be 16...exd4! 17 cxd4 ♘xd4 18 ♕xd4 ♗xf3 19 ♕d5+ ♔h8 20 ♗xf3 ♖xf3 21 ♗f4!? (trying to exploit the position of the rook; 21 ♗e3 with a very small advantage is of course possible) 21...♖xf4!? 22 gxf4 ♕g4+ 23 ♔f1 ♕h3+ 24 ♔e2 ♖f8. Maybe White is better here, but it would be hard to prove this with a chess clock ticking on the side.

17 d5!

Now the knight is in big trouble.

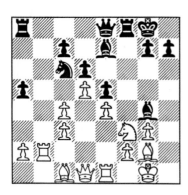

17...♘b8

17...♘d8 18 ♕d3 ♕h5 19 ♘h2 ♗c8 20 ♗e3 ♗g5 21 ♗xg5 ♕xg5 22 ♘f3 would give White a clear advantage. The break c4-c5 cannot be prevented forever, after which Black will have some weaknesses in his camp.

18 ♕d3 ♘a6 19 ♘h2 ♘c5 20 ♕c2 ♕h5

20...♗c8 21 ♗e3 ♗a6 22 ♗xc5 dxc5 23 ♘g4 would leave Black in big trouble too.

21 ♗e3 ♖f7 22 ♘xg4 ♕xg4 23 ♕d1

23 ♖eb1 ♗g5 24 ♗xc5 dxc5 25 ♖b8+ ♖f8 26 ♖xf8+ ♖xf8 27 ♖b7 is also very diffi-

cult for Black.

23...♕g6 24 ♗xc5 dxc5 25 ♗h3

From a positional point of view, White is winning. From here on the rest is easy for a player of Anand's greatness.

25...♔h8 26 ♗f5 ♕h6 27 ♔g2 g6 28 ♖h1 ♕g5 29 ♗e6 ♖ff8 30 ♕g4 ♕f6 31 ♕e2 ♔g7 32 ♖hb1 ♗d6 33 ♖b7 h5 34 ♖1b6 ♔h8 35 ♕e3 ♕xf2+ 36 ♕xf2 ♖xf2+ 37 ♔xf2 ♖f8+ 38 ♔g1 cxb6 39 ♖xb6 ♖d8 40 ♖a6 ♔g7 41 ♖xa5 ♔f6 42 ♖a6 ♔e7 43 ♖a7+ ♔f6 44 ♗d7 ♖f8 45 ♔g2 g5 46 a4 g4 47 a5 ♔g5 48 ♖a6 ♗c7 49 ♗f5 ♖f6 50 ♖a7 ♗d8 51 a6 ♖b6 52 ♖g7+ ♔f6 53 a7 ♖b2+ 54 ♔f1 ♖a2 55 ♖g8 1-0

Summary

Neither 8 ♖e1 nor 8 ♗g5 is really dangerous for Black. The real battle of the future is with 8 ♕c2. White looks better so far, but I have only been able to scratch a little on the surface. The real truth about this move is found deep down below – a place you cannot travel to alone! You need an opponent and tournament practice to know what is really going on.

A lot of these assessments are based solely on my analysis, as the Classical Dutch has been out of favour for such a long time and there are few games with top class players trying to defend the black side. Often what you see in published games in this opening is a strong Grandmaster beating a young ambitious player who does not quite back up his ambitious opening with good moves. This leads to a misconception of the real value of the opening.

1 d4 f5 2 c4 ♘f6 3 g3 e6 4 ♗g2 ♗e7 5 ♘f3 0-0 6 0-0 d6 7 ♘c3 a5 8 ♕c2

 8 ♖e1 ♘e4 (D)
    9 ♘d2 – *Game 22*
    9 ♕c2
        9...♘xc3 – *Game 19*
        9...♘c6
            10 ♘xe4 – *Game 20*; 10 ♗e3 – *Game 21*

 8 ♗g5 (D)
    8...♕e8 – *Game 17*
    8...♘c6 – *Game 18*

8...♘c6 9 e4 ♘b4 10 ♕e2 fxe4 11 ♘xe4 ♘xe4 12 ♕xe4 e5 (D) 13 g4

    13 dxe5 – *Game 16*

13...h5 – *Game 15*

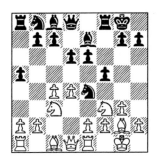
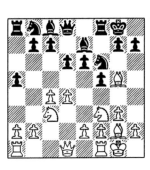
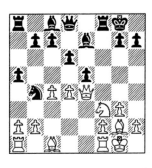

    8...♘e4   *8 ♗g5*   *12...e5*

CHAPTER THREE

Main Line: 7 ♘c3 ♕e8 and 7 ♘c3 ♘e4

---

1 d4 f5 2 c4 e6 3 g3 ♘f6 4 ♗g2 ♗e7 5 ♘f3 d6 6 0-0 0-0 7 ♘c3

In this Chapter we will look at the positions arising after the sequence 1 d4 f5 2 c4 ♘f6 3 g3 e6 4 ♗g2 ♗e7 5 ♘f3 0-0 6 0-0 d6 7 ♘c3

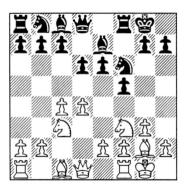

and now either of the moves 7...♕e8 or 7...♘e4.

First of all 7...♕e8 seems like a very viable option. The most dangerous lines are 8 b3 and 8 ♖e1, as after 8 ♕d3, 8 ♗g5 and 8 ♗f4, Black has no problems in gaining an easy equality. Actually, White can easily be fighting to keep the position level himself after these moves.

8 ♖e1 includes a trick so that after 8...♕g6 9 e4 fxe4 10 ♘xe4 ♘xe4 11 ♖xe4 (Games

23-25) the rook is immune – after 11...♕xe4 12 ♘h4! the queen quite surprisingly finds herself trapped in the middle of the board. So this line gives White the structure he is looking for and therefore presumably a very slight advantage, even though it is still a struggle. The line 8...♕h5 9 e4 (Game 28) also seems to be promising for White. But Black has had some success with 8...♘e4 (Games 26-27) and this might still prove to give him an equal game. This is certainly one of the critical positions for the Classical Dutch and its future life.

The move 8 b3 is a very natural way to play the position, but so far White has not been able to prove an advantage after the reply 8...♕h5. This position remains far from clear.

The move 7...♘e4 is slightly riskier than 7...♕e8, but also here it is not clear how White can gain an advantage. Both 8 ♕c2 ♘xc3 9 ♕xc3 ♗f6 10 b4 (Game 36) and 8 ♘xe4 fxe4 9 ♘e1 d5 10 f3 exf3 11 ♘xf3 ♘c6 12 b3 (Game 38) have been slightly worse for Black in games played, but I believe that 9...a5!? can be tried in the first line, should one consider the position really dangerous, and 12...b6! in the second line, after which the outcome of the opening battle is still undecided.

Game 23
Van Wely-Minasian,
European Team Ch., Batumi 1999

1 d4 e6 2 c4 f5 3 g3 ♘f6 4 ♗g2 ♗e7 5 ♘f3 d6 6 0-0 0-0 7 ♘c3 ♕e8

Here's a brief look at some other seventh move alternatives for Black:

a) 7...c6 8 ♕b3 (8 ♕c2 ♘bd7 9 e4 fxe4 10 ♘xe4 b6 11 ♘xf6+ ♘xf6 12 ♖e1 ♕c7 13 c5! ♘d5 14 cxd6 ♕xd6 15 ♘e5 gave White a minor advantage in Penrose-Mardle, England 1961) 8...♔h8 9 ♖e1 ♘a6 10 e4 fxe4 11 ♘xe4 ♘xe4 12 ♖xe4 and White is slightly better, Roos-R.Maric, Monte Carlo 1967.

b) 7...♘bd7 8 ♕d3 ♕e8 9 e4 ♕h5 10 exf5 exf5 11 ♗d2 c6 12 ♖ae1 ♗d8 13 b4 and White is somewhat better, Esing-Prins, Netherlands 1968.

c) 7...♘c6 8 d5! ♘e5 (8...exd5 9 cxd5 ♘e5 10 ♘d4 and White is better, Grünfeld-Tartakower, Viena 1921) 9 ♘d4! ♘xc4 10 ♘xe6 ♗xe6 11 dxe6 was good for White in Schweber-Torgalson, Argentina 1960.

8 ♖e1

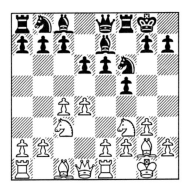

This is played with the idea of an early e2-e4 advance in the centre. The positional consequences of this are clearly illustrated in the games with 8...♕g6 (Games 23-25) and 8...♕h5 (Game 28). White wants to open a road down the centre to put pressure on the pawn on e6 and use his slight space advan-

tage to obtain more freedom for his pieces.

8...♕g6

Black has many alternatives here. Most of them are considered in the following games. But let us look at two lesser responses here:

a) 8...d5?! would be quite a good way to transpose into the Stonewall set-up, if there wasn't a tactical flaw connected to this move, as the knight on c3 is misplaced for the Stonewall: 9 cxd5! (White also achieved a little something with 9 ♘e5?! c6 10 f3 ♘fd7 11 ♘xd7 ♘xd7 12 cxd5 cxd5 13 e4 fxe4 14 fxe4 dxe4 15 ♘xe4 ♕g6 16 d5 in Bertok-Spassky, Varna 1958, but the main line is a simple refutation of the Black idea) 9...exd5 10 ♕b3 c6 11 e4! ♘xe4 12 ♘xe4 fxe4 13 ♖xe4 ♕d8 14 ♗f4 ♘a6 15 ♖e2 ♘c7 16 ♖ae1 and White had an overwhelming advantage in Iliwickij-Kotov, USSR Championship 1955.

b) 8...♘bd7?! is also not really a way to fight for central influence. After e2-e4 the knight is not very well placed on f6. Play may continue 9 e4 fxe4 10 ♘xe4 ♘xe4 11 ♖xe4 ♘f6 12 ♖e1 ♕h5 13 ♗d2 ♗d7 14 h3 h6!, when White has a small advantage. 14...♖ae8?! 15 ♘g5 was a minor disaster in Palermo-Pina, Argentina 1972.

9 e4

This is the main line of course. White has also tried 9 ♕d3 but this does not make a lot of sense after ♖e1, as this move is only justified if White plays e2-e4. 9...♘a6 10 ♗f4 c5 11 dxc5 ♘xc5 12 ♕c2 ♘fe4 13 ♖ad1 e5 14 ♘d5 ♗d8 15 ♗c1 was the continuation of Martin-Pelikan, Argentina 1954. Now Black can play quietly with 15...♗e6 with equality or go nuts with 15...f4!? with an unclear game.

9...♘xe4 10 ♘xe4 fxe4 11 ♖xe4

It should be stated that 11...♕xe4? 12 ♘h4, trapping the queen, is an important detail in the position!

11...e5!?

This move and the whole plan is very risky. In my opinion Black does not achieve equality.

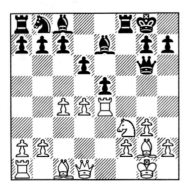

12 ♖e1

Critical might be 12 ♖e3!? ♘c6 13 dxe5 (13 d5 ♘b8 14 ♗d2 ♘d7 15 ♕e2 ♘f6 16 h3 gave White a small advantage in Chuchelov-Goldgewicht, Gifhorn 1992) 13...♗g4 14 exd6 ♗xd6 and now:

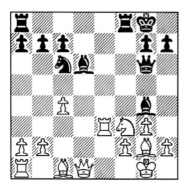

a) 15 h3? ♗xf3 16 ♗xf3 ♖ad8! and suddenly White's missing development is badly felt, for example:

a1) 17 ♗d2 ♗xg3 18 fxg3 (18 ♗d5+ ♖xd5 19 ♖xg3 ♕f6 gives Black a more or less winning position) 18...♕xg3+ 19 ♔h1 ♕xh3+ 20 ♔g1 ♕g3+ 21 ♔h1 ♕h4+ 22 ♔g1 ♘d4 23 ♗g2 ♕f2+ 24 ♔h2 ♖d6 gives Black a winning attack. Both ...♖h6 and ...♖g6 are deadly threats.

a2) 17 ♗e4 ♗c5! 18 ♕c2 (18 ♖xd8! ♖xd8 19 ♗xg6 ♖d1+ 20 ♔g2 ♗xe3 21 fxe3 hxg6 22 ♔f3 ♘e5+ 23 ♔e2 ♖h1 gives Black some chances to win the endgame, but it is by far

the best shot) 18...♕h5 19 ♗xc6? (19 ♔g2 ♗xe3 20 ♗xe3 with some compensation for the exchange was forced) 19...bxc6 (19...♖d1+!? 20 ♔g2 bxc6 gives a winning attack) 20 ♖e2 ♕xh3?? (20...♖d1+!! 21 ♕xd1 ♗xf2+ wins on the spot due to 22 ♔h2 ♗xg3+ 23 ♔g1 ♗f2+ 24 ♔h2 ♕f3 and the threat of mate forces White into giving up the queen) 21 ♗e3 and White was at least still alive, though in a crisis in Crispin-Wood, Seattle 1986.

b) 15 c5! is an important move to remember. The only game played in this line continued 15...♗e7 16 ♕b3+ ♔h8 (16...♕f7? 17 ♘e5 ♕xb3 18 axb3 ♘xe5 19 ♖xe5 ♗f6 20 ♖e4 gives White a winning advantage) 17 ♘e5 ♘xe5 18 ♖xe5 ♖ad8 (Bauza-Estrada Degrandi, Uruguay 1961) 19 ♗f4 ♗f6 20 ♖ee1 ♗d4. Black has some compensation for the pawn but it's not clear that it's enough.

12...♘c6 13 dxe5 ♗g4 14 h3

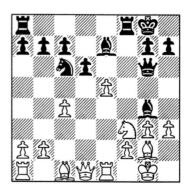

Here White has some serious alternatives:

a) 14 ♕b3! is a new strong invention that puts pressure on Black. Probably the best try is to force an endgame with 14...♕f7 (14...♗xf3?! 15 ♗xf3 ♘d4 16 ♗d5+ ♔h8 17 ♕d1 gives White a clear advantage, as does 14...♖xf3? 15 ♕xb7, while 14...dxe5? 15 ♘xe5 ♘xe5 16 ♖xe5 ♖ae8 17 ♕xb7 does not offer Black enough compensation for the material) 15 ♗f4 ♗xf3 (15...♘a5? 16 ♕b5 ♘xc4 17 ♖ac1! ♘b6 [17...d5 18 ♘g5!] 18

♖xc7 and White is winning) 16 ♗xf3 ♘d4 17 ♗d5 ♕xd5 18 cxd5 ♘xb3 19 axb3 dxe5 20 ♖ac1! (White is playing for the 7th rank) and now:

a1) After 20...exf4 21 ♖xe7 ♖ae8 22 ♖exc7 White has very good chances to win the endgame, even though Black has some counterplay with 22...f3!?. Then White has the antidote in 23 d6!. Exchanges will have to happen for Black to get rid of the annoying d-pawn.

a2) 20...b6! (Black takes control over c5 with this move and thereby keeps himself in the game) 21 ♗xe5 (after 21 ♖xe5 ♗d6 22 ♖e6 ♗xf4 23 gxf4 ♖f7 the white pawn structure is terrible, so Black will be able to make the draw after 24 ♖ec6 ♖d8 25 ♖xc7 ♖xd5 26 ♖xf7 ♔xf7 27 ♖c7+ ♔f6 28 ♖xa7 ♖b5; interesting though is 21 ♖xc7!? ♗d8 22 ♗xe5 ♗xc7 23 ♗xc7 ♖f7 24 d6 ♖d7 25 f4 with good compensation for the pawn) 21...♗c5 22 ♖c2 ♖fe8 23 ♔f1 ♖ad8 24 ♗xc7 ♖xe1+ 25 ♔xe1 ♖xd5 and Black has good chances to draw this endgame.

b) 14 exd6 only helps Black. Play continues 14...♗xd6

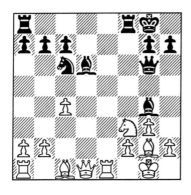

and now:

b1) 15 ♘h4 ♕f6 16 ♗d5+ ♔h8 17 f3 ♗d7 gives Black the advantage despite the pawn deficit. White is completely uncoordinated and will have trouble resisting an attack.

b2) 15 ♕d5+ ♔h8 16 ♗e3 ♖ad8 gives Black good counterplay. Also possible is 16...♗b4!? but Black should realise that he cannot solve all his problems with tactics after 17 ♖ed1 ♗xf3?! (17...♖ad8! would give Black the advantage) 18 ♗xf3 ♖f5 19 ♕e4 ♖e8. Now White has 20 ♖d5!! ♖xe4 21 ♗xe4 with a clear advantage.

b3) 15 c5!? ♗xf3 16 ♗xf3 ♗xc5! offers Black a good game too. The difference from 12 ♖e3 is of course that the f3-bishop is hanging now.

b4) 15 h3?? with a further split:

b41) 15...♗e6?? 16 ♕e2? (16 ♘g5 ♗xc4 17 ♗e4 ♕f6 18 ♕c2 ♔h8 19 ♘xh7 and White wins) 16...♖ae8 17 ♗e3 ♕h5? (17...♗b4 would have kept White's advantage to a minimum) 18 g4! ♕a5 19 ♘g5 ♔h8 20 c5 ♗xc5 21 ♕c2 1-0 Halasz-Forgacs, Ballerup 1985.

b42) 15...♗xf3! 16 ♗xf3

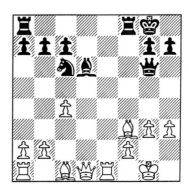

16...♗xg3!! 17 fxg3? (17 ♕d5+! ♔h8 18 ♖e6! ♗xf2+ 19 ♔xf2 ♖xf3+ 20 ♔xf3 ♕xe6 21 ♕xe6 ♘d4+ 22 ♔g4 ♘xe6 gives Black good chances to win the endgame, but White still has a lot of resistance to offer) 17...♕xg3+ 18 ♗g2 ♖ad8 19 ♕e2 (19 ♗d2 ♖f2!) 19...♘d4 and Black wins at least the queen.

14...♗xf3 15 ♗xf3 dxe5!

For 15...♘xe5 see Game 25.

16 ♗e4

White looks slightly better at the first glance, but in reality Black has good counterplay due to his control over the d4-square.

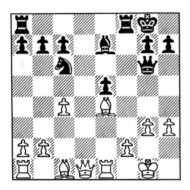

16...♕f6 17 ♗e3 ♖ad8 18 ♕c2 h6 19 ♖ad1 ♖xd1 20 ♖xd1 ♘d4!

This pawn sacrifice should perhaps be rejected, as it is impossible to find a white advantage after this.

21 ♗xd4 exd4 22 ♗xb7 c6!?

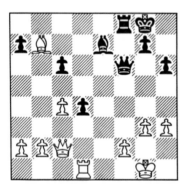

Keeping the bishop out of the game. Black has some compensation for the pawn, but after a move like 23 c5!?, with the idea of 23...♗xc5 24 ♗xc6!, a player like Karpov would give Black a very hard time. The move 22...♗c5! was for this reason the right way to prove compensation.

23 ♖d3

After 23 ♕e2!? ♗c5 24 ♖d3 a5 25 h4 ♔h8 I do not see how White can play for a win.

23...♕e6 24 ♖xd4

Safer is 24 c5 ♕e1+ 25 ♔g2 ♕e4+ 26

♔g1 ♕e1+, though Black is by no means forced to agree to a draw here.

24...♗c5 25 ♖d2?!

This is a very risky decision exposing White to a dangerous attack. Safer was 25 ♖f4 ♖xf4 26 gxf4 ♕xh3 27 ♗xc6, which gives White some extra pawns but they are all weak on the dark squares, so a draw is the most likely outcome.

25...a5!

Stopping White's winning plan before it has been conceived: ♗a6, a2-a3, b2-b4 and c4-c5. 25...♕e5!? was also possible, the idea being that after 26 ♔g2 ♕c7 27 ♗a6 ♕a5 28 ♗b7 ♕c7 the position is drawn.

26 ♔g2 ♖b8 27 ♗a6 ♖a8 28 ♖e2?

28 ♗b7 ♖b8, with a draw, was forced.

28...♕d7 29 ♖e5 ♗d4

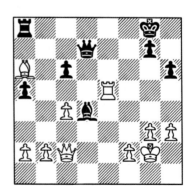

30 ♖xa5

White has now won a second pawn but he

has completely abandoned his kingside and will soon be under a bad storm.

30...♖f8 31 f3 ♕e7

White pieces are too far from the scene of the action.

32 h4?

After this White is in serious trouble. He could still defend with 32 c5! ♕e1 33 ♕c4+ ♔h8 34 ♕xd4! ♕xa5 35 ♗c4 ♖d8 36 ♕e5 ♖d2+ 37 ♔h1 ♖d1+ 38 ♔h2 ♕d2+ 39 ♗e2 ♖e1 and now White has a perpetual with 40 ♕e8+ ♔h7 41 ♕e4+. On 32 ♕d2 comes the reply 32...♗e3! 33 ♕e1 ♖d8 followed by ...♖d2+ with good chances to fight for an advantage.

32...♕e1 33 ♖f5

Not 33 ♖a3? when 33...♕g1+ 34 ♔h3 ♗f2 35 f4 ♕f1+ 36 ♔g4 h5+! 37 ♔xh5 ♕h3 wins for Black.

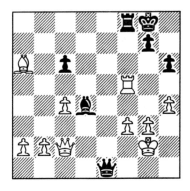

33...♖e8??

This logical move does not work. Black should have played 33...♖a8! 34 ♖f4 (34 ♗b7 ♖b8 35 ♕e4 ♕xe4 36 fxe4 ♖xb7 is probably a winning endgame for Black) 34...♕g1+ 35 ♔h3 ♖xa6 36 ♕f5 ♖a8 37 ♕e6+ ♔h8 38 ♕xc6 ♔g8 39 ♖f5! (39 a4?? h5 and White is mated) 39...♗xb2 and Black has good winning chances.

34 h5??

34 c5 ♕g1+ 35 ♔h3 ♗f2 36 ♕c4+ ♔h7 37 ♕f4 would let White escape with the full point. Now it goes the other way.

34...♕g1+ 35 ♔h3 ♗f2 0-1

1 d4 e6 2 c4 f5 3 g3 ♘f6 4 ♗g2 ♗e7 5 ♘f3 d6 6 0-0 0-0 7 ♘c3 ♕e8 8 ♖e1 ♕g6 9 e4 fxe4 10 ♘xe4 ♘xe4

Not very popular but quite interesting is 10...♘c6 and now:

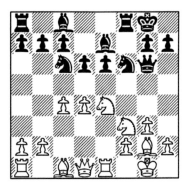

a) 11 ♘xf6+?! ♗xf6 12 ♗f4 does not promise White anything. 12...♘b4 (12...♕f5?! 13 ♕d2 ♔h8 14 d5 e5? – 14...♘e5 was much better – 15 dxc6! exf4 16 ♘d4 ♗xd4 17 ♕xd4 f3 18 ♖e7! gave White a big plus in Krogius-A.Zaitsev, USSR) 13 ♗f1 ♖d8! 14 a3 e5 15 axb4 exf4 16 ♗d3 ♗f5! equalises.

b) 11 d5! and now:

b1) 11...♘e5?! 12 dxe6 ♗xe6 (12...♘fg4 13 ♘xe5 ♘xe5 14 ♘c5! would promise White a clear advantage) 13 ♘eg5 ♗g4 14 h3 ♗xf3 15 ♘xf3 with a definite White plus.

b2) 11...exd5 12 ♘h4! ♕g4 13 ♗f3 ♕d7 14 ♘xf6+ ♗xf6 15 ♕xd5+ ♔h8 16 ♕h5 ♗xh4 17 ♗e4 g6 18 ♕xh4 and White has a large advantage, Greenfeld-Riedel, Munich 1992.

11 ♖xe4 ♘c6 12 ♖e1 e5

Also possible is 12...♗f6 13 ♗e3 e5 14 dxe5 and now:

a) 14...♘xe5 15 ♘xe5 ♗xe5 16 ♗d4 with a slight edge according to Yermolinsky.

b) I believe that after 14...dxe5! Black

should have a nice game. In the Ilyin-Zhenevsky the positions with the isolated e-pawns are usually good. Of course this implies that Black needs to avoid exchanging pieces. 15 ♘d2?! (15 ♕d5+! ♔h8 16 ♖ad1 ♗g4 gives an even game) 15...♖d8! and now:

b1) 16 ♗xc6? is a computer move! Humans are animals – they have instinct! 16...bxc6 17 ♕a4 c5 18 ♕c6 ♖b8 19 b3 ♗b7 gives Black a dangerous attack – the white position looks like a Swiss cheese.

b2) 16 ♕b1 ♗f5 17 ♗e4 ♘d4 with a comfortable position for Black.

13 dxe5 ♗g4 14 h3 ♗xf3 15 ♗xf3 ♘xe5?

For the superior 15...dxe5! see the previous game.

16 ♗e4 ♕f6 17 f4!

White has the advantage.

17...♘c6 18 ♗e3 ♖ae8

18...♕xb2?? 19 ♗xc6 bxc6 20 ♗d4 would drop a piece.

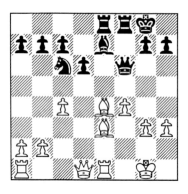

19 ♕d2?!

19 ♕h5! g6 20 ♕b5 would secure White a very large advantage. Black's position is very weak on the light squares.

19...♔h8 20 ♔g2?

This move allows counterplay. 20 ♗f2! ♕h6 (20...d5? 21 ♖xd5 ♕xb2? now loses to 22 ♕h5) 21 ♔g2 still gives White some advantage.

20...d5! 21 ♕xd5

21 cxd5 ♗b4 is one of the points behind the pawn sacrifice.

21...♕xb2+ 22 ♗f2 ♗b4 23 ♖ed1?

23 ♖eb1 ♕f6 24 a3 ♗a5 25 ♖a2 is probably still fine for White.

23...♗c3?

Now Black returns the favour. After 23...♖e5! we have:

a) 24 ♖ab1?? ♖xd5 drops material.

b) 24 ♕d3?! ♗c5 25 ♖f1 ♖xe4 26 ♕xe4 ♗xf2 27 ♖ab1 ♕d4 28 ♕f3 ♗e3 29 ♖fe1 ♗d2 30 ♖e4 (30 ♖ed1? ♘a5! and Black wins the c-pawn too) 30...♕d6 would give Black brilliant winning chances.

c) 24 ♖db1 ♕e2 25 ♗f3 ♖xd5 26 ♗xe2 ♖d2 and Black has the advantage, though nothing is decided yet.

24 ♖ab1 ♕xa2 25 ♕d3 ♖xe4?

This loses by force. It was still possible to play 25...♘d8 26 ♖bc1 ♗f6 27 ♗xh7 ♘f7 with problems, but still with a position to play.

26 ♕xe4 ♗d4 27 ♖xd4 ♘xd4 28 ♖xb7 ♘e2 29 ♖xa7 ♕b2 30 ♖a8 1-0

Game 25
Nielsen-Boe
Nyborg 2001

1 d4 f5 2 c4 e6 3 ♘f3 ♘f6 4 ♘c3 ♗e7 5 g3 0-0 6 ♗g2 d6 7 0-0 ♕e8 8 ♖e1 ♘c6 9 e4 fxe4 10 ♘xe4 ♘xe4 11 ♖xe4 ♕g6 12 ♕e2

This move looks logical, but it's most

likely that White will not be able to prove an advantage.

12...♗f6 13 ♗d2

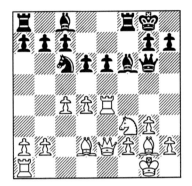

Also possible is: 13 d5 exd5 (13...♘e5 14 ♘d4 looks good for White) 14 cxd5 and now:

a) 14...♗f5 is bad because of 15 ♘h4! ♗xh4 16 dxc6 ♗xe4 17 ♗xe4 ♕f7 18 ♕c2! (18 cxb7? ♖ae8! 19 b8♕ ♖xb8 gives Black a clear advantage) 18...♗e7 19 cxb7 ♖ab8 20 ♗xh7+ ♔h8 21 ♗g6 and White has a clear advantage.

b) 14...♘e5 15 ♘d4 with a further split:

b1) 15...♗g4?! 16 f3 ♗f5 17 ♘xf5 ♕xf5 18 ♗e3 (18 g4! ♕g6 19 g5 ♗d8 20 f4 ♘d7 21 ♗e3 would have given White a strong attacking position) 18...♘d7 19 ♖c1 ♕xd5 20 f4? (20 ♖xc7 with a good position was better) 20...♘c5 21 ♖d4 ♕f5 22 ♖d5?! (22 ♖dd1! would still have kept White in a stronger position) 22...♕e6 23 ♕d2 ♔h8 24 b4 ♖ae8 25 ♗f2 ♘e4 26 ♖e1 (26 ♗xe4 ♕xe4 27 ♖xc7 was still unclear) 26...♘xd2 and Black won in P.Kostenko-Gavritenkov, Moscow 1999.

b2) Better is 15...♖e8 16 ♘e6 ♗xe6 17 dxe6 c5! (17...♖xe6 18 f4 d5 19 ♖e3 d4 20 ♖xe5 and White has a clear advantage) 18 f4 ♘c6 19 ♕c4 ♗d4+ 20 ♔h1 ♖e7 and the consequences are as hard to evaluate as the result is to predict.

13...e5 14 dxe5 ♘xe5

After 14...dxe5 15 ♗c3 ♗f5 (15...♗g4?!

16 ♘h4! ♗xe2 17 ♘xg6 ♗d3 18 ♘xf8 ♗xe4 19 ♗xe4 ♖xf8 20 ♗xc6 bxc6 21 ♖e1 gave White a winning advantage in Kauppila-Pessi, Finland 1998) 16 ♘h4 ♗xh4 17 ♖xh4 ♖ae8 18 ♕e3 White was slightly better in Knaak-Schmittdiel, Bad Wörishofen 1992.

15 ♘xe5 ♗xe5 16 ♗c3 ♗xc3 17 bxc3 c6?!

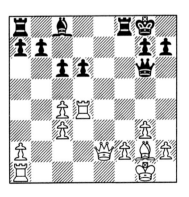

Here Black can equalise with 17...♗d7! 18 ♖e1 (or 18 ♖e7 ♖ae8 19 ♗xb7 c6! and, as Adorjan likes to say, Black is OK!) 18...♖ae8 (18...b6!? is provocative; 19 ♖e7 ♖ae8 20 ♕d2 ♖xe7 21 ♖xe7 ♕b1+ with a draw in Taylor-O'Neal, correspondence 1994) 19 c5 ♗c6 20 ♖xe8 ♖xe8 21 ♕c4+ ♔f8 22 ♖xe8+ ♕xe8 and a draw was agreed in Liebert-Farago, Szolnok 1975.

18 ♖d4

18 ♖e7!? ♕f6 19 ♕e3 with good attacking possibilities was also interesting.

18...≝f6 19 c5! dxc5?!

Here Black has a better defence: 19...d5! 20 c4 dxc4 21 ≝d8+ ≝f8 22 ≝xf8+ ♔xf8 and now:

a) 23 ≝e1 is too optimistic. After 23...≝f7 24 ≝e5 ♔g8 25 ≝d6 ≝f5! 26 ≝e7 ≝f8 27 ≝d5+ (27 ≝xb7? ≝xd6 28 cxd6 c3 would win for Black) 27...cxd5 28 ≝xd5+ ♔h8 29 ≝f7 ≝e8 White has some problems with the pawn on c3.

b) 23 ≝xc4 ≝f5 24 ≝e1 ≝d8 25 ≝b4 and White has a little pressure, but nothing more.

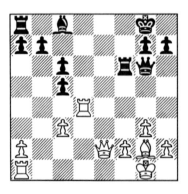

20 ≝d8+ ≝f8 21 ≝xf8+ ♔xf8 22 ≝e1 ≝f7 23 ≝e5! ≝f5??

This overlooks a simple win for White. 23...♔g8 24 ≝d6! (24 ≝xc5 ≝e6 would just be even) 24...≝f8 25 ≝c7! is much better for White, but Black would have some chances.

24 ≝xc5+ ♔g8 25 ≝e7 ≝f6 26 ≝xb7

White has now regained his material investment and has retained his positional advantage.

26...≝d8 27 h3 h5 28 ≝xa7 ≝d3 29 ≝a8+ ♔h7 30 ≝f8 1-0

Game 26
Flohr-Sokolsky
Moscow 1954

---

1 ≝f3 e6 2 c4 f5 3 g3 ≝f6 4 ≝g2 ≝e7 5 0-0 0-0 6 ≝c3 d6 7 d4 ≝e8 8 ≝e1 ≝e4

This is the main way to prevent e2-e4.

9 ≝c2

This is not a very dangerous move.

9...≝g6 10 b3

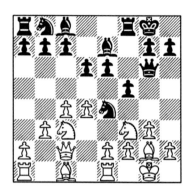

White should be careful not to fall for 10 ≝xe4? fxe4 11 ≝h4 (or 11 ≝d2 e3 and Black wins) 11...≝xh4 12 ≝xe4 ≝f7 and Black wins. 12 gxh4 e3! gives us the same result.

10...≝xc3 11 ≝xc3 ≝f6 12 ≝a3?!

In the game it quickly becomes apparent that the bishop is not placed well here, but belongs on the long diagonal. After 12 ≝b2 ≝c6 13 ≝d2 (with the idea of d4-d5) the position would be level.

12...≝c6

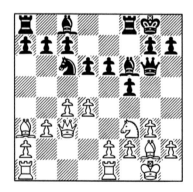

13 ≝ad1

Here it is also possible to play 13 c5 d5 14 ≝e5 ≝xe5 15 dxe5 ≝e7 with an unclear position – this is probably more in the spirit of 13 ≝a3. In this case Black should be careful not to fall for ...≝d7, which is met with c5-

c6! winning material.

13...♗d7 14 ♕c1

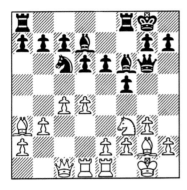

14...a5!

A strong and typical move in these lines, preparing to meet d4-d5 with ...♘c6-b4.

15 d5 ♘b4 16 dxe6 ♗xe6 17 ♕d2?

White is wasting his time. It was necessary to change the course of the game with 17 ♘d4 ♗xd4 (17...♗c8!? with unclear play was also an option) 18 ♖xd4 ♘xa2 19 ♕d2 ♘b4 20 ♗xb7 ♖ab8 21 ♗g2 with even chances.

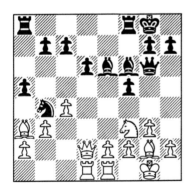

17...f4!

Black is fully mobilised and now starts a kingside attack.

18 ♖c1

The f-pawn is immune. 18 gxf4? ♗h3 19 ♘g5 ♗xg2 20 ♔xg2 h6 would drop a piece and 18 ♕xf4 ♗c3 wins the exchange for no compensation. Remember that the pawn on a2 is also hanging.

18...fxg3 19 hxg3 h5 20 ♗xb4 axb4 21 ♕xb4

Capturing this pawn is very risky and not at all appropriate. Black now has strong options for all his pieces and decides that White's queen departure is a good reason to increase the pace of the kingside attack with a pawn sacrifice.

21...h4 22 ♘xh4 ♗xh4 23 gxh4 ♕f6 24 ♖f1 ♖xa2 25 ♕xb7

White is in trouble. 25 c5 doesn't help: 25...d5 26 ♕xb7 ♖xe2 27 ♗xd5 ♕xh4 28 ♗xe6+ ♖xe6 29 ♕d5 ♖ff6 and the kingside cannot be defended.

25...♖xe2 26 ♕xc7 ♕d4 27 ♕e7 ♖fxf2 28 ♔h1!?

28...♗h3! 0-1

A killer. But Black should avoid 28...♖xg2 29 ♕e8+ ♔h7 30 ♕h5+, when White gets an undeserved perpetual.

Game 27
Reshevsky-Yee
Pasadena 1983

1 d4 f5 2 ♘f3 ♘f6 3 c4 e6 4 g3 d6 5 ♗g2 ♗e7 6 0-0 0-0 7 ♘c3 ♕e8 8 ♖e1 ♘e4 9 ♕c2 ♕g6 10 ♘d2 ♘xc3 11 ♕xc3 ♘c6 12 d5

This is the only ambitious move in the position. After 12 b4? ♘xd4! Black has just won a pawn for nothing. The tragedy could actually now continue with 13 e3? ♘e2+! 14

♖xe2 ♗f6 and Black wins the exchange and probably also the game.

12...♗f6 13 ♕c2 ♘d8?!

This is slightly passive and gives White time to take over the centre. After 13...♘d4! 14 ♕d3 exd5 15 cxd5 ♗d7 Black is fully mobilised and has equalised. 16 e3 ♖ae8! is not something he should fear. The knight will find time to get out of trouble. One trick is 17 ♖f1 ♗b5 18 ♘c4 f4! and White's position is falling apart.

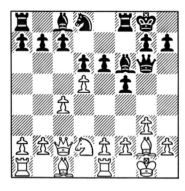

14 dxe6?

This move is silly and only helps Black to develop. Far better is 14 e4!, playing against the knight on d8. After 14...e5 15 exf5 ♗xf5 16 ♘e4 White has a tiny advantage.

14...♘xe6 15 ♘f3 ♗d7!

Black is simply developing his pieces to good and natural squares.

16 ♗d2 ♗c6

Black's pieces are harmoniously placed and are all potential attacking forces.

17 ♗c3 ♕g4

Here it was worth considering 17...♗xc3!? 18 ♕xc3 f4, starting a kingside offensive.

18 b3 ♗e4 19 ♕b2 ♗xc3 20 ♕xc3 ♖f6 21 h3 ♕h5 22 ♘d2?!

Here White misses 22 ♘d4! with the idea of exchanging minor pieces and arriving at an equal position. Play may continue 22...♗xg2 23 ♔xg2 ♖h6 24 h4 ♕g4 25 ♘xe6 ♖xe6 26 ♕f3 and the most likely outcome of this will be a draw.

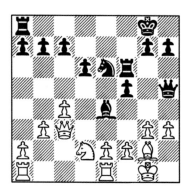

22...♗xg2 23 ♔xg2 ♖h6 24 h4 ♕g4 25 ♕f3 ♖xh4

A big difference from the line above.

26 ♕xb7 ♕h3+?

This move puts the rook on h4 en prise. The right continuation is 26...♖e8! 27 ♔g1 f4 28 ♘f1 fxg3 29 ♘xg3 ♘g5 and Black has very good chances of conducting a successful attack.

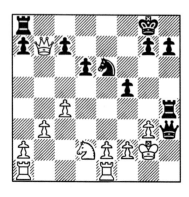

27 ♔g1 ♕h2+ 28 ♔f1 ♕h1+ 29 ♕xh1 ♖xh1+ 30 ♔g2 ♖xe1 31 ♖xe1 ♖e8 32 ♘f3 a5 33 e3 g6 34 ♖d1 ♖b8 35 ♘d4 ½-½

Game 28
Keres-Simagin
Moscow 1951

---

1 d4 f5 2 g3 e6 3 ♗g2 ♘f6 4 ♘f3 ♗e7 5 0-0 0-0 6 c4

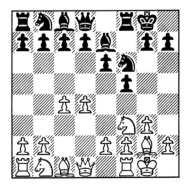

White can choose to either transpose to the main lines, or to play a less aggressive set-up with 6 b3 and now Black has tried:

a) 6...♘e4 is good only if Black is planning to play a Stonewall set-up. Otherwise he should attend to his remaining development first. 7 ♗b2 ♗f6 8 ♘bd2 d5 9 c4 ♘c6 10 e3 a5 11 a3 ♗d7 12 ♖c1 ♗e8 13 ♘e1 ♗f7 14 ♘d3 ♘e7 15 ♘f3 ♗h5 16 ♕c2 ♗xf3 17 ♗xf3 c6 and White had a small advantage in Shabalov-Spraggett, Torcy 1991. Of course, Black could have played differently a dozen times, but that lies beyond the realms of this book.

b) 6...d6! (we want to play the Ilyin-Zhenevsky!) 7 ♗b2 ♕e8 8 ♘bd2 a5 9 a3 ♘c6 10 e3 ♗d8 11 ♕e2 e5 and Black has already achieved full equality, Eperejsi-Ovetchkin, Budapest 1996.

c) 6...b6!? has some logic to it considering the pawn structure. Given his small positional advantage, White should probably hesitate to answer this provocation.

c1) 7 ♘e5?! c6 8 c4 ♗b7 9 ♗a3 (it is not easy to see what White is achieving by exchanging the bishops) 9...♗xa3 10 ♘xa3 d6 11 ♘d3 e5 12 ♘c2 (12 dxe5 dxe5 13 ♘xe5?? ♕e7 would fork the two knights and win the game) 12...♘bd7 13 ♕c1 ♕c7 (13...♕e7 looks more natural) 14 ♕b2 ♖ae8 15 dxe5 dxe5 16 ♖ad1 e4 17 ♘f4 ♘e5 and Black had a slightly more comfortable game in Bertok-Tolush, Baden-Baden 1957. The b7-bishop

might not look like much, but the g2-bishop also has a lot of problems finding a part to play.

c2) 7 ♗a3!? looks better. White has a chance to weaken Black's influence on the dark squares in the centre. However, 7...d6! still doesn't look bad for Black.

6...d6 7 ♘c3 ♕e8 8 ♖e1 ♘h5 9 e4

This is what White is heading for, so he should not hesitate to play it.

After 9 b3 ♘c6 10 d5 ♘e5 11 ♘xe5 dxe5 12 e4 ♕xd1 13 ♖xd1 exd5 14 ♘xd5 ♘xd5 15 cxd5 ♗d6 the players agreed a draw in Taimanov-Spassky, USSR 1958.

9 ♗g5 ♘c6 10 ♗xf6 ♗xf6 11 e4 fxe4 12 ♘xe4 ♗d7 13 ♖c1 ♖ae8 14 d5 ♘d8 15 ♘xf6+ ♖xf6 16 dxe6 ♖fxe6 was also agreed drawn in the game Malich-Hort, USSR 1972.

9...fxe4 10 ♘xe4 ♘xe4

After 10...♘c6 11 ♗f4 White is somewhat better. Really foolish is 11...h6 12 ♘c3 g5 13 ♗e3 e5?! 14 dxe5 dxe5 15 ♘d5, when White had a very large advantage in Gilgoric-Dueckstein, Zürich 1953.

11 ♖xe4 ♘c6 12 ♗f4 ♗f6

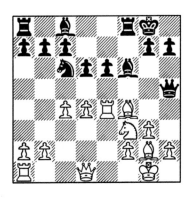

13 ♕d2

White has emerged from the opening with a slightly freer game. Alternatives to this natural move are the following:

a) 13 h4!? h6 14 ♖c1 was very slightly better for White in Winter-Mikenas, Lodz 1935.

b) 13 ♖c1 ♕f5 14 ♖e2 was played in Frey-Fridjonsson, Reykjavik 1982. Now Black could have played 14...♘b4! 15 ♖a1 ♘d3 16 ♗e3 e5 with an even game.

c) 13 d5 ♘d8 14 ♕d2?! (14 ♘g5 ♕xd1+ 15 ♖xd1 e5 would have been equal) 14...e5 15 ♗g5 ♗g4 gave Black the better chances in Kubicek-Lechetynsky, Bratislava 1967. The change in pawn structure benefits Black as the e6-pawn is no longer weak (or on e6!), and the pressure down the f-file is now the most important theme in the position.

13...♔h8 14 ♖ae1 ♗d7 15 c5!

White is quick to create extra weaknesses right after completing his development.

15...dxc5

15...d5?! 16 ♖4e2 ♖ac8 17 b4 would give White a large positional plus, with the e-file and the attack on the queenside.

16 dxc5 e5 17 ♘xe5

17 ♕xd7? exf4 18 ♖xf4 ♕xc5 is better for Black. Look at the f2-pawn – it is on a dark square just like Black's bishop.

17...♘xe5 18 ♗xe5 ♗c6 19 ♗xf6!

A very strong exchange sacrifice. After 19 ♖4e3 ♗xg2 20 ♔xg2 ♗xe5 21 ♖xe5 ♕f3+ 22 ♔g1 ♖ad8 Black has some counterplay, though not really enough to compensate for the pawn.

19...♗xe4

19...♖xf6 20 ♖e5 ♕g6 21 ♗xc6 ♖xc6 22 ♕d7 followed by ♖e8+ would win quite easily for White.

20 ♗xg7+ ♔xg7 21 ♕d4+ ♖f6 22 ♖xe4 ♖af8 23 h4

Maybe it was more exact to play 23 ♖g4+!? ♔h8 24 ♗xb7, when the bishop and three pawns defeat the rook.

23...♔h8 24 ♖e7 ♕f5 25 f4 ♕g6 26 ♔h2 ♖8f7 27 ♖e8+ ♔g7 28 ♗e4 ♕g4 29 ♗d5 ♕d7 30 ♕e5 h6 31 ♗xf7 ♔xf7 32 ♖f8+! ♔xf8 33 ♕xf6+ ♔g8 34 ♕g6+ ♔h8 35 ♕xh6+ ♔g8 36 ♕g6+ ♔h8 37 ♕f6+ ♔g8 38 h5 ♕d1 39 ♕g6+ ♔h8 40 ♕e8+ 1-0

Game 29
Botvinnik-Kan
Moscow 1931

---

1 d4 e6 2 c4 f5 3 g3 ♘f6 4 ♗g2 ♗e7 5 ♘f3 d6 6 0-0 0-0 7 b3 ♕e8 8 ♕c2 ♕h5 9 ♘c3 ♘c6 10 ♗a3 ♗d7

10...a5!, to make ...♘b4 a possibility, is the standard move here (see Game 13).

11 d5!

Now White uses the moment to seize the initiative in the centre.

11...♘d8

11...♘e5?? 12 ♘xe5 would leave the e7-bishop hanging, so the knight has to retreat.

12 ♘e5 dxe5 13 ♗xe7 ♖f7 14 ♗a3!

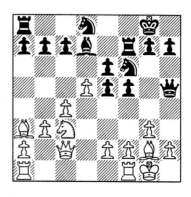

White keeps control over the dark squares with this move, thus making it hard for Black to coordinate his forces.

Less would have arisen from 14 ♗xd8?! ♖xd8 15 dxe6 ♗xe6 16 ♗xb7 ♘g4, when the b7-pawn is possibly less significant than

Black's attack on the kingside. Also 14 d6?! cxd6 15 ♗xd6 ♗c6 16 f3 e4 does not cause Black any concern.

14...exd5 15 ♘xd5 f4!

Black needs to create counterplay as soon as possible.

16 ♖ad1 ♘xd5

This move highlights the difference in development and coordination between the two armies in a very unfavourable way as far as Black is concerned. Better was 16...♗h3! 17 ♘xf6+ ♖xf6 18 ♗f3 ♛f7 19 ♖fe1 and White has only a small advantage.

17 ♗xd5 ♗e6 18 ♛d3!

White needs to keep his mobility and flexibility. After 18 ♛e4?! c6! 19 ♗xe6 ♘xe6 20 ♔h1 ♖e8 Black has good chances of creating a kingside attack.

18...♗xd5 19 ♛xd5

White needs to keep his pieces in dominating positions. After the weaker 19 cxd5?! ♖f6 20 ♛c4 ♘f7 White should be very careful:

a) Black wins after 21 ♛xc7? f3! 22 exf3 ♘g5 23 ♖d3 ♘h3+ 24 ♔h1 ♘f4!! 25 ♛xb7 ♖e8 26 ♛b5 ♖h6 27 h4 a6 28 ♛a4 ♘xd3.

b) 21 ♗e7! ♖h6 22 h4 g5! 23 ♛xc7?! (23 d6!? or 23 e3 is better, with a very unclear game ahead) 23...gxh4 24 ♛xb7 ♖e8 25 ♗xh4 ♛g4 and Black has the attack.

19...♘c6 20 ♗c5!

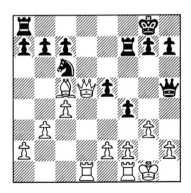

Taking control over d4, thereby keeping the advantage and preventing counterplay.

20...♖e8

After 20...♛xe2 21 ♛e6 ♛h5 22 ♖d7 ♛f5 23 ♛xf5 ♖xf5 24 ♖xc7 ♖f7 25 ♖xf7 ♔xf7 26 gxf4 exf4 27 ♖d1 White has excellent chances of winning the endgame.

21 b4 a6?!

This speeds up events on the queenside. The line 21...h6 22 b5 ♘d8 was the lesser evil, but of course Black is not singing in the rain here.

22 b5 axb5 23 cxb5 ♘a5

Or 23...♘e7 24 ♛d7 and White starts collecting his reward.

24 ♛e6!

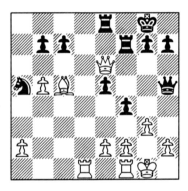

With this little tactic there begins an unstoppable invasion of the black position.

24...♖a8

Or 24...♖xe6 25 ♖d8+ and Black will be mated.

25 ♖d7 ♛g6 26 ♛d5 h6 27 ♖xc7 ♖e8 28 ♗b4 b6 29 ♗xa5 bxa5 30 b6 ♛e6 31 ♛xe6 ♖xe6 32 ♖b1 ♖e8 33 ♖xf7 ♔xf7 34 b7 ♖b8 35 gxf4 exf4 36 ♔g2 ♔e6 37 ♔f3 g5 38 ♔e4 1-0

Game 30
Botvinnik-Ryumin
Moscow 1936

In annotating this game, I have translated parts of the original annotations by Botvinnik.

1 ♘f3 f5

Botvinnik, who himself played the Stonewall in many important games, did not like this move order as it gives White a wide choice of set-ups. It also gives White the chance to go for the gambit line 2 e4!?, which is beyond the scope of this book.

2 g3 ♘f6 3 ♗g2 e6 4 0-0 ♗e7 5 c4 0-0 6 b3

Botvinnik: 'If Black plays 6...d5 then White can reply 7 d3, and later, with advantage, carry out a break with e4. Therefore Black chooses to employ the Ilyin-Zhenevsky set-up.'

6...♕e8 7 ♘c3 ♕h5 8 ♕c2 ♘c6 9 d4

Via a transposition of moves we are back into main lines.

9...d6 10 ♗a3 ♖f7

This move is played to avoid the trick with d5, ...♘d8 and ♘e5, when the bishop on e7 hangs after ...dxe5 (see Game 29).

11 ♖ad1 ♗d7

Botvinnik: 'Possibly slightly better was 11...e5 12 dxe5 dxe5 13 ♗xe7 ♖xe7 14 ♘d5 ♘xd5 15 cxd5 ♘d8 16 ♕c5 ♕e8 17 e4 ♘f7 and Black has somewhat freed his game at the cost of the weakened e5-pawn.'

12 d5 ♘d8

Black cannot play 12...♘e5 13 ♘xe5 dxe5 14 dxe6 ♗xe6 15 ♗xb7 as there is no compensation for the pawn. Botvinnik stops his line here. After 15...♘g4 16 h4 ♗xh4 17 ♔g2! (preparing ♖h1) 17...♗xg3 18 ♖h1 ♕g5 19 ♗xa8 ♗h4 20 ♔f1 ♘xf2 21 ♕d2! it seems that Black's attack has been repulsed.

13 dxe6

Black was planning to play 13...e5.

13...♘xe6

Botvinnik: 'Not 13...♗xe6, because of 14 ♘d4. In the 1931 USSR Championship, in a game against Kan, I employed this same system of development for White but did not play the important move 11 ♖d1, thanks to which Kan managed to equalise. Now, already with the rook on d1, White spoils Black's pawn formation with an interesting combination.'

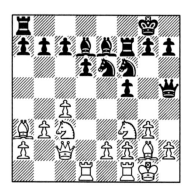

14 c5! dxc5

This is forced as 15 cxd6 would be a positional disaster for Black. Also unplayable is 14...♘xc5 15 ♗xc5 dxc5 16 ♘e5 and White wins material. Black cannot escape with 16...♘g4 as White wins after 17 ♘xg4 fxg4 18 ♖xd7.

15 ♘e5 ♘d4 16 ♕d3 ♘g4

This is forced by the circumstances. After most other moves White will exploit the pin on the d4-knight with 17 e3.

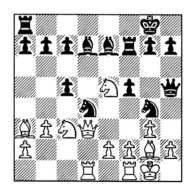

17 ♘xg4 fxg4

Botvinnik: 'Again forced as after 17...♕xg4 18 e3 White wins.' But this is not entirely true, as after something like 18...c4!? 19 ♕xc4 ♗e6 20 ♕xd4 ♕xd4 21 ♖xd4 ♗xa3 22 ♗xb7 ♖b8 23 ♗d5 White has a clear advantage, but it not too different from the ending arising in the game.

18 ♗xb7

After 18 e3? ♗f5 Black would be back in the game.

18...♖af8 19 ♗d5

Botvinnik: 'Exchanges are of course very favourable for White as the advantage of his better pawn structure must tell in the endgame.'

19...♗e6 20 ♗xe6 ♘xe6 21 ♘e4

Botvinnik: 'A very important move. Black threatened ...♖xf2, or even to transfer a rook via f6 to h6.'

Now Black tries to close the d-file with a knight, but even though the exchange of the white bishop for the black knight resurrects the black pawn structure, White has a large positional advantage as all the pawns in the centre are on the same colour as the bishop.

21...♘d4 22 ♗b2 ♖d8 23 ♛c4 ♛e5 24 ♗xd4 cxd4

Or 24...♖xd4 25 ♖xd4 cxd4 26 f3 gxf3 27 exf3 with a positional advantage for White. This was Black's best shot nonetheless.

25 f3 gxf3

Better here was 25...♖d5 (unpinning the ♖f7) 26 ♖d3 gxf3 27 exf3, but although Black has not suffered material loss, he can hardly move and would have few chances of saving the game against the great Botvinnik.

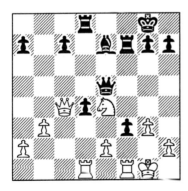

26 ♖xf3

Black now loses a pawn by force. After 26...♗f6 27 ♖f4! the pawn cannot be saved. The same goes for the move Black chose in the game.

26...♛d5 27 ♖xf7 ♔xf7

Or 27...♛xc4 28 ♖xg7+.

28 ♖xd4 ♛xc4 29 ♖xc4 c5 30 ♔f2 ♖d5 31 ♖a4 ♖d4

Black has no chances left to save the game, but still tries to fight on.

32 ♘c3 ♖xa4 33 ♘xa4 ♔e6 34 ♔e3 ♔f5 35 ♔f3 ♔e5 36 e3 ♗d6 37 ♘b2 ♔d5 38 ♘c4 ♗c7 39 ♔e2 ♔e4 40 ♘d2+ ♔f5 41 ♔f3 ♔e5 42 ♘c4+ ♔d5 43 ♔e2 ♔e4 44 ♘d2+ ♔f5 45 ♔f3 ♔e5

46 g4!

Taking the f5-square away from the Black king.

46...♔d5 47 h3 ♗d8 48 ♔e2 ♗c7 49 ♔d3 ♗g3 50 ♘e4 ♗e1 51 ♘g5

Botvinnik: 'Provoking an important weakening of the black position.'

51...h6 52 ♘e4 ♗h4 53 ♘c3+ ♔c6

Botvinnik: 'Forced. On 53...♔e5 follows 54 ♘b5 a5 and the black a-pawn is very weak. Now, however, the white king obtains the e4-square.'

54 ♔e4 ♗f6 55 ♘b1 ♔d6 56 ♘a3 ♔e6 57 ♘b5 a5 58 ♘c7+ ♔d7 59 ♘d5 ♗b2 60 ♘b6+ 1-0

Botvinnik: 'There might follow 60...♔e6 61 ♔d3 ♗a3 62 ♔c4 ♔e5 63 ♔b5 ♗b4 64 ♘c4+ ♔e4 65 ♘xa5 ♔f3 66 a4 ♔g3 67 ♘c6 ♗d2 68 a5 ♔xa5 69 ♔xa5 ♔xh3 70 ♘e5 and further struggle is useless. Or 60...♔c6 61 ♘c4 ♗c3 62 a3 g6 63 a4 and Black is in zugzwang.'

Game 31
Zinner-Flohr
Podebrady 1936

1 d4 f5 2 ♘f3 ♘f6 3 g3 e6 4 ♗g2 ♗e7 5 0-0 0-0 6 c4 d6 7 ♘c3 ♕e8 8 b3 ♕h5

Black has three alternatives here:

a) 8...c6 9 ♗b2 ♘a6 10 ♖c1 ♗d7 11 a3 ♘c7 12 b4 a5 13 ♕b3 axb4 14 axb4 ♕h5 15 b5 and White has a slightly better game, Sokolsky-Kofman, USSR 1947.

b) 8...♘bd7 9 ♗a3 e5 10 ♘b5 ♗d8 11 dxe5 ♘xe5 12 e3 ♔h8 13 ♘xe5 ♕xe5 14 ♕c2 a6 15 ♘c3 with advantage to White in Najdorf-Heidfeld, Torremolinos 1961.

c) 8...♘c6 9 ♕c2 (9 d5 should be investigated) 9...♕g6 10 ♗a3 ♘e4 11 ♘b5 ♗d8 12 d5 ♘b8 13 dxe6 ♗xe6 14 ♘d2 ♘xd2 15 ♕xd2 ♘c6 with an even game in Petrov-Keres, USSR 1938.

9 ♗b2 ♗d8!?

For 9...a5, see Chapter 1. Black has also tried 9...♘bd7 10 ♖e1

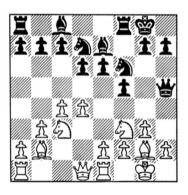

and now:

a) 10...♘e4 11 ♘xe4 (11 ♕d3 ♘df6 12 a3 ♘xc3 13 ♗xc3 ♘e4 14 ♗b2 ♗d7 15 ♘d2 would give White a minor advantage) 11...fxe4 12 ♘d2 with a further split:

a1) 12...d5 13 ♕c2 c6 (13...c5! 14 ♖ac1 ♘f6 15 ♘f1 cxd4 16 ♗xd4 e5, with good play for Black, was better) 14 f3 ♘f6 15 ♘f1 exf3 16 exf3 ♗d7 17 ♖e5 gave White a small

edge in Filip-Jezek, Prague 1953.

a2) 12...e3!? 13 fxe3 ♗g5 14 ♘f1 ♘f6 15 h3 e5 16 dxe5 dxe5 17 ♗xe5 ♗xh3 gave Black good attacking chances in the game Borisenko-Lazarevic, Leningrad 1964.

b) 10...a6?! (after this move Black is left with a weak pawn on e6) 11 e4 fxe4 12 ♘xe4 ♘xe4 13 ♖xe4 ♘f6 14 ♖e2 ♖b8 (with the idea of ...b7-b5 – there are no other viable plans for Black) 15 ♕d3 b5 16 ♖ae1 bxc4 17 bxc4 ♗d8 18 h3 ♕f5 19 ♕d2 (White has a positional advantage, but the game is not decided) 19...♘d7 20 c5!? (but not 20 ♖xe6? ♘b6 21 ♖6e2 ♘xc4 and Black is even better) 20...♘f6? (necessary was 20...♗b7! 21 ♘h4 ♗xh4 22 c6 ♗a8 23 cxd7 ♗xg2 24 ♔xg2 ♕f3+ 25 ♔h2 ♗f6 26 ♘c3 ♕c6 27 ♖xe6 and White only has a small advantage) 21 ♗a3! ♘e8 22 d5 e5 23 cxd6 ♘xd6 24 ♘xe5 with a close-to-winning position in the game Sulava-Sale, Kastel Stari 1997.

10 a3

After 10 e3 ♘bd7 11 ♘e2 ♘e4 12 ♘f4 ♕h6 13 b4 c6 14 ♕c2 g5 15 ♘d3 ♗c7 the position remains unclear.

10...♘bd7 11 ♕c2 e5 12 dxe5 dxe5 13 ♖ad1 c6?!

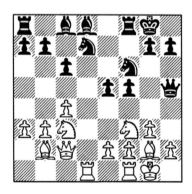

This move gives White the chance to seize the initiative in the centre. It was better to play 13...e4 14 ♘d4 ♘e5 15 ♘d5 c6! (15...♘xd5 16 cxd5 gives White an edge due to the pressure down the c-file, while after 16...e3?! 17 h3 f4 18 ♘e6! ♗xe6 19 dxe6

Black does not have a sufficient attack to compensate for his structural concessions) 16 ♘f4 ♕h6 17 h3 ♖e8 18 ♘de6 ♗xe6 19 ♗xe5 ♗f7 with excellent play for Black.

14 b4?!

Here White had the chance to play 14 e4! fxe4?! (not the best, but 14...f4 15 ♘e2 ♗c7 16 c5! also gives White the better chances) 15 ♘xe4 ♗c7 16 ♘fg5, when White is better in every way.

14...♗c7 15 e3

After 15 c5 a5 16 ♖d2 axb4 17 axb4 e4 Black is okay.

15...e4 16 ♘d4 ♘e5 17 ♘b1?!

One wonders what makes anyone play such a move. After 17 c5 ♖d8 18 f3 exf3 19 ♘xf3 ♗e6 20 ♖xd8+ ♖xd8 21 ♘b5!? cxb5 22 ♗xe5 ♗xe5 23 ♘xe5 ♘e4! the position is unclear. The point is, of course, that 24 ♗xe4? fxe4 25 ♕xe4 ♖d2 26 ♘f3 ♗d5 27 g4 ♕xh2+ 28 ♘xh2 ♗xe4 leaves Black with all the chances.

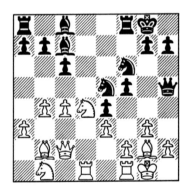

17...♘f3+?!

Forcing moves like this one are good for White in this position as he himself has no active play and can only sit and wait for Black to come running. Black probably wanted to play this before White got time to play ♘d2 (protecting f3), but stronger was 17...♘d3 with the idea of ...a7-a5 – Black is more than just slightly better here.

18 ♗xf3 exf3 19 ♘d2 f4!

This is a typical pawn sacrifice. Black has

compensation on the light squares and with this move he frees his bishop and weakens White's kingside.

20 exf4 ♗xf4 21 ♘2xf3 ♗g4 22 ♘h4?

White does not defend very well. After 22 ♖d3! ♗c7 23 ♘h4 ♖ae8 24 f3 ♗h3 Black has a lot of chances with his two bishops, but White is still in the game.

22...♗xd1 23 ♖xd1

23 ♕xd1 ♗e5 24 f4 ♕xd1 25 ♖xd1 ♗xd4+ 26 ♗xd4 ♖ad8 would give Black about a 90% chance of winning the endgame.

23...♗e5 24 ♘hf5

24 f3 ♖ae8 25 ♕d3 b6 is another line leading to a clear black advantage. Now Black has a direct win.

24...♖ae8

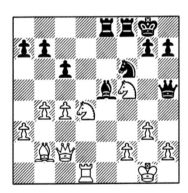

This move is of course okay, but better was 24...♘g4 25 f3 (or 25 h4 ♗xd4 26 ♘e7+ ♔h8 27 ♗xd4 ♘e5 with a winning position for Black) 25...♗xd4+ 26 ♖xd4 (26 ♘xd4 ♘e3 wins) 26...♘e5 27 ♖f4 ♘xf3+ and White should resign.

25 f4 ♗xd4+ 26 ♘xd4 ♘g4 27 c5 ♖f7 28 ♕d2 ♖fe7 29 ♘f3 ♘e3 0-1

Game 32
Arnson-Korchnoi
Leningrad 1951

1 d4 f5 2 ♘f3 ♘f6 3 g3 e6 4 ♗g2 ♗e7 5 0-0 0-0 6 c4 d6 7 ♘c3 ♕e8 8 ♕d3?!

Placing the queen in the centre is not advisable.

8...♘c6 9 ♗g5?!

This move is not particularly good. The alternatives are:

a) 9 ♗f4 ♗d7 10 a3 a5 11 ♖ab1 ♕h5 and here Black has two plans. Firstly, to prepare the advance in the centre with ...e6-e5 and secondly, to organise an attack on the kingside with ...h6 and ...g7-g5 etc. Overall, the position is unclear.

b) 9 e4?! ♕h5! 10 ♖e1 (after 10 exf5 e5! 11 c5 ♗xf5 12 ♕c4+ ♔h8 13 cxd6 ♗xd6 14 dxe5 ♘g4! 15 h4 [15 exd6?? ♘ce5 and the knight on f3 is overloaded] 15...♘gxe5 Black is better) 10...e5! 11 dxe5 dxe5 12 ♘d5 fxe4 13 ♘xf6+ ♗xf6 14 ♕xe4 ♗f5 and Black has equalised – at least.

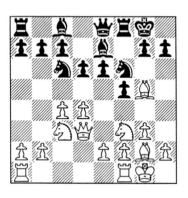

9...e5! 10 dxe5 dxe5 11 e4 fxe4

Even stronger is 11...♕g6! 12 ♖fe1 ♖d8 13 ♕e2 fxe4 14 ♘xe4 ♗g4 and Black has control over a lot of important squares in the centre.

12 ♘xe4 ♗e6

Black also has the following moves at his disposal: 12...♘xe4 13 ♕xe4 ♗f5 14 ♕d5+ ♔h8 15 ♗xe7 ♕xe7 16 ♖fe1 with equality and 12...♕f7 13 ♘xf6+ gxf6 14 ♗e3 ♖d8 15 ♕c2 ♗e6 with even chances.

13 ♘xf6+ ♗xf6

Not so good is 13...gxf6?! 14 ♗h6 ♕f7? (14...♖f7, with a slightly worse position, was forced) 15 ♗xf8 ♗xc4 16 ♕d7 ♗xf1 17

♘g5! and White has a clear advantage.

14 ♕e4 ♖d8

14...♕h5 15 ♗xf6 gxf6 (15...♖xf6?! 16 ♖fe1 would expose the e-pawn to attack) 16 ♖fe1 would be more or less even.

15 ♖ad1 ♕h5

Black also has 15...♖xd1 16 ♖xd1 ♗g5 17 ♘xg5 ♕h5 18 ♘f3 ♗g4 19 ♖d3 ♔h8, with a level position.

16 ♗xf6 gxf6 17 b3 ♗f5

Black has two alternatives here:

a) 17...f5?! 18 ♕h4! ♕xh4 19 ♘xh4 gives White a slight positional edge due to the weakness of the e5/f5 complex.

b) 17...♗g4 18 ♖xd8 ♖xd8 19 ♖e1 results in a level position.

18 ♕h4 ♕g6!

18...♕xh4?! 19 ♘xh4 ♗c2 20 ♖xd8 ♖xd8 21 f4! would give White the chance to gain the initiative.

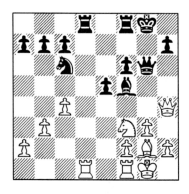

19 c5?!

19 ♖fe1 with an even game was better. Now Black gains time.

19...♗d3 20 ♖fe1 ♘d4!

White's queen is now clearly out of play on the edge of the board.

21 ♕h3 ♘c2! 22 ♘h4?

After this move White cannot offer any more resistance. Better was 22 ♕e6+!? ♔h8 23 ♘xe5! fxe5 24 ♕xe5+ ♕g7 (24...♖f6 25 ♕xc7 ♖df8 26 ♖e7 gives White a lot of unnecessary counterplay) 25 ♕xg7+ ♔xg7 26 ♖e7+ ♔f6 27 ♖xc7 ♗f5 28 ♖xd8 ♖xd8 29 h4 ♖d1+ 30 ♔h2 ♖d2 and Black has a some chances to win the endgame.

22...♕g7 23 ♗xb7 ♘xe1 24 ♖xe1 ♕d7

24...f5 25 ♗g2 ♕f6, with an overwhelming advantage, also seems natural.

25 ♕g2 e4!

25...♔h8 26 ♕c6 ♗b5 27 ♕xd7 ♗xd7 is also very good for Black, but this is more clean cut.

26 ♗xe4

This is forced, otherwise the bishop is lost.

26...♖fe8 27 ♗d5+ ♔h8 28 ♖xe8+ ♖xe8 29 h3 ♖e1+ 30 ♔h2 ♗f1!

A nice little tactic to finish the game. Of course it's h3 which is the problem.

31 ♗c6 ♕e6 32 ♗d5 ♗xg2 33 ♗xe6 ♗c6! 0-1

Game 33
Tregubov-Kobalija
St. Petersburg 1994

---

1 d4 e6 2 c4 f5 3 g3 ♘f6 4 ♗g2 ♗e7 5 ♘c3 0-0 6 ♘f3 d6 7 0-0 ♕e8 8 ♗g5

This move is not at all dangerous for Black.

8...♕g6!?

The natural move, but Black also has alternatives:

a) 8...♘bd7 9 ♕b3 ♕h5 10 c5! d5 11 ♕a4 h6 12 ♗xf6 ♘xf6 13 ♘e5 with a small advantage to White in Grivas-Palma, Thessalo-

niki 1984.

b) 8...♘e4!? 9 ♗xe7 ♘xc3 10 bxc3 ♕xe7 11 ♕d3 (11 ♖b1 ♘d7 12 ♘d2 ♖b8 13 ♕a4 a6 seems to hold the position on the queenside together – the position is unclear) 11...♘c6 12 ♘d2 e5 13 e3 ♗d7 with an even game in Rossolimo-Pachman, Hilversum 1947.

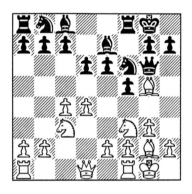

9 ♖e1 ♘c6 10 d5

After 10 ♘b5 ♘e8 11 ♗xe7 ♘xe7 White has no advantage.

10...♘e5

10...♘d8? 11 ♘b5! would make Black suffer severely.

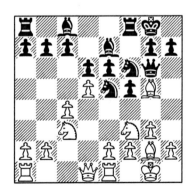

11 ♗xf6

11 ♘xe5 ♕xg5 12 ♘f3 ♕g4 13 dxe6 ♕xc4 14 ♘d4 f4!? is unclear, but 14...♗xe6? 15 ♖c1! would expose the bad position of the black queen. The line 14...c5 15 ♘xf5 ♕xe6 16 e4 is also comfortable for White.

11...♘xf3+ 12 exf3

After 12 ♗xf3!? ♛xf6! (12...♗xf6?! 13 dxe6 ♗xc3 14 bxc3 ♗xe6 15 ♗xb7 ♖ae8 16 ♗d5 would secure a white advantage) 13 ♘b5 (13 dxe6 c6! 14 e3 ♗xe6 is slightly better for Black) 13...♗d8 14 dxe6 ♗xe6 15 ♗xb7 ♖b8 16 ♗d5 f4 the position is unclear.

12...♗xf6 13 ♘b5 ♛f7

13...♖f7? is completely wrong; 14 dxe6 ♖e7 15 f4 would give White a distinct advantage.

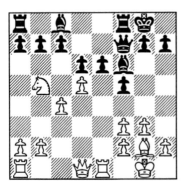

14 f4?!

This allows Black to solve all his problems. After 14 dxe6 ♗xe6 15 ♘xc7! ♛xc7 16 ♖xe6 ♛xc4 17 f4! White still has some pressure.

14...e5 15 c5

Worse would be 15 fxe5?! ♗xe5 16 ♛c2 a6 and the bishop on e5 dominates the board.

15...a6 16 cxd6 axb5 17 fxe5 ♗xe5!

Maybe White had not really realised that Black would simply return the bishop. 17...♗g5? 18 e6 ♛g6 19 dxc7 would give White an overwhelming advantage with three passed pawns on the 5th, 6th and 7th ranks.

18 ♖xe5 cxd6 19 ♖e3

The rook is exposed here. Better is 19 ♖e1!? f4 20 ♛d2 f3 21 ♗f1 with an unclear position.

19...f4 20 gxf4 ♖a4! 21 ♛e2 ♖xf4

This is simply a perfect position for Black! White can only sit and wait to see how Black

will irritate him.

22 ♖f1 b4 23 ♖g3

23 ♖e7 ♛g6 24 ♔h1 ♛h6 gives Black a chance to attack the weakest spot in White's position: h2.

23...h5! 24 ♗h3?

24 h3 was necessary. Now White is in trouble.

24...♖e8!

24...♗xh3 25 ♖xh3 ♖f5 26 ♛d2 ♛xd5 27 ♛xb4 ♖f4 28 ♛b3 ♖g4+ 29 ♖g3 ♛xb3 30 axb3 ♖f3 31 ♖xg4 hxg4 32 b4 ♖b3 33 ♖d1 ♖xb4 would give White some, though not many, chances to win the endgame.

25 ♖e3 ♖xe3 26 fxe3 ♖xf1+ 27 ♗xf1 ♛xd5 28 b3 ♛g5+ 29 ♔f2 ♛h4+ 30 ♔g1 ♛g5+ 31 ♔f2 ♗e6 32 ♛f3 ♛f5 33 e4 ♛e5 0-1

Black would eventually win this ending, but I assume that here White lost the game on time.

Game 34
Szily-Farago
Budapest 1967

---

1 d4 e6 2 g3 f5 3 ♗g2 ♘f6 4 c4 ♗e7 5 ♘c3 0-0 6 ♘f3 d6 7 0-0 ♛e8 8 ♗f4

It is very hard to see exactly what the positional justification is for putting the bishop here. All I can think of are some ideas involving c4-c5 to try to weaken Black's queenside.

ter 19...♗d7 Black looks okay.

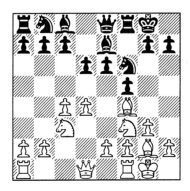

8...c6

8...♘h5 9 ♗g5 ♗xg5 10 ♘xg5 h6 11 ♘f3 (11 ♘xe6!? ♗xe6 12 ♗xb7 ♘d7 13 d5 ♗f7 14 ♗xa8 ♕xa8 would give an unclear position) 11...♘c6 12 d5 ♘d8 13 dxe6 ♗xe6 14 b3 ♘f6 15 ♘d4 gave White a slight edge in R.Byrne-Rossolimo, US Championship 1962/63. However, maybe Black can play 8...♘c6!? with the standard development plan of ...♗d7, ...♕h5 and ...♖ae8. After 9 d5 ♘d8 10 dxe6 ♘xe6 Black should be equal. In this line the bishop on f4 is clearly exposed.

9 ♕b3 ♘bd7

9...♕h5 would allow White to obtain an advantage after 10 ♕a3! ♖d8 11 ♖fe1, when Black's pieces are somewhat passively placed.

10 a4 a5

After the premature 10...♘e4?! 11 ♘xe4 fxe4 12 ♘d2 d5 (12...e5? 13 dxe5 dxe5 14 ♗e3 is just bad for Black) 13 f3! White would have the advantage as he is better prepared for the opening of the centre.

11 ♘g5 e5 12 ♗e3?

Here White misses his chance. The line 12 c5+! ♔h8!? (12...d5 13 ♗xe5! ♘xe5 14 dxe5 ♘g4! 15 ♘xd5 cxd5 16 ♗xd5+ ♔h8 17 ♘f7+ ♖xf7 18 ♗xf7 ♕c6 19 e6 ♖a6 20 ♖ad1 and the position is anything but clear) 13 cxd6 ♗xd6 14 dxe5 ♘xe5 15 ♖fd1 ♕e7 would probably give White an advantage, but he cannot force matters with 16 ♖xd6 ♕xd6 17 ♗xe5 ♕xe5 18 ♘f7+ ♖xf7 19 ♕xf7 as af-

12...♕h5!

Suddenly all kinds of threats start to arise around White's king.

13 ♘e6 ♘g4 14 h3 ♘xe3

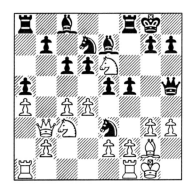

15 ♘xf8?

Probably a miscalculation. 15 fxe3 ♖f6 16 ♘c7 ♖b8 17 ♔h2 e4 would give Black good possibilities to create an attack, but this was still White's best path.

15...♘xf1 16 ♘xd7 ♘d2 17 ♕d1 ♘xc4 18 b3?!

This is too slow. The best chance is 18 ♕b3 ♗xd7 19 ♕xc4+ ♕f7 20 d5 and White is still kicking and screaming his way to his execution.

18...♘b2 19 ♕d2 exd4!

Now Black just wins everything.

20 ♘b6

20 ♘d5 ♗g5 21 ♕xb2 ♗xd7 22 ♘b6

♖d8 23 ♘xd7 ♖xd7 24 b4 would give White some chances to offer resistance.

20...dxc3 21 ♕e3 ♗g5 22 f4 ♗f6 23 ♘xa8

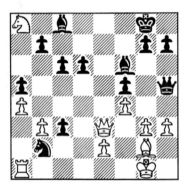

White is an exchange up, but his position is beyond help.

23...d5 24 ♕c5 ♕xe2 25 ♗xd5+ ♗e6 26 ♗xe6+ ♕xe6 27 ♖f1

Or 27 ♘c7 ♕d7!.

27...♕e4 0-1

Game 35
Marin-Hamdouchi
Sitges 1994

---

1 d4 e6 2 c4 f5 3 g3 ♘f6 4 ♗g2 ♗e7 5 ♘f3 0-0 6 0-0 d6 7 ♘c3 ♘e4!?

This is the move that, besides 7...a5, holds the best prospects for Black.

8 ♕c2 ♘xc3 9 bxc3 ♘c6 10 d5

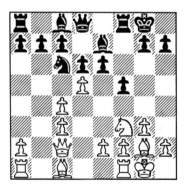

Here it is important to note the following lines after 10 e4:

a) 10...♘a5 11 ♕a4 b6 12 exf5 ♗d7 13 ♕c2 exf5 14 ♖e1 ♗f6 15 ♘d2 c6 16 ♕d3 ♖e8 17 ♖xe8+ ♕xe8 18 ♘b3 was agreed drawn in Cs.Horvath-Bricard, Bischwiller, 1999.

b) 10...e5! (Black has already equalised) 11 ♗a3 f4! (This structure is perfect for Black. The bishop on e7 will do his part defending the structure, while the bishop on c8 gets to have all the fun.) 12 c5 ♔h8 13 ♖ad1?! (Here White is drifting. The structure is, in the long run, very dangerous for him. Correct is 13 d5! ♘a5 14 c4, an attempt to use the misplacement of Black's knight to his own advantage.) 13...♕e8! 14 d5 ♘d8!. Black has obtained a perfect version of the King's Indian Defence's main lines, where the race on opposite flanks is the main agenda. Here White has trouble creating weaknesses on the queenside, While Black is only a few moves away from a deadly attack on the kingside. I have left this game in as an illustration of the way things can go wrong for White. 15 c4 b6 16 cxd6 cxd6 17 ♗b4 ♕h5 18 ♖d3 ♗g4 19 ♕c3 ♘b7 20 ♖b1 ♖f7 21 a4 ♖af8 22 ♖b3 ♔g8 23 ♔h1 g5 24 ♘g1 ♖f6 25 gxf4 ♖h6 26 h3 ♖xf4 27 f3

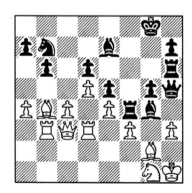

27...♗xh3! 28 ♘xh3 ♖h4 29 f4 exf4 30 ♔g1 ♗f6 31 ♕d2 ♗e5 32 a5 g4 33 a6 ♘d8 34 ♘xf4 ♖h1+ 35 ♔f2 ♖f6 36 ♗xh1 ♕xh1 37 ♔e2 ♖xf4 38 ♕e1 ♕g2+ 39 ♔d1 ♖f1 40

♖e3 ♘f7 41 ♗d2 ♗d4 0-1 Hanko-Ovetchkin, Pardubice 1996.

10...♘a5 11 ♛a4 c5

Here Black should have preferred 11...b6!?. The point is that after 12 ♘d4 e5 13 ♘c6 ♗d7! (13...♘xc6 14 dxc6 e4 15 f3 exf3 16 exf3 ♗e6 17 f4 would give an equal game) 14 ♘xd8 ♗xa4 15 ♘e6 ♖fc8 Black has a better position. Black also enjoys a good position after 12 dxe6 ♗xe6 13 ♘d4 ♗xc4! 14 ♗xa8 ♛xa8. The control over the light squares combined with a pawn is worth more than the exchange.

12 dxc6 ♘xc6 13 ♘d4 ♗d7?

This changes the evaluation of the position. After 13...♘e5! 14 f4 (but not 14 ♛b3? ♛c7 15 ♗e3 ♛xc4 16 ♗f4 ♛xb3 17 axb3 ♘g6 and Black is a pawn up for nothing) 14...♘g4 15 ♛b4 ♘f6 Black has the better chances.

Worse would have been 13...♘a5?! 14 ♘b3 ♘c6 (14...♘xb3 15 axb3 is better, but White still has a favourable position) 15 c5 d5 16 c4 dxc4 17 ♛xc4, when White has a distinct advantage.

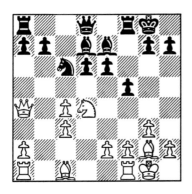

14 ♘xc6

White has no reason to reject the offer.

14...bxc6 15 ♗xc6 ♗xc6 16 ♛xc6 ♖c8 17 ♛a4 ♛c7 18 ♗a3 ♛xc4?!

This gives away a vital pawn. After 18...♖fd8 Black is slightly worse. Now he is in trouble.

19 ♛xa7 ♖f7 20 ♗b4!

With the obvious idea of a2-a4.

20...♛xe2

Black has problems dealing with the pawn: 20...f4 21 a4 ♗f6 22 ♛b6 fxg3 23 hxg3 ♛xe2 24 a5 ♗xc3 25 ♗xc3 ♖xc3 26 a6 ♛f3 27 a7 ♖c8 28 ♛xd6 and White has excellent winning chances.

21 ♖fe1

21 ♛d7 ♛c4 22 ♗xd6?? ♗f6 would be a foolish way for White to lose a good position.

21...♛c4 22 ♛d4 d5?!

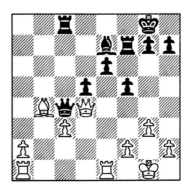

This more or less loses on the spot. 22...♛xd4 23 cxd4 d5! (23...♖c4 24 a3 ♗f6 25 ♖xe6 ♖d7 26 ♖d1 d5 27 ♗c5 leaves White in control) 24 ♗xe7 ♖xe7 25 a4 ♖c6 26 a5 ♖a7 27 ♖eb1 ♔f7 gave Black good chances to scrape a draw.

23 ♛xc4 ♖xc4 24 ♖xe6 ♗xb4 25 cxb4 ♖xb4 26 ♖e8+ ♖f8 27 ♖xf8+! ♔xf8 28 a4

This endgame is without any chances for Black. In order to stop the passed pawn he will have to leave his rook in a very passive place, after which the white king marches into the centre.

28...♖b6 29 a5 ♖a6 30 f4 ♔e7 31 ♔f2 ♔d6 32 ♔e3 ♔c5 33 ♔d3 h5 34 ♖a2 g6 35 ♖a1 d4 36 ♖a4 ♔b5 37 ♖a2 ♔c5 38 ♖a1 ♔d5 39 ♖e1 ♖d6 40 ♖b1!

Precise play. White is toying with the idea of 40...♔c5 41 ♖b6!? as the pawn ending would win easily. After the reckless 40 ♖e7?

♔c6 41 a6 ♔c5 42 ♖c7+ ♔d5 43 a7 ♖a6 Black's rook would suddenly have achieved a perfect active position, from where it could irritate White's king.

40...♔c5 41 ♖c1+

41 ♖b6!? would not win on the spot as after 41...♖d7 42 ♖xg6 ♖b7 43 ♖b6 ♖e7 44 ♖f6 ♖e3+ 45 ♔d2 ♖a3 46 ♖xf5+ ♔c4 47 ♖xh5 ♖a2+, the d-pawn will give Black enough counterplay to give White a serious headache.

41...♔b5

After 41...♔d5 42 ♖c4 the d-pawn is lost.

42 ♖a1!

Threatening just to push the a-pawn. Now Black has no choice but to leave the king as a blockader.

42...♔a6 43 ♖a2 ♖d8 44 ♖a4 ♖b8

Black cannot defend the d-pawn in the long run and decides to get some counterplay with an active rook as soon as possible. Still, it is too late to make any difference.

45 ♖xd4 ♖b2 46 ♖d6+ ♔xa5 47 ♖xg6 ♖xh2 48 ♖g5 ♔b6 49 ♖xf5 ♖h3 50 ♔e4 ♖xg3 51 ♖xh5 ♔c6 52 ♖e5 ♔d6 53 ♔f5 ♖g8 54 ♖e6+ ♔d5

54...♔d7 55 ♔e5 ♖g1 56 ♔f6 ♖h1 57 f5 ♖h6+ 58 ♔f7 ♖h7+ 59 ♔g6 ♖h3 60 ♖e2 ♖g3+ 61 ♔f7 ♔d6 62 f6 would eventually lead to a theoretically winning position.

55 ♖a6 ♖e8 56 ♔g5 ♖g8+ 57 ♔g6 ♖e8 58 f5 ♖a8 59 ♖b6 ♖g8+ 60 ♔f6 ♖g1 61 ♔f7 ♔e5 62 f6 ♖a1 63 ♔f8 1-0

Game 36
San Segundo-Vega Holm
Cala Galdana 1999

1 ♘f3 e6 2 c4 f5 3 g3 ♘f6 4 ♗g2 ♗e7 5 0-0 0-0 6 ♘c3 d6 7 d4 ♘e4 8 ♕c2 ♘xc3 9 ♕xc3

This recapture is more natural than 9 bxc3.

9...♗f6 10 b4!?

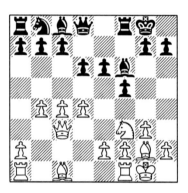

White is playing the full-blown and quick attack on the queenside. As this might give White an edge, Black should seriously consider 9...a5!? as a way to play the position. As the centre is quite closed, development is of less importance and Black might still have time for some prophylaxis.

10...c5

Black has also tried 10...♕e7 11 ♗b2 and now:

a) 11...g5?! is too soon and does too little. You cannot organise an attack when half of your pieces are still, if not in the box, in their starting positions: 12 ♕b3 g4 13 ♘e1 ♘c6 14 e3 ♘d8 15 f4! gxf3 16 ♘xf3 e5 17 dxe5 dxe5 18 e4! fxe4 19 ♘d2 and White has a large positional advantage. Irzhanov-Langier 1997.

b) 11...♘c6 12 b5 ♘d8 13 ♖fe1 g5 14 e4 fxe4 15 ♖xe4 ♕g7 16 h3 and White is a little better, Tartar-Langier, Rogue 1997.

11 bxc5 dxc5 12 e3 ♘c6 13 ♗b2

White has a slightly more pleasant position, but Black should not despair. He is very close to equality. It is simply a question of who plays the best chess from here!

13...♕c7 14 ♕a3

14 ♖ad1 b6 15 ♕a3 ♗b7 would give Black time to equalise with normal developing moves.

14...b6 15 ♖ab1!

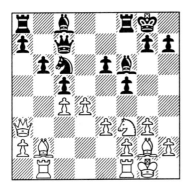

This is something that Nimzowitsch would have called a mysterious rook move. There is more than one idea. First of all, there is an x-ray effect on the b7-square. Secondly, after dxc5 White does not have to recapture on b2 with the queen. And thirdly, there is pure logic. There is nothing to attack in the d-file, so why should the rook go there?

15...♘a5 16 ♖fc1 ♗b7?!

Here Black should have played 16...♗e7! with the idea 17 ♘e5 ♗b7 18 ♗xb7 ♘xb7 19 d5 ♗f6 20 ♘c6 ♘d8! 21 ♘xd8 ♖axd8 and Black has equalised. But maybe 17 d5!? is better.

17 dxc5 ♗e4?!

Black has no idea of what he is doing. The alternatives are:

a) 17...♗xb2 18 ♖xb2 ♖fc8 19 ♖b5! (19 cxb6 axb6 20 ♕b4 ♘xc4 21 ♖bc2 ♕d6 22 ♕xd6 ♘xd6 would let Black escape with a draw) 19...♕e7 20 ♖c3 ♖xc5 21 ♖xc5 ♕xc5 22 ♕xc5 bxc5 23 ♘e5 ♗xg2 24 ♔xg2 ♘b7 25 ♖d3 and the superior placement of White's pieces gives him good chances to win the game.

b) 17...♗e7! is again the best try. After 18 cxb6 axb6 19 ♕c3 ♗f6 20 ♕b4 ♘c6 21 ♕b3 ♘a5 22 ♕b5 ♗a6 23 ♗e5 ♗xb5 24 ♗xc7 ♗xc4 25 ♘d4 ♗xa2 26 ♖xb6 White would only have a slight initiative to show for his efforts.

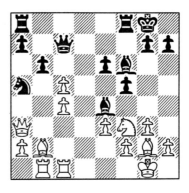

18 ♗xf6 ♖xf6 19 ♖b5

It is hard to see why White is not just a pawn up for nothing.

19...♖ff8 20 cxb6 axb6 21 ♕b4 ♘b7?!

This is a bad square for the knight. The idea is ...♘c5-d3, but this is not dangerous. 21...♘c6 22 ♕b2 would give White an extra pawn and good chances to win the game, but no more.

22 ♖xb6 ♘c5 23 ♖a1!

Why give away the extra material?

23...e5?

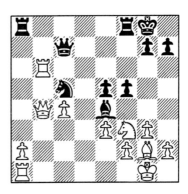

This is played with little or no planning. 23...♖a4 24 ♕b5 ♖xc4 25 ♕xc4 ♕xb6 26 ♘d4 ♗xg2 27 ♔xg2 is technically winning for White, but such positions are not always easy to play in practice so Black should have given it a try.

24 ♖b5 ♘d3 25 ♕c3 f4

Steinitz said that the player with the advantage has to attack or he will lose his advantage. Black must have misunderstood something, or perhaps he is just hoping for miracles.

26 ♘xe5 fxg3 27 ♘xd3 gxh2+ 28 ♔h1 ♕c6 29 ♖g5 ♖f7 30 ♘e5 ♕f6 31 ♗xe4 ♕xg5 32 ♘xf7 1-0

After 33 ♗xa8 Black is in trouble...

Game 37
Czebe-Varga
Zalakaros 2001

1 d4 f5 2 c4 d6 3 g3 ♘f6 4 ♗g2 e6 5 ♘f3 ♗e7 6 0-0 0-0 7 ♘c3 ♘e4 8 ♕c2 ♘xc3 9 ♕xc3 ♗f6 10 ♖d1?!

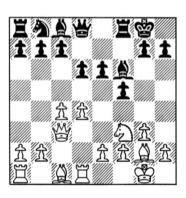

Other White tries are:

a) 10 b4!? was seen in Game 36.

b) 10 ♗e3 ♘c6 (10...♕e7 with the idea e5 should give Black excellent play) 11 ♖ad1 ♕e7 12 b4 ♘d8 13 ♕b3 ♘f7 14 c5 g5 15 ♘e1 and White was slightly better in Khasin-Simagin, USSR 1956.

c) 10 b3 ♕e7 (10...♘c6 11 ♗b2 e5 with unclear play seems logical) 11 ♗a3 ♘c6

(11...c5!? is interesting) 12 c5 d5 13 b4 a6 14 ♗b2 ♗d7 15 a4 ♘d8 16 e3 ♕e8 17 ♕b3 b5 18 cxb6 (18 a5 with a slight advantage is more logical. After 18...♘c6 19 ♘e1 ♕h5 20 ♘d3 White has the plan f3+e4.) 18...cxb6 19 ♖fc1 b5 20 axb5 ♗xb5 21 ♘e5 ♗xe5 22 dxe5 ♘c6 23 ♗f1 ♗xf1 24 ♔xf1 ♖b8 25 ♖xa6 ♘xb4 and the position is level. Gulkov-Ovetchkin, Duban 2000.

10...♕e7 11 b3 e5! 12 e3 e4 13 ♘e1 c5

Black is already close to being better.

14 ♘c2 ♘c6 15 ♕e1 a5 16 a3 ♗d7 17 ♖b1 ♗e8 18 ♕e2 ♗f7 19 h4 ♖fd8 20 ♗h3 g6 21 d5 ♘e5

White has not been able to show anything. The black advantage is now undisputed.

22 ♘e1

22 ♗b2 b5! 23 cxb5 ♘f3+ 24 ♔h1 ♗xb2 25 ♖xb2 ♕e5 26 ♘e1 ♗xe1 27 ♖xe1 ♗xd5 would give Black an overwhelming advantage and a very strong centre.

22...h5?

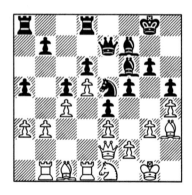

This weakens the kingside for no reason. After 22...b5! 23 cxb5 ♕b7 24 ♕d2 ♕xb5 Black has a clear advantage due to all the white weaknesses.

23 f3 exf3 24 ♘xf3 ♘xf3+

24...♘g4 would give White hope: 25 e4! ♖e8 26 ♗xg4 hxg4 27 ♘g5 ♗xg5 28 ♗xg5 ♕xe4 29 ♕xe4 ♖xe4 30 ♗f4 ♖a6 31 ♖e1 ♖xe1+ 32 ♖xe1 ♖b6 33 ♖e3 and a draw is the most likely result.

25 ♕xf3 ♖e8 26 a4 ♕e4 27 ♕xe4 ♖xe4

28 ♔f2 ♖ae8 29 ♗g2 ♖4e7 30 ♗h3 ♔g7

This is not very ambitious. After 30...♗g7! 31 ♖d3 ♗h6 Black has some practical chances too and can play for a win. The idea of ...g6-g5 sometime in the future is the only active plan on the board.

31 ♖e1 ♗c3 32 ♗b2 ♗xb2 33 ♖xb2 ♔f6
½-½

Game 38
Relange-Bricard
Besancon 1999

---

1 d4 e6 2 c4 f5 3 ♘c3 ♘f6 4 ♘f3 d6 5 g3 ♗e7 6 ♗g2 0-0 7 0-0 ♘e4 8 ♘xe4!

This is the right way to fight for an advantage for White.

8...fxe4 9 ♘e1

After 9 ♘d2 d5 10 f3 exf3 11 ♘xf3 (11 ♖xf3 ♗f6 12 e3 ♘a6 13 ♕c2 b6 14 b3 ♘b4 15 ♕c3 c5 seems to give Black good counterplay; the knight is not well placed on d2 and therefore the natural recapture is with the knight) 11...♘c6 we are back in the main game.

9...d5 10 f3 exf3 11 ♘xf3 ♘c6 12 b3!

This is the most precise move. Black's pawn structure in the centre is already wrecked, so after 12 ♗f4?! dxc4! (12...♗f6 gives Black counterplay according to Marin, but after 13 ♖c1! White is somewhat better) 13 e4 b5 there is possibly not enough for the pawn. 12 cxd5?! exd5 leaves Black with a better pawn structure – the e-pawn is ugly.

12 ♗e3 is more complex, for example:

a) 12...dxc4? 13 ♕a4 ♘b4 14 ♘e5 ♖xf1+ 15 ♖xf1 c6 16 ♗e4 gives White a strong attacking position.

b) 12...♗d7? 13 cxd5 exd5 14 ♕b3 gives Black major problems in the centre.

c) 12...b6 13 ♖c1 ♕d7!? (natural development with 13...♗b7 14 ♗f4 ♕d7 15 ♕d2 leaves White slightly better) 14 ♗f4 ♗a6! gives Black good counterplay.

d) 12...♗f6 13 ♗f2 ♔h8 (13...b6!? is also possible – see 12...b6 for the ideas) 14 ♕c2

♕e8 15 ♖ac1 ♗d7 16 e4 ♘b4 with an unclear position, Bromberger-Dobos, Bechofen 1998.

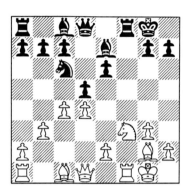

12...e5?

This is a very reckless pawn sacrifice. The right way is: first development, then attack. The line 12...♗f6 13 ♗b2 b6 14 ♘e5 ♗b7 15 ♘g4 ♗e7 16 ♖xf8+ ♗xf8 17 ♕d2 would leave White with a small edge, but after 12...b6! 13 ♗b2 ♗b7 14 ♕d2 ♕d6 it's not obvious that White has an advantage.

13 ♘xe5 ♘xe5

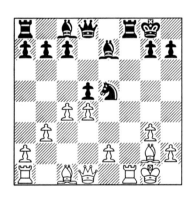

14 dxe5

After 14 ♖xf8+ ♕xf8 15 dxe5 dxc4 16 ♕d5+ ♔h8 17 ♕xc4 ♗c5+ 18 ♔h1 ♕e7 we are back to the game, only with a different number of moves played.

14...♖xf1+ 15 ♔xf1 ♕f8+ 16 ♔g1 dxc4 17 ♕d5+ ♔h8 18 ♕xc4 ♗c5+ 19 ♔h1 ♕e7 20 ♗b2?!

White misses the chance to exploit his lead in development. Much better is 20 ♗g5! ♕xe5 21 ♖d1 ♗e6 22 ♗f4! ♕f5 (or 22...♗xc4 23 ♗xe5 ♗xe2 24 ♖d7 ♗f8 25 ♖xc7 ♖e8 26 ♗d4 b5 27 ♗xa7 and White should win) 23 ♕b5 ♗b6 24 ♕xf5 ♗xf5 25 ♗xb7 and White has a healthy extra pawn in the endgame.

20...c6 21 ♗d4

The position is still much better for White. The question is: 'Is it enough to win?' In my opinion the answer is, 'Yes'.

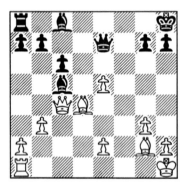

21...♗a3 22 ♖d1 ♗e6 23 ♕c2 a5 24 ♗e4 h6 25 ♗f3 ♖f8 26 ♗c3 ♕c7 27 ♕g6 ♗f5 28 ♕h5 ♗b4 29 ♗b2 ♗e6 30 ♗e4 ♕f7 31 ♕xf7 ♖xf7 32 ♗g6

Here White misses the chance to play 32 ♖d8+! ♖f8 33 ♖xf8+ ♗xf8 34 ♔g2, when he should win this endgame, or at least try to do so until the end of the world.

32...♖f8 33 e4??

This is an awful blunder that costs White an exchange. After a normal move like 33 h4 he would have kept a clear advantage and had good chances to win the game.

33...♗g4 34 ♖d3 ♗c5! 35 ♗f5 ♗e2 36 ♗d4!

White is still able to make the draw after this move due to his passed pawns in the centre. After 36 ♖c3 ♗d4 37 ♔g2 ♗xc3 38 ♗xc3 b6 39 e6 the bishop would be less well placed.

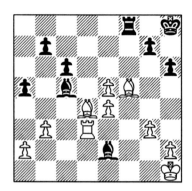

36...♗xd3 37 ♗xc5 ♖e8 38 ♗d6 c5 39 ♔g1 ♗b5 40 e6 g6 41 ♗h3 c4 42 bxc4 ♗xc4 43 e7 ♗b5 44 ♔f2

44 ♗e6 ♔g7 45 ♗e5+ ♔h7 46 ♗d6 is a forced draw. Still, Black cannot win.

44...♔g7 ½-½

> ## Game 39
> ## Porat-Lys
> *Pizen 2001*

1 d4 f5 2 g3 ♘f6 3 ♗g2 e6 4 ♘f3 ♗e7 5 0-0 0-0 6 c4 d6 7 b3 ♕e8 8 ♗b2 ♘bd7 9 ♖e1 ♕g6 10 e3 ♘e4 11 ♘c3 ♘df6

After 11...♗f6 12 ♘e2! b6 13 ♘f4 ♕f7 14 ♘d2 ♗b7 15 ♕c2 White has a small advantage.

12 ♘d2

The alternative knight move 12 ♘e2!? is also a possibility.

12...d5?!

I'm not convinced that this is the best solution. If Black wants to play the Stonewall, he should do so directly in the opening. 12...♘xc3 13 ♗xc3 ♘e4 14 ♗b2 ♗d7 15 f3 ♘xd2 16 ♕xd2 ♗f6 would have equalised the position.

13 f3 ♘g5?

13...♘xc3 14 ♗xc3 ♗d7 15 e4 is better, when White has a small advantage. The knight is not well placed on g5.

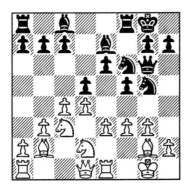

14 e4

14 ♘e2, with some advantage, is also possible.

14...f4

This does not look good, but there are no real alternatives. 14...c6? 15 exd5 cxd5 16 cxd5 and there is a problem with the bishop on e7.

15 exd5 fxg3 16 hxg3?!

Here White misses 16 h4! ♘f7 17 dxe6 ♘d6 18 ♘f1, with an overwhelming advantage.

16...♘h5 17 ♘de4?

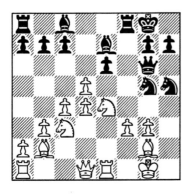

White continues to carelessly let Black set up an attacking position. After 17 ♕b1! ♕xb1 (17...♘h3+? 18 ♗xh3 ♕xg3+ 19 ♗g2 ♘f4 – 19...♗d6 20 ♘f1! – 20 ♖e2 exd5 21

♕e1 ♘xe2+ 22 ♕xe2 ♗d6 23 ♘f1 repulses the attack and gives White the advantage) 18 ♖axb1 ♘xg3 we reach an unclear position.

17...♘xg3!

A brilliant sacrifice.

18 ♘xg5

White loses after 18 ♘xg3? ♘xf3+ 19 ♗xf3 ♕xg3+ 20 ♔h1 (or 20 ♗g2 ♖f2!) 20...♕h3+ 21 ♔g1 ♖xf3.

18...♗xg5 19 dxe6

19 ♘b5? ♗f4! would leave White's king all alone amongst the wolves.

19...♗xe6 20 ♘e4?

This move gives Black time to develop a winning attack. The last chance was 20 f4! ♕f5 21 ♖xe6 (21 fxg5? ♕f2+ 22 ♔h2 ♖f4 and Black wins) 21...♕xf4 (21...♕xe6?? 22 ♗d5) 22 ♕e1 (22 ♘d5? ♕f2+ 23 ♔h2 ♕xb2 and Black is winning) 22...♕xd4+ 23 ♔h2 ♕h4+ 24 ♗h3 ♗f4 25 ♔g2 ♕g5, when Black has a strong attack for the piece, but still the game is undecided.

20...♘xe4 21 ♖xe4 ♗f5

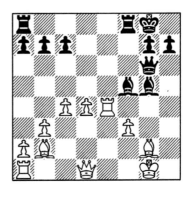

22 ♖e5

This only forces the bishop to f4. Not impressive play!

22...♗f4 23 ♖e7 ♗d6 24 ♖e2 ♕g3 25 ♖d2 ♗h3 26 ♖f2 ♕h2+ 27 ♔f1 ♖ae8 0-1

The move ...♕h1+ is coming.

Summary

As we have seen, White has not yet proven beyond reasonable doubt that he has an advantage after either 7...♕e8 and 7...♘e4. It is true that both lines are risky for Black, but that is the nature of the opening as a whole. In general, White is probably doing best in systems with b3 and ♗b2, but Black does not appear to have anything to fear.

1 d4 f5 2 c4 ♘f6 3 g3 e6 4 ♗g2 ♗e7 5 ♘f3 0-0 6 0-0 d6 7 ♘c3

    7 b3 ♕e8 8 ♗b2 ♘bd7 9 ♖e1 ♕g6 10 e3 ♘e4 11 ♘c3 – *Game 39*

7...♕e8

    7...♘e4

        8 ♘xe4 – *Game 38*

        8 ♕c2 ♘xc3

            9 bxc3 – *Game 35*

            9 ♕xc3 ♗f6 (D)

                10 b4 – *Game 36*; 10 ♖d1 – *Game 37*

8 ♖e1

    8 ♕d3 – *Game 32*; 8 ♗g5 – *Game 33*; 8 ♗f4 – *Game 34*

    8 b3 ♕h5

        9 ♗b2 – *Game 31*

        9 ♕c2 ♘c6 10 ♗a3

            10...a5 – *Chapter 1*; 10...♖f7 – *Game 30*; 10...♗d7 11 d5 – *Game 29*

8...♕g6 (D)

    8...♕h5 – *Game 28*

    8...♘e4 9 ♕c2 ♕g6

        10 b3 – *Game 26*; 10 ♘d2 – *Game 27*

9 e4 fxe4 10 ♘xe4 ♘xe4 11 ♖xe4 (D) e5

    11...♘c6

        12 ♖e1 ♗f6 – *Game 24* (notes)

        12 ♕e2 ♗f6 – *Game 25*

12 ♖e1 ♘c6 13 dxe5 ♗g4 14 h3 ♗xf3 15 ♗xf3 dxe5 – *Game 23*

    15...♘xe5 – *Game 24*

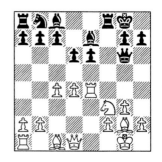

      9...♗f6   *8...♕g6*   *11 ♖xe4*

CHAPTER FOUR

Main Line: White Plays b2-b4

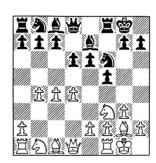

1 d4 f5 2 c4 e6 3 g3 ♘f6 4 ♗g2 ♗e7 5 ♘f3 0-0 6 0-0 d6 7 b4

The b4 system against the Classical Dutch has never been considered a main line, but it is nonetheless one of the most dangerous ideas that White can employ. By advancing quickly on the queenside, White forces Black to create counterplay in the centre or the queenside with great pace, or else White will take over the initiative and Black will find himself struggling.

Games 40-42 deal with White playing b2-b4 as early as move seven, so that Black is not able to prevent this idea with ...a7-a5 (as in Chapters 1-2). Games 43-45 see the move order 7 ♘c3 ♕e8 8 b4, while Games 46-48 concentrate on the line 7 ♘c3 ♕e8 8 ♕c2 ♕h5 9 b4.

Game 40
Baburin-Heidenfeld
Kilkenny 2000

---

1 d4 e6 2 c4 f5 3 g3 ♘f6 4 ♗g2 ♗e7 5 ♘f3 0-0 6 0-0 d6 7 b4

This is an interesting but not very popular move. In my opinion it is White's best chance to fight for an advantage. After 7 ♘c3 Black can play both 7...a5 and 7...♘e4 with good chances for equality.

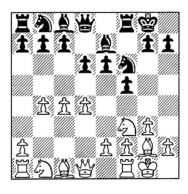

7...♕e8

Black has also tried:

a) 7...e5 8 dxe5 dxe5 9 ♘xe5 and now:

a1) 9...♗xb4 10 ♕b3 c5 (this is forced; after 10...♗c5? 11 ♗xb7 ♗xb7 12 ♕xb7 ♗d4 13 ♗b2 ♗xb2 14 ♕xb2 White is just a pawn up, while following 10...♘a6? 11 c5+ ♔h8 12 ♘f7+ ♖xf7 13 ♕xf7 Black does not have compensation for the exchange) 11 a3 ♕e7 12 axb4 ♕xe5 13 ♗b2 and White is a good deal better.

a2) 9...♕xd1 10 ♖xd1 ♗xb4 11 ♘d3 ♗e7 12 ♗f4 and White has the advantage, Levitt-Williams, British League 2000.

b) 7...c6 8 ♗b2 and now:

b1) 8...d5 is somewhat of a misunderstanding. Black played the Ilyin-Zhenevsky, not the Stonewall! What Black did not realise is that White can play a queenside advance in the Stonewall, even though this is not his usual plan. 9 c5 b6 10 ♘bd2 a5 11 a3 axb4 12 axb4 ♖xa1 13 ♕xa1 ♗a6 14 ♖e1 ♕c7 15 ♗c3 and White can play for a win without any risk. In Smyslov-Letzelter, Monaco 1968, the former World Champion shows us how: 15...♖e8 16 ♘g5 ♗f8 17 f3! 17...bxc5 18 bxc5 f4? (18...e5 19 e4 dxe4 20 fxe4 exd4 21 ♗xd4 and White is only a little better) 19 ♗a5 ♕e7 20 gxf4 ♘h5 21 e3 e5 22 dxe5 ♕xc5 23 ♘b3 ♕a7 24 ♔h1 ♗c4 25 ♘d2 ♗d3 26 ♗h3 h6 27 ♘e6 ♕d7 28 ♕d4 and Black resigned. White wins after 28...♗a6 29 ♘xg7 ♘g3+ 30 ♔g2 ♕xg7 31 hxg3.

b2) Much stronger is 8...♕e8 9 ♘c3 ♘bd7 10 b5 ♕h5 11 a4 e5! 12 e3 e4 13 ♘d2 ♕h6 with unclear play. Black's plan is the following: ...♖f7, ...♘f8, ...g7-g5, ...♗d7, ...♘g6 and then he is ready for the big breakthrough.

8 ♗b2 ♘bd7

This is probably not a good path. The right move appears to be 8...♘c6, as shown in Game 46. Black has also tried 8...♕h5 and now:

a) 9 ♘bd2 ♘bd7 10 ♕c2 e5 11 dxe5 dxe5 12 c5 e4 13 ♘d4 ♘e5 (13...♘d5!? is a possible improvement) 14 f4 ♘eg4?! (14...♘f7 15 ♘c4 would have kept White's advantage to a minimum) 15 ♕b3+ ♔h8 16 h3 ♘h6 17 ♖fd1 c6 18 ♘c4 and White is certainly better, Birukov-Vager, St. Petersburg 1997.

b) 9 ♘c3 (the most natural) 9...g5!? 10 e3 ♘e4 11 ♘d2 ♕xd1 12 ♖axd1 ♘xc3 13 ♗xc3 ♗f6 14 f4 ♘d7 15 e4 gxf4 16 exf5 exf5 17 ♖xf4 ♗g5 18 ♖ff1 and White has a small advantage, Mandl-Bocksberger, Germany 1995.

9 ♘bd2

9 ♘c3!? looks more logical, while also possible is 9 ♕b3 ♗d8!? (I find that this move is usually way too slow; 9...♕h5 10 c5, with an edge to White, is probably better) 10 ♘c3 ♔h8 11 c5 d5 12 a4 c6 13 ♘a2 ♗c7 14

♘c1 e5 15 ♘xe5 ♘xe5 16 dxe5 ♗xe5 17 ♘d3 ♗xb2 18 ♕xb2 and White has a clear advantage, Moskalenko-Sizykh, Alushta 1997.

9...♘e4 10 ♘xe4

In a rare game of mine from this book, Black escaped trouble after the sequence 10 ♕b3 ♕h5?! (10...♘df6 11 a4 ♕h5 12 e3 g5, with an unclear game, was better) 11 d5 (11 ♘xe4! fxe4 12 ♘d2 ♕xe2 13 ♘xe4 gives White the advantage) 11...exd5 12 cxd5 ♗f6 13 e3 ♗xb2 14 ♕xb2 ♘df6 15 ♕d4 ♕f7 16 ♘xe4 fxe4 17 ♘g5 ♕xd5 18 ♕xd5+ ♘xd5 19 ♗xe4 (19 ♘xh7?! does not work: 19...♖f5 20 ♗xe4 ♖e5 21 ♗g6 [or 21 ♗b1 ♘c3 22 f4 ♖xe3 23 ♘g5 a5 and Black has the initiative] 21...♘e7 22 ♗b1 ♖h5 23 h4 ♖xh7 24 ♗xh7+ ♔xh7 and the endgame favours Black) 19...♘f6 20 ♗g2 h6 21 ♘e4 ♘xe4 22 ♗xe4 c6 with complete equality in Ehrenfeucht-Pinski, Warsaw (rapid) 2002.

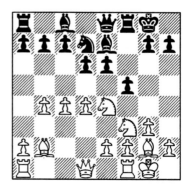

10...fxe4 11 ♘d2 d5 12 ♕b3 c6 13 b5 ♔h8

Black needs to keep the control over the b8-square. After 13...♘f6 14 bxc6! (14 f3!? 14...exf3 15 ♖xf3 dxc4 16 ♘xc4 cxb5 17 ♘e5 with compensation is an interesting alternative) 14...bxc6 15 ♖ab1 White would have the advantage.

14 f3

14 bxc6 bxc6 15 ♖ab1 ♖b8 16 ♕a4 ♕h5 would give Black sufficient counterplay.

14...♗g5

14...exf3 15 ♖xf3 ♖xf3 16 ♕xf3 would leave White too much in control.

15 e3

15 f4 ♗f6 (15...♗e7?! 16 ♗a3! gives White a positional advantage) 16 bxc6 bxc6 17 ♕c2 ♗a6 would result in an unclear position.

15...exf3 16 ♘xf3

The alternatives are not dangerous for Black:

a) 16 ♖xf3 ♖xf3 17 ♗xf3 cxb5 18 cxb5 ♘f6 19 ♖c1 ♗d7 20 a4 ♖c8 and the position is completely even.

b) 16 ♗xf3 cxb5 (16...e5?! does not work tactically: 17 cxd5 exd4 18 ♗xd4 c5 19 ♗c3 ♗xe3+ 20 ♔g2 and after ♖ae1, Black will find himself in major trouble) 17 cxb5 (17 cxd5 exd5 18 ♖ae1 ♘f6 19 ♗xd5 ♗h3 20 ♗g2 ♗xg2 21 ♔xg2 ♗h6! gives Black good counterplay against the white centre) 17...♘f6 with a balanced position.

16...dxc4?

This move should have been punished. After 16...♗h6 (the natural square for this bishop, keeping an eye on e3) 17 bxc6 (17 g4 dxc4 18 ♕c3 cxb5 19 g5 ♖xf3 20 ♖xf3 ♗xg5 21 a4 bxa4 22 ♕xc4 ♘b6 would give Black three pawns for the exchange and a better position) 17...bxc6 18 ♗a3 (18 g4? ♗a6! immediately puts White in his own coffin) 18...♖f7 19 ♘d2 ♗a6 an unclear struggle lies ahead.

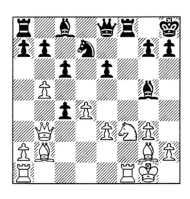

17 ♕xc4?

Here White should have played in a less forcing fashion with 17 ♕c3! and now Black has two possibilities:

a) 17...♗h6?! 18 bxc6 bxc6 19 g4! with a further split:

a1) 19...♗b7 20 g5 ♖xf3 21 ♖xf3 ♗xg5 22 ♖af1 is just very good for White.

a2) 19...♕d8 20 h4 and White has a strong initiative. In fact, Black has no better move than 20...♖xf3.

a3) 19...♕g6? 20 ♘e5! just wins after 20...♖xf1+ 21 ♖xf1 ♕e8 22 ♗xc6 ♖b8 23 ♗a3.

a4) 19...♘f6 20 g5 ♘e4 21 ♕a3 also exposes the problems of the back rank. The main line is 21...♘xg5 22 ♘xg5 ♖xf1+ 23 ♖xf1 ♗xg5 24 ♕f8+ and Black is getting mated.

b) 17...♗f6 18 bxc6 bxc6 19 ♘d2! (19 ♕xc4 c5 20 ♘e5 with a strong initiative for White is also possible) 19...♘b6 20 ♗a3 ♖f7 21 ♘xc4 gives White a clear advantage.

17...♗xe3+ 18 ♔h1 cxb5 19 ♕xb5 ♗h6!

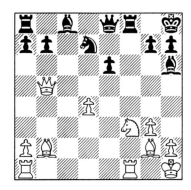

Excellent defence. After 19...♘f6? 20 ♕e2! ♗h6 21 ♗a3 ♖g8 (or 21...♖f7 22 ♘e5 and White wins the exchange) 22 ♘e5 White is close to winning. Black simply cannot develop freely.

20 ♖ae1

This rook needs to enter the scene of action. After 20 ♘e5?! ♗xe5 21 ♕xe5 ♗d7 22 ♖xf8+ ♕xf8 23 ♗xb7 ♖c8! Black is suddenly ahead in development and on his way to taking over the initiative. Note that 24 ♗xc8 ♕f3+ 25 ♔g1 ♗e3+ is not an option for White.

20...♘f6 21 ♕b3

21 ♕xe8 ♖xe8 22 ♘e5 with good compensation for the pawn was another viable option.

21...♗d7 22 ♗a3 ♗a4 23 ♕xe6 ♕xe6 24 ♖xe6 ♖fe8 25 ♖xe8+ ♖xe8 26 ♘e5 ♗e3 27 ♘f7+ ♔g8 28 ♘d6 ♖d8 29 d5

White should not be tempted into 29 ♖xf6?? gxf6 30 ♗d5+ ♔g7! 31 ♘f5+ ♔g6 32 ♘xe3, when Black has the counter-combination 32...♖xd5! 33 ♘xd5 ♗c6. Not only is the knight lost but also the pawn on a2, giving Black a realistic hope of converting an extra pawn into a full point.

29...b6 ½-½

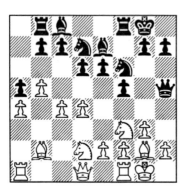

Game 41
Edvardsson-Grivas
Panormo 2001

1 d4 f5 2 g3 d6 3 ♗g2 ♘f6 4 ♘f3 e6 5 c4 ♗e7 6 0-0 0-0 7 b4 a5 8 b5 ♕e8 9 a4 ♘bd7 10 ♗b2 ♕h5 11 ♘bd2 ♖b8

This move makes good sense as it takes care of the development of the c8-bishop. The alternatives are less attractive:

a) 11...♘e4 12 ♘xe4 fxe4 13 ♘d2 d5 14 ♗a3! ♗xa3 15 ♖xa3 and White has a structural advantage.

b) 11...g5 12 ♕b3 ♖f7 13 e3 ♘f8 14 ♘e1 ♘g6 15 f4! and White's queenside offensive seems to move faster than Black's on the kingside.

12 ♖c1 b6

Also interesting is 12...c5!? 13 e3 b6 with unclear play.

13 ♗a3 ♗b7 14 ♘e1 ♗xg2 15 ♔xg2 f4?!

Black underestimates White's reply. The position would have remained unclear after 15...e5 16 dxe5 ♘xe5 17 ♘d3 ♖be8 18 ♘f4 ♕f7 19 ♕c2, when Black can go for three results after 19...g5!? 20 ♘d3 ♕h5.

16 e4 ♕g6

16...♕xd1 17 ♖xd1 fxg3 18 hxg3 is better for White as Black has space problems and a bad bishop.

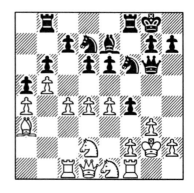

17 e5 ♘g4 18 ♘ef3 ♖be8 19 exd6 cxd6 20 ♕e2 e5 21 ♕e4 ♕xe4 22 ♘xe4 d5

Black should probably have tried 22...fxg3 23 hxg3 exd4 (23...♖xf3?! 24 ♔xf3 ♘h2+ 25 ♔e3 ♘xf1+ 26 ♖xf1 exd4+ 27 ♔xd4 would give White very good chances to win the endgame) 24 ♘xd4 (24 ♘xd6 ♗xd6 25 ♗xd6 ♖xf3 26 ♔xf3 ♘h2+ 27 ♔g2 ♘xf1 28 ♔xf1 d3 29 ♖d1 ♖e4 30 ♖xd3 ♖xc4 gives Black good counterplay) 24...♗f6 25 ♘xf6+ ♖xf6, when Black has good practical chances, even if White is slightly better.

23 ♗xe7 dxe4 24 ♗xf8 exf3+ 25 ♔h3 h5 26 ♗d6 exd4 27 gxf4

Black does not have enough compensation for the sacrificed exchange.

27...♘df6 28 c5 ♘e4

After 28...d3 29 cxb6 d2 30 ♖a1 ♘e4 31 ♗c7 ♘gxf2+ 32 ♔h4 d1♕ 33 ♖axd1 ♘xd1 34 ♖xd1 White's b-pawn decides the game.

29 ♗c7 ♘xc5 30 ♗xb6 ♘d3

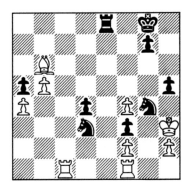

31 ♗xd4!

The simplest. Now the endgame becomes easier for White to control. That said, White also wins after 31 ♔g3! ♘xc1 32 ♖xc1 d3 33 ♗xa5.

31...♘xc1 32 ♖xc1 ♖e4 33 b6!

Winning the exchange again.

33...♖xd4 34 b7 ♘xf2+ 35 ♔g3 ♘e4+ 36 ♔xf3 ♖b4 37 ♖c8+ ♔h7 38 b8♕ ♖xb8 39 ♖xb8 ♘c3 40 ♖a8 ♘xa4 41 ♖xa5 ♘b6 42 ♖xh5+ ♔g6 43 ♖c5 ♘d7 44 ♖c6+ ♘f6 45 ♖a6 ♔f5 46 h3 ♔g6 47 ♖a7 ♔h6 48 ♔g3 ♔g6 49 ♖a5 ♔h6 50 ♔h4 ♔g6 51 f5+ ♔h6 52 ♖a6 ♔h7 53 ♖b6 ♔h6 54 ♖e6 ♔h7 55 ♔g5 ♘d5 56 h4 ♔g8 57 ♖d6 1-0

Game 42
Krush-N.Pert
Hastings 2001/02

---

1 d4 e6 2 c4 f5 3 g3 ♘f6 4 ♗g2 ♗e7 5 ♘f3 0-0 6 0-0 d6 7 b4 ♘e4 8 ♗b2 a5

8...♗f6 is not a good plan at all. A good illustration are the following games:

a) 9 ♕b3 ♔h8 10 ♘c3 c6 11 ♘xe4 fxe4 12 ♘d2 d5 13 f3. Black's pieces are not de-

veloped, so White has a clear advantage, Levtchouk-Charbonneau, Quebec 1997.

b) 9 ♘bd2 ♕e7 10 ♘xe4 fxe4 11 ♘d2 d5 12 ♕b3 c6 13 b5! ♕f7 14 f3 dxc4 15 ♘xc4 ♕d7 16 bxc6 ♘xc6 17 e3 b5 18 ♘d2 exf3 19 ♗xf3 ♖b8 20 ♖ac1 ♖b6 21 ♘e4 ♘a5 22 ♘xf6+ ♖xf6 23 ♕c3 and White again has a clear advantage, Stefansson-Heidfeld, Panormo 2001.

c) 9 ♘c3! (the simplest) 9...♘xc3 10 ♗xc3 ♘d7 11 ♕c2 ♘b6 12 ♘d2 d5 13 c5 ♘d7 14 b5 and White has a very large advantage, Milos-Pelikan, Sao Paulo 2000.

9 a3?!

This is slow. It is better simply to play 9 b5 ♕e8 10 ♘fd2 d5 11 ♘xe4 fxe4 12 ♘c3 c6 13 a4 with a small advantage.

9...axb4 10 axb4 ♖xa1 11 ♗xa1 b5!?

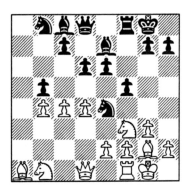

This pawn sacrifice is positionally unjustified as Black cannot keep control of the light squares in the centre and has problems protecting the c7-pawn. But there is a tactical justification.

12 cxb5 ♘d7 13 d5!?

White is afraid of the d5-square, but after 13 ♕c2!? ♘b6 14 ♘fd2 (14 ♖c1 ♘d5 15 ♘fd2?! does not really work because the obvious 15...♗g5! 16 e3 [16 f4 ♗xf4 17 gxf4 ♗xf4 18 ♘xe4 fxe4 with the idea of ...♕h4 is terrible for White] 16...♘xe3 17 fxe3 ♗xe3+ 18 ♔f1 ♗d7! gives Black good play for the piece) 14...d5 15 ♖c1 ♘xd2 16 ♘xd2 ♗d7, Black is also in the game.

13...e5 14 ♘fd2

14 ♕c2 ♘b6 15 ♖d1 ♗d7 16 ♘a3 ♕a8! looks good for Black.

14...♘xd2 15 ♕xd2 ♘b6 16 ♘c3

Interesting is 16 e4!? ♗g5! (16...fxe4 17 ♘c3 ♗g5 18 ♕e2 e3! gives Black a pleasant game too) 17 f4 (17 ♕c2 f4 is dangerous for White) 17...♗h6 with an unclear position. But not 17...exf4?! 18 gxf4 ♗h6 19 e5 dxe5 20 ♗xe5 ♖e8 21 ♕c3, which would give White the advantage.

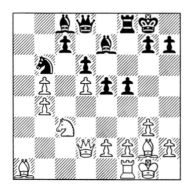

16...♗d7 17 e3 ♕a8 18 ♗b2 ♘c4 19 ♕e2 ♘xb2 20 ♕xb2 e4 21 ♖a1 ♕b7 22 ♗f1 ♗f6 23 ♖a5 ♖b8 24 ♕a3 ♕c8

Black prepares to answer ♖a7 with ...♖b7 because 24...♗e5 25 ♖a7 ♕c8 26 ♗h3! would give White the better chances. Then 26...♖b7 27 ♘xe4! ♖xa7 28 ♕xa7 fxe4 29 ♗xd7 ♕xd7 30 b6! wins for White.

25 ♗c4

25 ♖a7 ♖b7 26 ♖a8 ♖b8 is a draw. Maybe White should start thinking along those lines...

25...♕e8 26 ♖a7 ♖c8 27 ♖a5

27 ♗f1 ♗xc3 28 ♕xc3 ♗xb5 29 ♗xb5 ♕xb5 30 ♕c6 was another possibility. After 30...♕e2!? Black would keep the balance.

27...♖b8 28 ♖a7 ♖c8 29 ♖a5 ♖b8 30 ♘e2

30 ♖a7, with a draw, should be considered.

30...♗xb5 31 ♗xb5 ♖xb5 32 ♘f4

After 32 ♖xb5! ♕xb5 33 ♘f4 ♔f7 34

♕c1 White has a very small advantage, but generally the position is drawish.

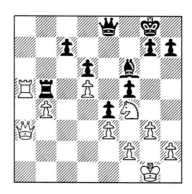

32...♖b8 33 ♘e6 h6 34 ♖a7 ♕h5?!

Both players are probably running short of time around here. Better was probably 34...c5!, with the idea of 35 bxc5 ♖b1+ 36 ♔g2 ♖a1 37 ♕xa1 ♗xa1 38 ♖xa1 dxc5 39 ♖a7 g5 40 ♘xc5 ♕d8 41 ♘d7 ♕e7 42 ♖b7 ♕d6 and Black might have some winning chances.

35 ♕a4 ♔h7 36 ♘xc7 ♕e2 37 b5 ♗c3 38 ♘e6??

A terrible blunder. After 38 ♕a2 Black has nothing better than 38...♕d1+ 39 ♔g2 ♕f3+ with a perpetual check.

38...♖xb5 39 ♕a2 ♖b2! 0-1

Game 43
G.Buckley-N.Pert
British Championship, Torquay 1998

---

1 d4 e6 2 c4 f5 3 g3 ♘f6 4 ♗g2 ♗e7 5 ♘f3 d6 6 0-0 0-0 7 ♘c3 ♕e8 8 b4 ♘bd7

Alternatively:

a) 8...a5!? 9 b5 ♘bd7 10 a4 e5 11 c5 h6? (11...exd4 12 cxd6 ♗xd6 13 ♘xd4 ♘c5 14 ♗a3 would have given approximate equality) 12 dxe5 dxe5 13 c6 bxc6 14 bxc6 ♘b6 15 ♕b3+ ♔h7 16 ♘xe5 ♗b4 17 ♘d7! and White has a clear advantage. Sarkisian-Hobart, Houston 1999.

b) 8...♗d8 (this plan is too slow) 9 c5! (9 ♕c2 would miss the chance; after 9...e5 10 dxe5 dxe5 11 ♖d1 c6 the position is equal) 9...e5 10 dxe5 dxe5 11 e4! ♔h8?! (it was better to play 11...fxe4 12 ♘g5 – 12 ♘xe4 also gives White some advantage – 12...♘c6 13 ♘gxe4 ♘xe4 14 ♘xe4 with some advantage to White) 12 exf5! ♗xf5 13 ♖e1 e4 14 ♘g5 ♘c6 15 ♘gxe4 ♘xe4 16 ♘xe4 with an extra pawn for White in Pezerovic-Rasidovic, Bihac 1999.

9 ♕b3 h6?!

This is too slow. When Black wants to play ...g7-g5, he normally plays something like ...♕h5 or ...♘e4 first. The move ...h7-h6 does nothing to enhance Black's position.

After 9...c6 White has the following two paths:

a) 10 ♗f4 ♕h5 (10...♘e4 11 ♘xe4 fxe4 12 ♘d2 d5 13 f3 would give White the initiative in the centre) 11 b5 ♘e4 12 ♘xe4 fxe4 13 ♘d2 cxb5 14 cxb5 d5 with an unclear position.

b) 10 ♗b2 ♕h5 11 a4 ♘e4 12 a5 ♘df6 13 b5 ♘xc3 14 ♗xc3 cxb5 15 cxb5 ♗d7 with even chances in a rather unbalanced position.

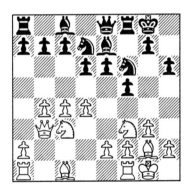

10 d5?

This is simply a positional mistake. After the typical 10 c5! Black has serious problems. Play may continue 10...♗d8 (10...d5 11 ♘b5 ♗d8 12 ♗f4 gives White a clear advantage too) 11 cxd6 cxd6 12 a4 and Black has no good plan, while White can improve his position with ♗a3, b4-b5, ♖fc1 and ♘f3-d2-c4 with heavy pressure on Black's centre and

queenside.

10...e5 11 c5 ♖f7?!

This is too passive. Better is 11...♕f7 12 ♘b5 (12 cxd6?! ♗xd6! 13 ♖d1 ♘b6 would give Black a superior structure and therefore a small advantage) 12...e4!? (Fritz wants to see the proof! 12...♘e8 13 ♗b2 ♗f6 14 cxd6 cxd6 15 ♘d2 a6 16 ♘c3 e4 17 ♖ac1 b6 would give an interesting position with chances for both players.) 13 ♘fd4 ♘xd5 14 ♘xf5 ♘7f6 15 ♘xe7+ ♕xe7 16 cxd6 cxd6 17 ♘c3 ♗e6 18 ♘xe4 ♘f4 19 ♘xf6+ ♖xf6 20 ♕d1 ♘xg2 21 ♔xg2 ♗c4 and Black has good compensation for the sacrificed material.

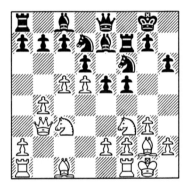

12 ♗a3?

This is silly – White loses a pawn without compensation. After 12 ♘b5! ♕d8 13 ♗b2 a6 14 cxd6 cxd6 15 ♘c3 White would be slightly better.

12...dxc5 13 bxc5

After 13 ♘b5 c4! (probably this is what White overlooked) 14 ♕c2 (14 ♕xc4?? 14...♘b6 would drop a piece) 14...♗d8 15 ♘c3 ♘b6 16 ♖ad1 ♗d7 Black has a close-to-winning advantage.

13...♘xc5 14 ♕c4 ♘ce4 15 ♗xe7 ♕xe7 16 ♖ac1 ♘d6 17 ♕b3 ♗d7 18 ♖fd1 ♖e8

Now Black is in full control.

19 ♘a4 ♗xa4 20 ♕xa4 a6 21 ♘e1 ♕d7 22 ♕xd7

White's position is of course lost, but he should still have kept the queens in order to create some counterplay later.

22...♖xd7 23 ♘d3 b6 24 f4 ♘f7 25 fxe5 ♘xe5 26 ♘f4 ♘eg4 27 ♖d3 ♘e3 28 ♗f3 g5 29 ♖c6 ♖d6 30 ♖xd6 cxd6 31 ♘e6 ♘exd5 32 ♖xd5 ♖xe6 33 ♖xf5 ♔g7 34 ♔f2 ♖e7 35 ♗g2?!

This invites the knight into the position. 35 g4 ♖c7 would give Black a 90% chance of winning the endgame. Now it's much higher than that!

35...♘g4+ 36 ♔e1 ♘e3 37 ♖f2 ♘xg2+ 38 ♖xg2 ♖e3!

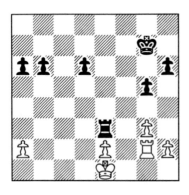

White is completely dominated.

39 ♔d1 ♖a3 40 e4 ♔f6 41 ♖e2 ♔e5 0-1

White loses a second pawn and the game.

Game 44
Vaganian-Andersson
Groningen 1969

---

1 d4 e6 2 c4 f5 3 ♘f3 ♘f6 4 g3 ♗e7 5 ♗g2 0-0 6 0-0 d6 7 ♘c3 ♕e8 8 b4 ♕h5

This move is risky as White has a free hand on the queenside. Black could also try the following moves:

a) 8...a5 9 bxa5 (9 b5 with a slight advantage is more logical) 9...♘c6 10 d5 ♘xa5 11 dxe6 c6 12 ♘d4 ♕h5 13 h3 ♘xc4 14 ♕d3 d5 15 ♘xf5 ♗b4 gave an unclear game in Kluger-Farago, Hungarian Championship 1998.

b) 8...♘e4 9 ♗b2 ♗f6 10 ♕d3 ♕g6 11 ♘d2 ♘xd2 12 ♕xd2 c6 13 e4 e5! 14 exf5

♗xf5 15 ♖ae1 ♗g5 was equal in Cs.Horvath-Danner, Budapest 1994.

9 ♕b3

A good alternative is 9 c5!? a5! (9...a6?! would give White too much space; 10 ♖b1 ♘e4 11 ♕c2 ♕g6 12 ♗f4 with an advantage for White) 10 cxd6 ♗xd6 11 bxa5 ♖xa5 12 ♕b3 ♘c6 13 a4 with an unclear position, Dus Chotimirsky-Rovner, Vilnius 1947.

9...♔h8 10 c5 ♘c6

After 10...♘e4 11 ♗b2 ♗f6 12 cxd6 cxd6 13 ♖ac1 White stands a little better.

11 b5 ♘d8 12 ♗a3 ♘f7

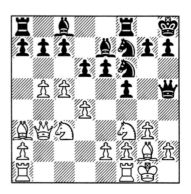

13 ♖ac1?!

Here White misses the most dangerous continuation: 13 c6! ♘e4 (13...♘d8 14 ♕a4 ♘e4 15 ♖fc1 ♗f6 16 ♖ab1 looks very dangerous for Black) 14 ♕c2 bxc6 15 bxc6 with a complex position, where White possibly has the better chances.

13...g5 14 cxd6

14 c6!? is still a good move.

14...cxd6

14...♗xd6 15 ♖c2 g4 16 ♘d2 would be slightly better for White.

15 ♘d1 f4!

Black is playing the attack with great precision – now ♘e3 is impossible. After 15...♘d5 16 ♘e3! ♘xe3 17 ♕xe3 g4 18 ♘d2 ♗g5 19 ♕d3 the exchange favours White, who is slightly better.

16 ♕b2 ♘d5 17 ♘c3 g4!

Black does not want to give up the control

over d5, even if it means putting a pawn there.

18 ♘xd5 exd5 19 ♘e1

19 ♘d2 ♗g5 would be unclear, but 19 ♘e5? ♘g5! 20 ♗xd5 ♖f6! would not be to White's benefit.

19...♘g5 20 ♖c7??

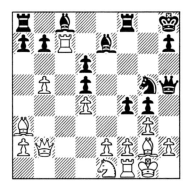

This is a terrible move. After 20 gxf4 ♖xf4 (20...♘h3+ 21 ♗xh3 gxh3 22 ♔h1 ♖xf4 with an unclear game is also possible, but normally Black should not exchange pieces before an attack) 21 ♖c7 ♘h3+ 22 ♗xh3 gxh3 23 ♔h1 ♗d8 24 ♖c3 the consequences are unclear.

20...f3?

Here Black misses a chance: 20...♗d8! 21 ♖xc8 (21 ♗xd6 ♗xc7 22 ♗xc7 f3 wins as the bishop can never go to h1!) 21...♖xc8 22 ♗xd6 fxg3 23 hxg3 ♖f5 24 ♘d3 ♗f6 gives Black a clear advantage.

21 ♖xe7 fxg2 22 ♔xg2 ♖f6 23 h4?

Better was 23 ♕c1, even though after 23...♗d7! 24 ♔h1 (24 ♖xd7 ♕h3+ 25 ♔g1 ♖h6 would lose on the spot) 24...♗xb5 25 ♘g2 ♖af8 Black has a very dangerous attacking position.

23...gxh3+ 24 ♔h2 ♗f5?

Here Black could have ended it all with 24...♘e4! 25 ♘d3 ♕g6! 26 e3 ♘xg3! 27 ♖g1 ♘f1+ 28 ♔h1 ♕xg1+!! 29 ♔xg1 h2+ 30 ♔h1 ♖g6 31 ♖e8+ ♔g7 32 ♖e7+ ♔h6 and there is no defence!

25 ♕c3 ♖g8

25...♖e8 26 ♕c7 ♘e4 with an unclear game was better.

26 ♕e3 ♕g6 27 ♘f3 ♘e4

After 27...♘xf3+ 28 exf3 ♗d3 29 ♖c1 ♖gf8 30 f4 ♗c4! 31 ♕f3 White is slightly better. This shows how quickly the game can turn in the Classical Dutch.

28 ♘h4 ♕h5 29 ♘xf5?!

This exchange does not make any sense. After 29 ♖g1 White should feel good about his position.

29...♕xf5 30 ♖xe4!

White needs to get rid of the knight now as after a careless move like 30 ♖xb7, then 30...♖xg3! would decide the game in Black's favour.

30...dxe4 31 d5!

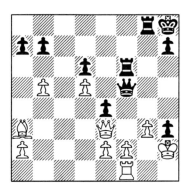

Unleashing the a3-bishop.

31...♕e5

Also possible was 31...♕xd5 32 ♗b2 ♖gf8 33 ♕h6 ♕f7 34 ♕xh3 ♔g8 35 ♗xf6 ♕xf6 with equality.

32 ♖b1

Now Black needs to pay attention. After 32...♕xd5 33 ♗b2 ♖gf8 34 ♕xa7 ♔g8 35 ♗xf6 ♖xf6 he would still have a level position. After Black's choice, however, White begins to take over.

32...♖gf8 33 ♗b2 ♕f5 34 ♖c1 ♔g8 35 ♗xf6 ♕xf6?!

Black should not leave the e-pawn undefended. After 35...♖xf6 36 ♕xa7 ♕xf2+ 37 ♕xf2 ♖xf2+ 38 ♔xh3 ♖xe2 39 ♔g4 ♖xa2 40

♗f4 White is better in the endgame, but it is not a lot and Black should be able to draw.

36 ♔xh3?!

This gives the wrong pawn away. After 36 ♕xe4! ♕xf2+ 37 ♔xh3 ♕f7 38 ♕g4+ ♔h8 39 e4 ♕f6 40 ♕h4 ♕f3 41 a4 b6 42 ♕g4 White has a clear extra pawn and good chances to win the game.

36...♕f5+ 37 ♔g2 ♕xd5 38 ♖c7!

38...♖f7 39 ♖c8+

Here the best is 39 ♖xf7 ♔xf7 40 a4 b6 41 ♕h6 ♔g8 42 e3 ♕e5 43 ♕h3 with a minimal advantage in the endgame.

39...♖f8 40 ♖c7 ♖f7 41 ♖c8+?!

Still 41 ♖xf7!.

41...♔g7?

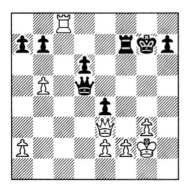

This mistake is truly amazing. After 41...♖f8 42 ♖xf8+ (or 42 ♖c7 ♖f7 and it is time to call in the arbiter and claim a draw!) 42...♔xf8 43 ♕xa7 ♕xb5 44 ♕d4 ♕xe2 45 ♕xd6+ ♔f7 46 ♕d5+ ♔g6 47 ♕e6+ ♔g7 48 ♕e7+ ♔g6 the game is a draw.

42 ♖e8!

Had Black forgotten about this move?

42...♖f5 43 ♖e7+ ♔g6 44 ♕xa7 ♖f7 45 ♖e8 ♕xb5 46 ♖xe4 ♕f5 47 ♕d4 ♖f6 48 ♖f4 1-0

Game 45

Postl-Moser

Austrian League 2000

1 d4 e6 2 c4 f5 3 g3 ♘f6 4 ♗g2 ♗e7 5

♘f3 d6 6 0-0 0-0 7 ♘c3 ♕e8 8 b4 e5!? 9 dxe5

After 9 ♖b1!? e4 10 ♘g5 h6! (10...c6?! would be too slow; after 11 f3! h6 12 ♘h3 d5 13 cxd5 cxd5 14 fxe4 fxe4 15 ♘f4 Black has problems with d5 and his entire structure in the centre) 11 ♘h3 ♕f7 12 d5 ♘bd7 13 ♘f4 ♘e5 the game would be unclear.

9...dxe5

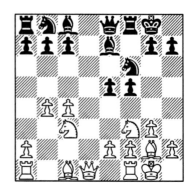

10 ♕b3

White could also try:

a) 10 c5?! e4 11 ♘d4 a5! (11...♕f7?! 12 f3! exf3 13 ♖xf3 ♖d8 14 ♖d3 ♘a6 15 a3 was better for White in Sheldon-Spice, British League 1996) 12 ♘cb5 ♘a6 13 a3 ♔h8! and Black is slightly better. One line is 14 ♘c3 b6 15 cxb6 axb4 16 axb4 ♗xb4 17 ♘a2 ♗c5 18 bxc7 ♘xc7 and Black is better coordinated.

b) 10 ♘d5 ♗d8 11 ♗b2 c6 12 ♘xf6+ ♗xf6 13 e4 f4! (13...fxe4 14 ♘d2 is better for White) 14 ♕d6 ♗g4 15 b5 cxb5 16 ♕d5+ ♔h8 17 cxb5 ♘d7 18 ♖ac1 ♕h5 19 ♖c7 was played in Herndl-Weinzettl, Austrian League 1990. Now 19...♘b6! 20 ♕b3 ♖ac8! 21 ♖xc8 (21 ♖xb7? ♘c4! with the threat of ...♘a5 and ...♘xb2 would not be in White's interests) 21...♖xc8 would have given Black full equality.

10...e4 11 ♘d4

White should not blunder with 11 ♘e5? ♗xb4 12 ♕xb4 (12 c5+ ♕e6! is an important detail, but not 12...♔h8 13 ♕xb4 ♕xe5 14 c6 and White wins) 12...♕xe5 13 ♗f4 ♕e6, when Black is clearly better as 14 ♗xc7 allows 14...♘a6! 15 ♕d6 ♕xc4.

11...c5! 12 bxc5 ♗xc5

12...♘a6?!, with the idea of ...♘xc5, would be met with 13 c6! bxc6 14 ♕a4 and White still has some pressure.

13 ♘db5 ♘a6 14 ♗a3 ♗e6

Also possible is 14...♗xa3 15 ♕xa3 ♕c6 16 ♖ab1!? b6! with equality (16...♕xc4!? 17 ♖fc1 would give White good compensation for the pawn).

15 ♖fd1 ♕c6?!

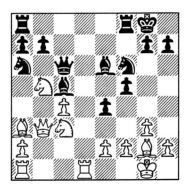

This is careless. After 15...♗xa3! 16 ♕xa3 ♕c6 Black has equalised.

16 ♘d5 ♔h8 17 ♘d4!

White is slightly better here.

17...♗xd4

After 17...♕d7 18 ♘xe6 ♕xe6 19 ♗b2 White has a strong attack on the a1-h8 diagonal.

18 ♖xd4 ♘c5 19 ♕e3 b6

19...♘g4!? 20 ♕d2 b6 21 ♖d1 ♘e5 22 ♕c3 was perhaps better, even though White keeps a small advantage.

20 ♖ad1 ♘g4 21 ♕c1!

From here the queen takes care of the a3-bishop and the c4-pawn.

21...♖fd8 22 f3?!

This is not well prepared. Better is 22 ♗b2! ♖d7 23 f3! and Black has to lose a pawn: 23...♘e5 (23...exf3? 24 exf3 ♘e5 25 f4 would open up the deadly g2-a8 diagonal) 24 fxe4 fxe4 25 ♗xe4 and White has good

chances for the full point.

22...♘e5 23 fxe4?!

23 ♗b2!, to put pressure on the long diagonal, is the most logical move.

23...♘xe4 24 ♗xe4 fxe4 25 ♖xe4 ♗xd5 26 cxd5 ♖xd5 27 ♖xd5?!

After this there is no advantage for White. 27 ♖f1! is the right move.

27...♕xd5 28 ♕e3 ♘c4 29 ♖e8+ ♖xe8 30 ♕xe8+ ♕g8 31 ♕xg8+ ♔xg8 32 ♗c1 ♔f7 33 ♔f2 ♔e6 34 ♔f3 ♔e5 35 g4 b5 36 ♗f4+ ♔d4 37 ♗c7 a5 38 e3+ ♔d3 39 ♔f4 b4 40 e4 a4 41 e5 ♘e3 42 ♗d6 b3 43 axb3 axb3 44 ♗a3 ♘c4 45 e6 ♘xa3 46 e7 b2 47 e8♕ b1♕ 48 ♕e3+ ♔c4 49 ♕xa3 ♕b8+ 50 ♔e4 ♕e8+ 51 ♔f3 ½-½

Game 46
Geller-Milic
Leningrad 1957

---

1 c4 e6 2 ♘c3 f5 3 g3 ♘f6 4 ♗g2 ♗e7 5 ♘f3 0-0 6 0-0 d6 7 d4 ♕e8 8 ♕c2 ♕h5 9 b4 ♘c6

This plan is the most dangerous that White can face. Who will be fastest? I think that White has better chances, something that could be defined as a small advantage, but Black has a nice position to play. Why? Because he is attacking the king! That is the way it is with the Classical Dutch, and I would be dishonest if I tried to tell you otherwise. White has a small positional advantage, but the games are exiting and Black often gets good chances to attack the king. So, if you decide to play the Classical Dutch, you let go of the idea of the perfect game, and instead indulge yourself in a terrible fight. You will lose more games than in the Queen's Gambit Declined, but I promise you that you will win many more too, and you will have more fun doing so! No opening really promises Black even chances in all the critical lines. It is the nature of the game.

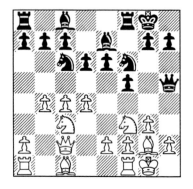

10 b5

White has also tried 10 ♖b1 ♗d7 11 d5?! (I do not know why, but in the Ilyin-Zhenevsky this move is very often not good for White; 11 b5 ♘d8 12 ♖d1 ♘f7 with an unclear game is more to the point) 11...♘d8 12 dxe6 (otherwise Black simply plays ...e6-e5) 12...♘xe6 13 ♘d5 ♗d8 14 ♖d1 ♘e4 15 ♗b2 and in this even position the players agreed a draw, Geller-Franz, Dresden 1959.

10...♘d8 11 a4 ♘f7 12 ♗a3 g5 13 ♖ad1

13 a5!?, to put immediate pressure on the queenside, was worth a consideration.

13...f4 14 ♕c1 ♕h6

Protecting the f-pawn as after 14...g4?! 15 ♘e1 fxg3 16 fxg3 e5 17 ♕e3!, White has a positional advantage.

15 h3 g4

After 15...♘h5 16 g4 ♘f6 17 e4 ♖e8 18 e5 White would have a dangerous initiative in the centre.

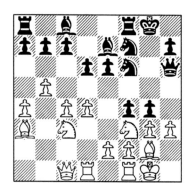

16 ♘e5?

This combinatorial move does not work out. Better is 16 hxg4 ♘xg4 17 gxf4 (17 ♕xf4? ♘g5 18 ♕xg4 e5 would put White's queen in an embarrassing situation) 17...♖h8! 18 f5 ♕h5 19 e4 ♘g6 20 ♖fe1 ♘h4 with a very unclear position.

16...gxh3 17 ♘xf7 ♖xf7 18 ♗f3

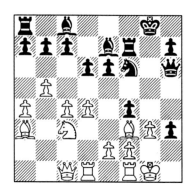

18...♘h5?!

Not the best. After 18...♘d7! 19 ♘e4 (19 ♔h2 ♘b6 20 c5 fxg3+ 21 fxg3 ♗g5 22 ♕a1 ♘c4 would give White a winning advantage) 19...d5 20 ♘c5 ♕g6 Black has an overwhelming positional advantage.

19 ♔h1 h2?!

This move makes little sense. The idea is to prevent ♖g1, but more to the point was 19...♗g5! 20 gxf4 ♗xf4 21 ♖g1+ ♘g7 22 ♕c2 ♕h4 and Black is clearly better.

20 ♖d3 e5?

Black has no idea of what he is doing. After 20...♘g7 21 c5 d5 he would remain slightly better. Now it is less clear.

21 dxe5 ♗f5!?

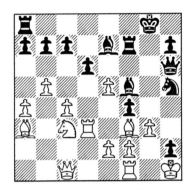

This gives White the opportunity to grab the initiative. But after 21...dxe5 22 ♗xe7 ♖xe7 23 ♖d8+ ♔g7 24 ♕a3 ♖f7 25 ♗d5 White has the advantage.

22 exd6 ♗g5

22...♗xd6 23 ♖xd6 cxd6 24 g4 is quite clearly better for White.

23 ♘e4

This loses time and allows Black to reorganise his attack. Time is of the greatest importance here, and after 23 g4!? there would follow 23...♗xd3 24 gxh5 ♗xc4 25 ♘e4 ♗d5 26 dxc7 ♖c8 27 ♘f6+, when White would have the advantage.

23...♗xe4 24 ♗xe4 fxg3 25 ♕d1 cxd6

Or 25...♖xf2 26 ♖xf2 gxf2 27 dxc7 and it's White's passed pawn which is the most dangerous.

26 fxg3 ♗e3 27 ♗xd6 ♖xf1+ 28 ♕xf1 ♕xd6! 29 ♖xe3

White should not fall for 29 ♗xh7+? 29...♔g7 (29...♔xh7 30 ♕f7+ and White wins) 30 ♕a1+ ♕f6 31 ♕xf6+ ♘xf6 32 ♖xe3 ♔xh7 33 ♖e7+ ♔g6 34 ♔xh2 b6, which gives Black good chances to win the endgame.

29...♘xg3+ 30 ♖xg3+ ♕xg3 31 ♗d5+ ♔h8

31...♔g7 32 ♕f7+! (32 ♕a1+ ♔g6 33

♕b1+ ♔f6 would allow Black's king to dance away) 32...♔h6 33 ♕f6+ ♕g6 is a minor improvement over the game, but it's hardly enough for Black to save it.

32 ♕f6+ ♕g7 33 ♕xg7+ ♔xg7 34 ♗xb7

I doubt if Black can save this position.

34...♖e8 35 ♗f3 ♖c8 36 ♗d5 ♔f6 37 a5 ♔e5 38 a6

Now the a-pawn queens.

38...♔d4

38...♖c7 39 b6 axb6 40 ♗b7! is an important variation.

39 b6 axb6 40 a7 ♔c5 41 e4 ♖f8 42 ♔xh2 ♖f2+ 43 ♔g3 ♖a2 44 a8♕ ♖xa8 45 ♗xa8 ♔xc4 46 e5 ♔c5 47 e6 ♔d6 48 ♗d5 1-0

Game 47
Ponomarenko-Gavritenko
Tula 1998

---

1 ♘f3 e6 2 c4 f5 3 g3 ♘f6 4 ♗g2 ♗e7 5 0-0 0-0 6 ♘c3 d6 7 d4 ♕e8 8 ♕c2 ♕h5 9 b4 ♘c6 10 b5 ♘d8 11 a4 ♘f7 12 ♗b2

The following game proves that humans make mistakes...

12 ♗a3 g5 13 a5 f4 14 ♕d2 ♘h6? (14...fxg3 15 fxg3 ♗d7 16 ♗c1 h6 17 e4 with unclear play was the right choice) 15 c5? (here 15 gxf4! gxf4 16 ♕xf4 ♘g4 17 ♕g3 ♘f5 18 ♕h3 ♕g6 19 e4 would give White an overwhelming position) 15...♘fg4? (15...dxc5

---

16 dxc5 ♖d8 17 ♕c2 g4 18 ♘d2 fxg3 19 hxg3 ♗xc5 20 ♘de4 gives unclear play) 16 h3 ♘xf2 17 ♔xf2 (17 ♖xf2 should repulse the attack) 17...g4 18 hxg4 ♘xg4+ 19 ♔e1 (19 ♔g1 fxg3 20 cxd6 cxd6 21 ♘e4 ♘h2 22 ♖fd1 ♘xf3+ 23 exf3 ♕h2+ 24 ♔f1 ♗d7 25 ♖ab1 and there is no attack) 19...♘e3 20 ♖g1 (20 ♖f2 ♕g6 21 ♖c1 is best for White) 20...♕g6 21 gxf4?? (21 ♗h1 still wins) 21...♕g3 mate (!), Rausch-Klawa, Germany 1997.

12...e5 13 dxe5

Also possible is 13 a5 e4 14 ♘d2. Now why does Black not play ...a7-a6 in this position? Well, there is one thing you should know. In these kind of positions you should avoid playing where you are weakest (the queenside), and try to direct your efforts to exploiting your strengths (the kingside). The continuation 14...♘g5! 15 h4 ♘e6 16 ♘d5 ♗d8 17 ♘b3 g5 leads to an unclear position.

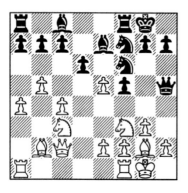

13...dxe5 14 ♘d5?

This is a grave positional mistake as Black does not have problems closing the queenside after this. 14 ♗a3 ♗xa3 15 ♖xa3 ♖d8 16 ♖d1 ♖xd1+ 17 ♕xd1 ♗e6 18 c5 ♖d8 would be better for Black too, but after 14 ♖fd1 the game would still be open.

14...♘xd5 15 cxd5 ♗d6 16 ♗a3?

16 e3 f4 17 ♕c3 fxe3 18 fxe3 ♗g4 looks good for Black, but the position is still not so clear. After the text move White is in trouble.

16...f4 17 ♗xd6 cxd6 18 ♘d2

Black has obtained his perfect position. He will swiftly create an attack on the kingside.

18...♗f5

18...♗g4!? was also very annoying for White.

19 ♗e4 ♗h3 20 ♗f3 ♕h6 21 ♖fc1 ♘g5 22 ♕d1

After 22 ♕d3? ♗f5! 23 ♕c3 (or 23 ♕a3 fxg3 24 hxg3 ♘h3+ 25 ♔f1 ♕xd2) 23...♘h3+ 24 ♔f1 ♘xf2! Black has a winning attack.

22...♗f5

After 22...♘xf3+!? 23 ♘xf3 (23 exf3! ♖ac8 is more resilient) 23...e4 24 ♘d4 fxg3 25 hxg3 e3 Black should win – the attack is very strong.

23 ♗g2 ♖f6!

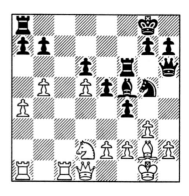

Black is slowly including all his pieces in the offensive.

24 ♖a3

Another line that illustrates Black's potential is 24 ♖c7 ♗h3! 25 ♗h1 ♖af8 26 ♖a3 fxg3 27 ♖xg3 ♔h8! (27...♖xf2 28 ♗f3! would help only White) 28 f3 ♘e6 29 ♖c3 ♘f4 and White's pieces look ridiculous.

24...♖af8 25 e4

25 gxf4 ♘h3+ 26 ♗xh3 ♗xh3 27 f5 ♖xf5 28 ♘e4 ♖f4 29 f3 ♕g6+ 30 ♘g3 h5 would give Black a winning initiative.

25...♗h3 26 g4

This is pure frustration. After 26 gxf4 ♖xf4! 27 f3 ♖4f6 28 ♖c2 ♗xg2 29 ♔xg2

♖g6 30 ♔h1 ♘h3 White is taken to the cleaners.

26...f3!

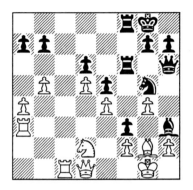

This little tactic undermines all White's hopes of building up a defence.

27 ♘xf3 ♗xg2 28 ♘xg5 ♖xf2 29 ♖c2 ♖xc2 30 ♕xc2 ♕xg5 31 ♔xg2 ♕xg4+ 32 ♖g3 ♖c8!

Bringing another friend to the party.

33 ♕f2?

33 ♕d3 puts up more resistance, although it does not change the outcome.

33...♕xe4+ 34 ♔h3 ♖f8 35 ♕xa7 ♕f5+ 36 ♔h4 g6 37 ♕xb7 ♕h5 mate

---

Game 48
Baburin-Pert
British League 1999

I have based the annotations to this game on those used by Baburin in *Chess Informant 75*.

1 d4 e6 2 c4 f5 3 g3 ♘f6 4 ♗g2 ♗e7 5 ♘f3 d6 6 0-0 0-0 7 ♘c3 ♕e8 8 ♕c2 ♕h5 9 b4 ♘bd7

This move is not as good as 9...♘c6 (see Game 47).

One should not open the position before one has developed, as shown by the following miniature: 9...e5?! 10 dxe5 dxe5 11 ♘xe5 ♗xb4 12 ♘d5 ♗d6 13 ♘d3 c6 (13...♘xd5 14 ♗xd5+ ♔h8 15 c5 would have given Black a very difficult game too) 14 ♗f4 ♗xf4 15 ♘e7+! ♔h8 16 ♘xf4 ♕e8 17 ♘xf5 ♗xf5 18 ♕xf5 ♘d5

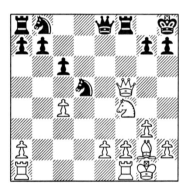

19 ♘g6+! 1-0 Petrosian-Rantanen, Tallinn 1979. After 19...hxg6 20 ♕h3+ ♔g8 21 cxd5 White is a pawn and a position ahead.

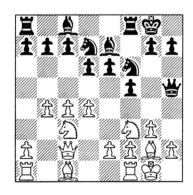

10 ♗b2

This is a little slow – the game is a race!

Better is 10 c5! a5 11 cxd6 cxd6 (11...♗xd6 12 bxa5 ♖xa5 13 ♕b3 ♘b6 14 ♘b5 looks good for White) 12 bxa5 ♖xa5 13 ♕b3 and White is slightly better.

10...c6 11 c5!

After 11 e4 fxe4 12 ♘xe4 ♘xe4 13 ♕xe4 ♘b6 Black is okay. The same goes for 11 b5 e5 12 bxc6 bxc6 13 dxe5 dxe5, when the c6-pawn is a hard to attack. White should not fall for 14 ♕a4?! ♘c5 15 ♕xc6 ♗d7 16 ♕c7 e4 17 ♘e5 ♖fc8 18 ♕a5 ♘b7 19 ♕a6 ♘c5 and Black has at least a draw.

11...♘d5 12 cxd6 ♗xd6 13 b5 ♘xc3 14 ♕xc3 cxb5 15 ♗a3 ♗xa3 16 ♕xa3 ♘f6 17 ♖ac1 ♗d7

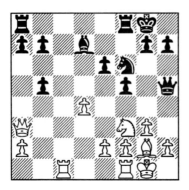

18 ♘e5!

White should be careful. After 18 ♖c7?! ♗c6 19 ♕e7 ♕f7 20 ♕xf7+ ♖xf7 21 ♖xf7 ♔xf7 22 ♘e5+ ♔e7 23 ♘xc6+ bxc6 24 ♗xc6 ♖b8 Black has a better endgame with a chance of a distant passed pawn and his more active king.

18...♗c6 19 ♘xc6 bxc6 20 ♗xc6 ♖ad8 21 ♗f3?!

This is unnecessary. After 21 ♕xa7! ♕xe2 22 ♖fe1 White has a very clear advantage.

21...♘g4 22 ♗xg4 ♕xg4 23 e3 f4 24 exf4 ♖xf4 25 ♕xa7 ♖fxd4 26 ♕b6 ♕f5??

This seems to be just a blunder. After 26...♕e2 27 ♖fe1 ♕xa2 Black will draw.

27 ♖c5 ♕e4

27...♖4d5 28 ♖xb5! might have been what Black overlooked. 27...♕h3 28 ♖e1 ♖d1 29 ♖ce5 also leaves him with little hope.

28 ♖xb5 ♖4d6 29 ♕b7 ♕c4

29...♕xb7 30 ♖xb7 ♖d2 31 ♖c1! 31...♖d1+ 32 ♖xd1 ♖xd1+ 33 ♔g2 ♖a1 34 ♖a7 gives White a winning rook endgame.

30 ♖g5 ♕c3 31 ♕e4 ♕f6 32 ♖e5 ♖d4 33 ♕e3 ♖d3 34 ♕c5 ♖d2 35 a4

White is steadily making improvements to his position...

35...h6 36 a5 ♖a2 37 ♕e3 ♕f7 38 h4 ♖d6 39 h5 ♖d5 40 ♖xd5 exd5 41 ♖c1 ♕xh5?

...not that it really matters!

42 ♖c8+ ♔h7 43 ♕d3+ ♕g6

Or if instead 43...g6 44 ♕d4 and White wins.

44 ♖h8+ ♔xh8 45 ♕xg6 ♖xa5 46 ♔g2 ♖c5 47 ♕d6 ♖b5 48 ♕c6 1-0

Summary

With the b4 system White has put Black face to face with a difficult task in the fight for equality. Black needs to act quickly with the break ...e6-e5 or with a kingside offensive in order to keep the balance. It is probably not a good idea to play ...a7-a5 as after b4-b5 White wins a tempo for his march on the queenside, and Black has lost some control over the dark squares. The right paths seem to be the ones chosen by Moser in Game 45 and Milic in Game 46. After this it should be possible for Black to equalise.

1 d4 f5 2 c4 ♘f6 3 g3 e6 4 ♗g2 ♗e7 5 ♘f3 0-0 6 0-0 d6 7 b4

     7 ♘c3 ♕e8

        8 b4

            8...♘bd7 – *Game 43*

            8...♕h5 – *Game 44*

            8...e5 – *Game 45*

        8 ♕c2 ♕h5 9 b4 (D)

            9...♘bd7 – *Game 48*

            9...♘c6 10 b5 ♘d8 11 a4 ♘f7 (D)

                12 ♗a3 – *Game 46*; 12 ♗b2 – *Game 47*

7...♕e8

     7...a5 – *Game 41*

     7...♘e4 – *Game 42*

8 ♗b2 ♘bd7 9 ♘bd2 ♘e4 (D) – *Game 40*

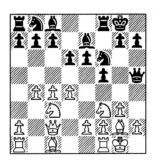
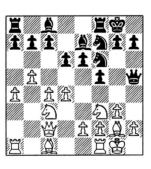
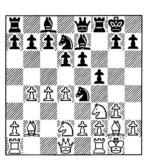

     9 b4   *11...♘f7*   *9...♘e4*

CHAPTER FIVE

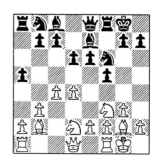

Main Line: White Plays ♘bd2

1 d4 e6 2 ♘f3 f5 3 g3 ♘f6 4 ♗g2 ♗e7 5 0-0 0-0 6 c4 d6 7 b3 a5 8 ♗b2 ♕e8 9 ♘bd2

In this Chapter we will study some games in which White plays ♘bd2 against both 7...a5 and 7...♕e8. For some reason, especially against 7...a5 (Games 49-52), this is quite popular, even though the knight gets no additional options on d2 rather than c3. The minor differences from the critical lines in Chapter 1 are to Black's advantage. Nevertheless, Game 51 does offer an independent idea, after which Black needs to play energetically in order not to gradually slip into a worse position (as he indeed does in this game).

Game 49
Averbakh-Boleslavsky
Zürich 1953

1 d4 e6 2 ♘f3 f5 3 g3 ♘f6 4 ♗g2 ♗e7 5 0-0 0-0 6 c4 d6 7 b3 a5 8 ♗b2 ♕e8 9 ♘bd2 ♘c6 10 a3 ♗d8

In this position Black has no problems at all. Very often this move is not very good (it's slow after all), but in here White has been very peaceful too, and cannot really answer this with anything active. This is a drawback of the knight development on d2.

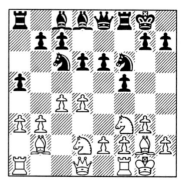

11 ♘e1 e5 12 e3

Another idea is 12 d5 ♘e7 13 ♘b1, heading for b5, but after 13...b5! Black is fine.

12...♗d7 13 ♘c2 exd4 14 ♘xd4

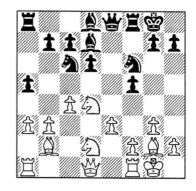

This is more or less forced. After 14 exd4?! f4! Black has good attacking chances on the kingside. One possible line is 15 ♖e1 ♕g6 16 d5 ♘e5 17 ♗xe5 dxe5 18 ♖xe5 ♘g4 with a serious initiative and the two bishops in return for the sacrificed pawn.

14...♘xd4 15 ♗xd4?!

Safer was 15 exd4 c6 16 ♖e1 ♕g6 17 ♕f3 f4! 18 h3 fxg3 (18...♗c7?! 19 ♕xf4 ♕c2 20 ♖ab1 ♘g4 looks tempting, but White has the computer move 21 ♗e4!, securing a clear advantage) 19 ♕xg3 ♕xg3 20 fxg3 with an even game.

15...♗c6 16 ♘f3?!

White plays this move to avoid exchanging the bishop and thereby exposing the light squares around his king to an attack. But now the bishop on c6 is the stronger of the two and Black is therefore on his way to obtaining a small advantage. 16 ♗xc6 ♕xc6 17 f3 ♘d7 18 b4 would have been completely level.

16...♗e4 17 ♘e1 b6

This is very solid. However, 17...b5!? looks strong. White would have to be careful not to be lumbered with serious weaknesses on the queenside.

18 a4 ♘d7 19 ♘d3 g5!

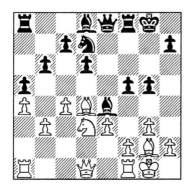

Taking the f4-square away from the knight.

20 ♘c1 ♘e5?!

This lets White escape into an acceptable endgame. 20...♗f6! 21 ♗xe4 fxe4 22 ♖a2

♘e5 would give Black some chances to fight for an advantage.

21 ♗xe4 fxe4 22 ♗xe5 ♕xe5 23 ♕d5+ ♕xd5 24 cxd5 ♖b8!?

24...♖f5 25 ♖d1 ♗f6 26 ♖a2 ♖f8 27 ♖c2 is equal too.

25 ♖d1 b5 26 g4 ♗f6 27 ♖a2 ♗e5 28 ♔g2 ♖f7 29 axb5 ♖xb5 30 ♖a4 ♗b2 31 ♖xe4 ½-½

> ### Game 50
> ## Chuchelov-Krings
> *Eupen 1994*

1 d4 e6 2 c4 f5 3 g3 ♘f6 4 ♗g2 ♗e7 5 ♘f3 d6 6 0-0 0-0 7 b3 a5 8 ♗b2 ♕e8 9 ♘bd2 ♘c6 10 ♖e1 ♘e4!

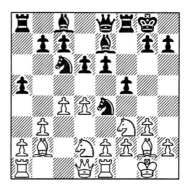

Black quite sensibly prevents e2-e4. After 10...♕g6 11 e4! fxe4 12 ♘xe4 ♘xe4 13 ♖xe4 ♗f6 (13...♕xe4? 14 ♘h4! is an old favourite) 14 ♕e2 ♗d7 15 ♗h3 White can put Black under some pressure.

11 ♘xe4

This is the only active plan that is immediately apparent, but 11 a3 is also possible. After 11 d5 ♘d8 12 ♕c2 ♘xd2 13 ♕xd2 (or 13 ♘xd2 e5 14 e3, when only White can have problems in this position) 13...e5! Black has some chances to mobilise an attack on the kingside. He could also choose to play 13...♗f6 14 ♗xf6 ♖xf6 15 dxe6 ♘xe6 with a typical equality.

11...fxe4 12 ♘d2 d5

Here Black should seriously consider 12...e3!? 13 fxe3 ♗g5 14 ♘f1 and now:

a) 14...e5! is the logical advance. 15 c5 ♕f7 16 ♔h1 ♗g4 and Black has achieved a lot of activity for his investment of a pawn.

b) 14...♕f7 15 ♗f3 ♕f6 (15...♘e7 is too slow; after 16 e4 ♘g6 17 e5 dxe5 18 dxe5 White's positions looks promising) 16 a3 e5 also gives Black good play for the pawn.

13 f3 exf3?!

After this White has a slightly better structure. The right move was 13...e3! and now:

a) 14 ♘b1 is too passive. After 14...dxc4 15 bxc4 ♗f6 16 ♘a3 ♕f7 (or 16...♕d7 17 ♘b5 ♖d8 18 ♕b3 ♘xd4 19 ♘xd4 a4 20 ♕xe3 ♗xd4 21 ♗xd4 ♕xd4 22 ♕xd4 ♖xd4 and Black has regained his pawn with equality) 17 ♘b5 ♘xd4! 18 ♗xd4 ♖d8 19 ♕b3 ♗xd4 20 ♘xd4 ♖xd4 21 ♖ed1 the position is equal.

b) I believe White should sacrifice the exchange for good compensation with 14 ♘f1! ♗b4 15 ♘xe3 ♗xe1 16 ♕xe1 ♕f7 17 f4 ♖d8 18 a3!. The game is rather unclear.

14 exf3 ♕f7?!

Black continues without a plan. Better was 14...♘b4!? 15 ♕b1 c5 16 f4 cxd4 17 ♗xd4 ♘c6 18 ♗b2 ♕f7 19 ♘f3, even though White remains slightly better because of the weak e6-pawn.

15 f4 ♗f6?!

Still too slow. The line 15...a4 16 bxa4 ♗f6 17 cxd5 exd5 18 ♘f3 ♗g4 19 h3 ♗xf3 20 ♗xf3 g5! was the last chance to create complications.

16 ♘f3 ♘e7

16...dxc4?! 17 bxc4 ♖d8 18 ♖e2! ♘xd4 19 ♘xd4 c5 20 ♖d2 cxd4 21 ♗xd4 ♗d7 22 ♗b6! (22 ♗xb7? ♗a4! 23 ♕xa4 ♖xd4 would give Black good counterplay) 22...♗a4 23 ♖xd8+ ♗xd8 24 ♕xa4 ♗xb6+ 25 ♔h1 would give Black a tough time defending the light-squared weaknesses all around his position. White has a clear advantage.

17 ♗a3!

The black knight is the only piece that has

a good square.

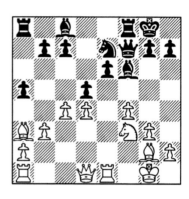

17...♖d8 18 ♗xe7 ♗xe7 19 ♘e5 ♕f8

19...♕f5 20 c5 is also clearly better for White.

20 c5! b6 21 ♘c6 bxc5

Black is trying to complicate. After 21...♖e8 22 ♘xe7+ ♖xe7 (22...♕xe7? 23 ♗xd5! cannot be recommended) 23 ♖c1 White has a major plus.

22 ♘xd8 ♕xd8 23 ♖c1 cxd4 24 ♕xd4 c5 25 ♖xc5!

Putting a stop to all ideas of compensation and tactics. White is positionally winning and this is the simplest way to exploit it.

25...♗xc5

Or 25...♕b6 26 ♖xc8+! and White wins.

26 ♕xc5 ♕f8 27 ♕c7 ♕b4

27...a4 28 bxa4 ♖xa4 29 ♖c1 ♖a8 30 ♗h3 also gives White, who threatens ♕xc8, a clear advantage.

28 ♖c1 ♗b7 29 ♕d7 ♕b6+ 30 ♔h1 1-0

Why did the game end here? Perhaps time? Or maybe Black couldn't face the idea of ♖c7, which apparently cannot be prevented.

Game 51
Latzel-Oestreich
Detmold 1958

This game is not marked by excellent play, but White's plan is rather interesting.

1 c4 f5 2 d4 e6 3 g3 ♘f6 4 ♗g2 ♗e7 5 ♘f3 0-0 6 0-0 d6 7 b3 ♕e8 8 ♗b2 a5 9

♘bd2 ♘c6 10 ♘e1!?

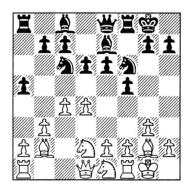

Evidently Black does not really understand this move at all. The knight is on its way to d3 in some cases, but is also clearing the path for the g2-bishop. Black should react immediately not to be worse.

10...♕g6?

This does not do Black any good. Instead I suggest 10...e5!. If this move is really possible then Black is okay! Now 11 ♗xc6?! seems very risky. After 11...♕xc6 12 dxe5 dxe5 13 ♗xe5 f4! 14 ♘ef3 (14 ♗xf4 ♗h3 15 ♘ef3 giving up the exchange is possibly better; the game is unclear but Black's rooks have good files at their disposal) 14...fxg3 15 hxg3 ♗h3 16 ♖e1 ♘g4 there are many black pieces crowded around the White king.

10...♕h5!? also deserves a practical test.

11 ♘d3!

After this move Black is a little worse.

11...♗d7 12 ♖e1

12 f4?! would be premature because of 12...♘g4 13 ♖f3 ♗f6!, when ...e6-e5 is on the way.

12...♕h6 13 e4

13 ♕c2!? was also good.

13...fxe4 14 ♘xe4 ♘xe4 15 ♗xe4!

After 15 ♖xe4 ♗f6 16 ♕e2 a4 Black has counterplay – the rook is not really well placed on e4. Following 17 ♗c3 axb3 18 axb3 ♖xa1+ 19 ♗xa1 ♖a8 20 ♗c3 ♘d8 Black is fine.

15...♖ae8?!

This is too passive. The move 15...a4! was the last chance to find some counterplay. 16 bxa4 ♗f6 17 ♘f4 ♘d8 gives White the better chances, but nothing is decided.

16 f4!

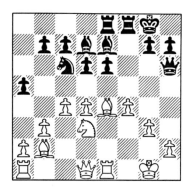

After this White has complete control over the centre. 16 h4 was also possible, and after 16...♘d8 (16...♗f6?? would lose to 17 ♗c1 g5 18 hxg5 ♗xg5 19 ♕g4) 17 ♕g4 would give White some advantage.

16...♗f6?!

16...♘d8 is better.

17 ♘f2 e5?

Black is desperate and tries to gain counterplay. In the end this gives him some chances, but really it should lose on the spot.

18 dxe5 ♗xe5 19 fxe5?

This is tactically unsound. White should play 19 ♗xe5 ♘xe5 20 ♕d5+! ♔h8 (or 20...♗e6 21 ♕xb7 and White will win on pawns instead of pieces) 21 ♕xb7 ♘g4 22 ♘xg4 ♗xg4 23 ♗c6, when Black has no visible counterplay for his material investments.

19...♖xf2!

This trick is as old as the world.

20 ♔xf2 ♕xh2+ 21 ♔e3 ♕xb2 22 ♕d2

After 22 exd6 Black plays actively with 22...♘e5! 23 ♖e2 ♘g4+ 24 ♔d3 ♘f2+ 25 ♖xf2 ♕xf2 26 ♕g1 ♕f6 27 dxc7 ♗f5 28 ♖e1 ♖xe4 29 ♖xe4 (29 c8♕+ ♖e8+ 30 ♕xf5 ♕xf5+ would only be good for Black) 29...♗xe4+ 30 ♔xe4 ♕c6+ and the game should be drawn.

22...♕a3?

22...♕xe5 23 ♔f2 ♕f6+ 24 ♕f4 gives White a very minor advantage, but this is what Black should do. After the text move he is in trouble.

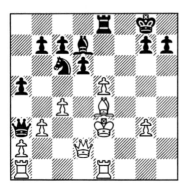

23 ♗xh7+??

This combination might be dangerous for the black king, but White is removing all the pieces sheltering his own king, which is still stuck in the centre. 23 exd6 ♕c5+ 24 ♔f3 ♕h5+ 25 ♔g2 ♕h3+ 26 ♔g1 ♕xg3+ 27 ♗g2 would have secured White a large plus.

23...♔xh7 24 ♖h1+ ♔g8 25 ♕h2 ♕c5+

Now all the black pieces will deal with the white king

26 ♔d2 ♕d4+ 27 ♔c1 0-1

Game 52
Eliskases-Larsen
Mar del Plata 1958

The annotations to this game are based on those by Bent Larsen in his excellent book *50 Selected Games*.

1 d4 f5 2 ♘f3 ♘f6 3 g3 e6 4 ♗g2 ♗e7 5 c4 0-0 6 0-0 d6 7 b3 ♕e8 8 ♗b2 a5 9 a3 ♘bd7

This knight manoeuvre is probably slightly inferior to 9...♘c6, as two knights shouldn't normally head for the same squares. Of course there are exceptions, but in this case it is clear that both knights cannot be on the e4-square at the same time. From c6 the knight is more active and fights for control of the dark squares in the centre full-heartedly.

10 ♘bd2 ♕h5 11 ♖e1

The following concept is important to remember: 11 e3 g5 12 ♘e1 ♕xd1! (12...♕h6?! 13 ♘d3 ♘b6 14 ♕e2 would give White a more pleasant position as Black does not have an immediate plan) 13 ♖xd1 ♖b8 (this is not a defensive move; Black prepares the advance ...b7-b5) 14 f4 g4 15 ♘d3 b5! and Black is not worse.

11...♘e4 12 e3 ♘df6 13 ♘xe4 fxe4!

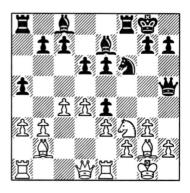

The position after 13...♘xe4 14 ♘d2 ♕g6 15 ♕c2 ♘xd2 16 ♕xd2 ♗f6 17 b4 a4 18 ♖ad1 is considered better for White by Larsen. It is easy to see why – Black has no real counterplay. 14...♕xd1 15 ♖axd1 ♘xd2 16 ♖xd2 ♖b8 is also slightly worse for Black.

14 ♘d2 ♕g6 15 f3?!

By recapturing on e4 with the pawn, Black has agreed to sacrifice a pawn after 15 ♕c2 d5 16 cxd5 exd5 17 ♕xc7 ♖f7. It's uncertain if Black has enough compensation for the pawn, though to me it seems very likely. In the game White is supposedly better, but my analysis suggests that Larsen overestimated his opponent's resources.

15...exf3 16 ♘xf3 ♘g4 17 e4 e5! 18 ♗c3

The pawn is taboo. After 18 dxe5? dxe5 White has only succeeded in opening a line towards his own king (the a7-g1 diagonal). And after 19 ♘xe5? (or 19 ♗xe5 ♖xf3!) 19...♕b6+ 20 ♗d4 ♗c5 he can simply resign.

18 d5?! ♗g5 would not put Black under any pressure.

18...♗g5 19 ♘xg5 ♕xg5

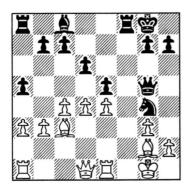

20 ♖a2!

The idea behind 18 ♗c3. The rook joins the game.

20...♕h6 21 ♗f3?

According to Larsen, White would be slightly better after 21 h3 exd4 22 ♗xd4 ♘e5 23 ♗xe5 dxe5 24 ♕d5+. First of all, Black should not be shy about playing 24...♗e6 with the idea of 25 ♕xe5 a4!, when Black has a very active position – probably the chances are equal. But 24...♖f7 also seems to be fine, while 21...♘e3!? is also worth a look. All in all, Black should have good chances.

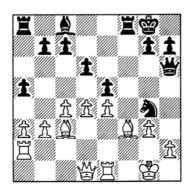

21...exd4 22 ♗xd4 ♘e5 23 ♗xe5 dxe5

24 ♕d3 ♗e6 25 a4 ♖ad8

This position is clearly better for Black because of one very important factor: all White's queenside pawns, plus the one in the centre, are on the same colour as the bishop. Probably White should not enter the endgame, but the position would be very hard to save no matter what.

26 ♕e3 ♕xe3+ 27 ♖xe3 ♗h3! 28 ♖a1 ♖d2 29 ♖b1 h5?!

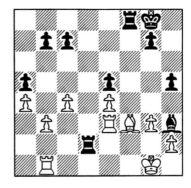

Black unnecessarily employs tactics. After 29...♖f6, with the plan ...♔f8-e7, Black is improving his position steadily without White having the chance to do the same.

30 ♗xh5 ♖g2+ 31 ♔h1 ♖ff2 32 ♗f3 ♖xh2+ 33 ♔g1 g5?

Black is doing really well in a positional sense, so the best move would have been 33...♔f8! to be prepared to invade the queenside the moment the rooks are exchanged.

34 ♖be1 ♖b2 35 ♖1e2 ♖hxe2 36 ♗xe2 ♗e6 37 ♔f1 ♔f8 38 ♔e1 ♔e7 39 ♔d1 ♔d6 40 ♔c1 ♖a2 41 ♔b1 ♖d2 42 ♔c1 ♖d4 43 ♔c2 ♔c5 44 ♔c3 c6 45 ♗f3 ♖d8 46 ♗e2 ♖h8 47 ♗f3 ♖h3 48 ♗g2 ♖h2 49 ♗f3 ♗f7

Because of his small mistakes earlier, Black is now forced to exchange his good bishop for White's bad one if he wants to play for a win.

50 ♗g4 ♗h5 51 ♗c8

White chooses activity.

51...♗e2 52 ♗xb7 ♗g4

Also possible was 52...g4!? 53 ♗c8 ♖g2 54 ♗d7 ♗d1 and Black plans ...♖c2+ followed by the winning ...♖b2 and ...♔b4.

53 ♖d3 ♖g2

54 ♗xc6

White simply surrenders under the pressure. But Black also wins after 54 ♖e3 ♗d1 55 ♗c8 ♖c2+ 56 ♔d3 ♔b4. White achieves nothing with 57 ♖e1 ♖c3+.

54...♔xc6 55 b4 axb4+ 56 ♔xb4 ♖b2+ 57 ♔c3 ♖e2 58 a5 ♖xe4 59 a6 ♗e6 60 ♔b2 ♖xc4 61 ♖a3 ♖b4+ 62 ♔c3 ♖b8 63 a7 ♖a8 64 ♖a6+ ♔d5 65 ♔b4 ♗d7 66 ♖a1 e4 67 ♔c3 ♗b5 68 ♔d2 ♔d4 69 ♖a3 g4 70 ♖b3 ♗a6 71 ♖b4+ ♗c4 72 ♖a4 e3+ 73 ♔c2 e2 74 ♔d2 ♔c5 75 ♖a1 ♔b6 0-1

Game 53
Villa Izquierdo-Gonzalez Velez
Sant Boi 1996

---

1 d4 f5 2 c4 ♘f6 3 ♘f3 e6 4 g3 ♗e7 5 ♗g2 0-0 6 0-0 d6 7 b3 ♕e8 8 ♗b2 ♕h5 9 ♘bd2

This move is, of course, harmless. Why on earth should the knight be better placed on d2 than on c3? The answer is, of course, that it is not.

9...♘c6

9...♘bd7!? 10 e3 c6 11 ♘e1 ♕xd1 12 ♖xd1 e5 with equality is also possible.

10 a3!?

Alternatively:

a) 10 ♘e1!? g5 (This is too soon – 10...e5! is better. After 11 e3 ♕h6 12 ♗xc6 bxc6 13 dxe5 ♘g4 14 ♘ef3 c5 15 ♕e2 ♗b7 Black has excellent compensation for the pawn.) 11 ♘d3 ♗d7 12 e4 ♕xd1 13 ♖axd1 fxe4 14 ♘xe4 ♘xe4 15 ♗xe4 with a small advantage for White in Salo-Dueckstein, Moscow 1956.

b) 10 e3 ♗d7 (Black should develop. After 10...g5 11 ♘e1 ♕h6 12 ♘d3 ♗d7 13 ♖e1 ♖ae8 14 d5 ♘d8 15 f4 White has a structural advantage, Eliskases-Pelikan, Mar del Plata 1956) 11 ♘e1 and now:

b1) 11...♕xd1 12 ♖xd1 ♖ae8 13 ♘d3 ♘d8 with the following plan: ...♘f7, ...♗d8 and ...e6-e5, reaching an even position.

b2) 11...♕h6 (this move means that Black is hoping for an attack, but defending against a coming attack is exactly what White has prepared himself for) 12 ♘d3 ♖ae8 13 h3 ♘d8 14 ♖c1 ♘f7?! (this is too committal) 15 f4 ♗c6?! (15...g5 was probably better) 16 ♗xc6 bxc6 17 ♔g2 g5 18 ♘b4 e5 (Goldin-Naumkin, Moscow 1992) and now 19 fxe5! dxe5 20 ♘xc6 would give White a very clear advantage. Better is simply 14...♗c6! 15 ♗xc6 (15 ♘f3 g5 would now be justified as White cannot play f2-f4) 15...♘xc6 16 ♔g2 ♘e4, which would keep the position unclear.

11...♗d7

Another good move was 10...a5!? to restrain White play on the queenside.

11 ♕c2

11 b4 was stronger. It is not obvious that the white queen belongs on c2. Maybe b3 or even a4 could come into consideration.

11...♖ae8 12 b4

It would help Black should White decide to test 12 e4?! e5! 13 d5 (13 dxe5 dxe5 14 ♘xe5 ♘xe5 15 ♗xe5 ♘g4! is an important detail to notice) 13...♘d8 14 exf5 ♗xf5 15 ♕c3 ♘f7. In this position all the black pieces are gathered on the right side of the board, near the enemy king. Here White should start to be careful and not fall for temptations like 16 ♕a5?! ♗d3 17 ♖fe1 e4 18 ♘d4 ♘g5!, when Black has a devastating attack.

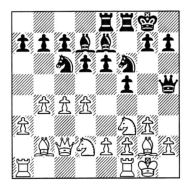

12...♘d8 13 ♖ad1?!

White is stalling. The right strategy was to proceed on the queenside as soon as possible (to have something else to do other than defending). The continuation 13 b5 ♘f7 14 a4 g5 would have given chances for both players.

13...♘g4!?

Black sees that White is not going to hurry, so he wastes a little time on provoking a weakness. Possibly White should just have ignored the knight for now, and proceeded with his own business.

14 h3 ♘f6 15 b5 g5 16 ♘e1?!

It is too late to generate a successful attack on the queenside. But now Black has played ...g7-g5, he has left a lot of weak squares behind the kingside pawns. To get access to these, White should have opened the centre with 16 e4! g4 (16...fxe4?! 17 ♘xe4 would only help White and 16...f4?? 17 e5 would be quite embarrassing) 17 hxg4 and now:

a) 17...fxg4!? would be met with 18 ♘e5! dxe5 19 dxe5 ♗c8 20 exf6 ♗xf6 21 ♗xf6 ♖xf6 22 c5 e5 with an unclear position. White should now take care of the threat of ...♖h6, ...♕h2+ and ...♖h3, when the g3-pawn cannot be defended. So probably the right move is 23 f4!.

b) 17...♘xg4! 18 exf5 exf5 19 ♖fe1 f4 and Black is about to organise a serious attack on the kingside. Still, the chances are level.

16...g4 17 h4

This is more or less forced as 17 hxg4 ♘xg4 18 ♘ef3 f4 19 gxf4 ♖xf4 20 e3 ♖f6 21 e4 e5, followed by moves like ...♖g6 and ...♖h6, would leave White in great trouble.

17...f4 18 ♘d3 ♕g6!

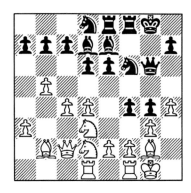

A nice move, pinning the knight.

19 ♕b3 ♘h5 20 ♗e4 ♕h6 21 ♘e1 c6!

Preparing ...d6-d5 and ...♗d6, so White now has to react.

22 bxc6 bxc6 23 d5

This is forced. 23 ♗g2 d5 24 ♗c1 ♗d6 25 ♘b1 ♕g6 would give the Black an attack with very good chances of success.

23...cxd5 24 cxd5 e5 25 ♘g2 a6 26 ♗xe5?

This is a pseudo-combination that just does not work. White could still stay in the game with 26 ♗c2! ♘f7! (bringing all the pieces to the scene; after 26...♗b5?! 27 ♖fe1 ♘b7 28 ♘e4 ♘a5 29 ♕b4 ♘c4 30 ♗d3 White still has some counterplay, so the right route for the knight is surely via the kingside) 27 ♘c4 ♖b8 28 ♕d3 ♖fc8 29 ♖b1 ♗b5 30 ♗b3 ♕g6!, although Black keeps a clear advantage.

26...dxe5 27 d6+ ♗e6

White must have underestimated something here.

28 dxe7

This is not really resistance. White could have offered more with 28 ♕d3 ♗f6 29 ♘b3, even though Black will most likely win in the end. 28 ♘c4 also does not save White as after 28...♗xd6! 29 ♖xd6 fxg3, White cannot let Black capture on f2 without going under. However, after 30 fxg3 ♖xf1+ 31 ♔xf1 ♕c1+ 32 ♖d1 ♕xc4 he can only resign.

28...♗xb3

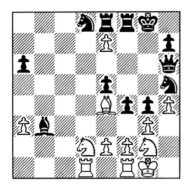

There is, of course, no real compensation for the queen.

29 exf8♕+ ♖xf8 30 ♘xb3 fxg3 31 ♗d5+ ♔h8 32 ♘c5 gxf2+ 33 ♖xf2 ♖xf2 34 ♔xf2 ♕f8+ 0-1

Game 54
Umanskaya-Stepovaia
Orel 1995

---

1 d4 f5 2 g3 e6 3 ♗g2 ♘f6 4 c4 d6 5 ♘f3 ♗e7 6 0-0 0-0 7 b3 ♕e8 8 ♗b2 ♗d8

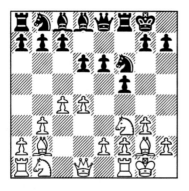

This move is not well timed. True, sometimes the bishop is well placed here, but sometimes it is also well placed on f6. And sometimes it's simply in the way on d8. Black should play as in Game 53 with 8...♕h5.

9 ♘bd2

White should pay attention to how passive his set-up can become, for example 9 ♕c2 ♘c6 10 ♘bd2?! (10 ♘c3, to cover d5 and b5 as well, is better here) 10...♕h5 11 e4 e5! 12 dxe5 dxe5 13 ♖ae1 f4 14 a3? (14 gxf4? ♗h3 15 ♗xh3 ♕xh3 16 ♗xe5 ♘g4 gets White mated, while 14 c5! fxg3 15 ♕c4+ ♔h8 16 fxg3 would keep the game unclear) 14...fxg3 15 hxg3?! (15 fxg3, with a slightly worse position, was better) 15...♘g4 and Black had serious attacking chances in Kozlowski-Pytel, Creon 1998.

9...♘bd7 10 ♕c2 ♕g6 11 d5?!

Here White misses the chance that has arisen from Black's slow play. After 11 ♖ae1! (improving the worst placed piece!) 11...c6 12 e4 ♘xe4 13 ♘xe4 fxe4 14 ♕xe4 ♕xe4 15 ♖xe4 ♘f6 16 ♖e2 the weak pawn on e6 gives White the better chances, while 11...♘e4?! 12 ♘xe4 fxe4 13 ♘d2 d5 14 f3 would give White a clear advantage.

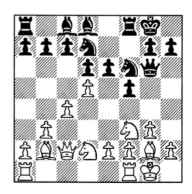

11...exd5 12 ♘h4 ♕f7

More accurate was 12...♕h5! and now:

a) 13 ♕xf5 ♕xe2 14 ♗xd5+ ♔h8 15 ♕g5 (15 ♕f4? ♘xd5 16 ♘g6+ does not work due to 16...♔g8! 17 ♕d4 ♘5f6 18 ♘xf8 ♘xf8 19 ♖ae1 ♕g4 and Black is winning) 15...♘e5 16

♗xe5 ♕xe5 17 ♕xe5 dxe5 and the two bishops secure Black a small advantage.

b) 13 ♘xf5 ♘e5 14 ♘e3 dxc4 15 ♘dxc4 (15 ♗xe5 ♕xe5 16 ♘dxc4 ♕h5 does not really improve White's chances – in the long run he will miss the bishop) 15...♘eg4 16 ♘xg4 ♘xg4 and Black has a dangerous attack.

13 ♘xf5 dxc4

13...♘b6!? was also possible.

14 ♘xc4 ♘c5

Black has managed to equalise completely. The knight on f5 is temporarily annoying, but it will go away.

15 ♘ce3 a5

Black needs to guard his knight. After 15...♕h5?! 16 ♗f3 ♕g5 17 b4! ♘cd7 18 ♖ad1 White controls the centre.

16 ♗d4 ♘e6 17 ♗c3 ♕g6

Black should not get too optimistic with 17...d5?! 18 ♖fd1 c6 19 ♘d6 ♕d7 20 ♘xc8 ♕xc8 21 ♘f5, when White has a distinct advantage because of his superior bishop.

18 ♘d4 ♘xd4 19 ♗xd4 ♕xc2 20 ♘xc2 ♖e8 21 ♘e3?!

More elastic was 21 ♖fe1.

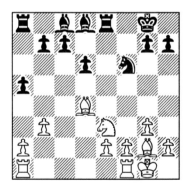

21...c6! 22 ♖ac1 d5 23 ♖c2 ♘g4 24 ♘xg4 ♗xg4

The opening has finished and the middle-game is also almost over. Black has a better structure in the centre and can attack down the a-file and against e2. Overall, his chances

are better.

25 ♖e1 ♗f5 26 ♖cc1 ♗e7

26...♗g5!?, trying to provoke 27 f4, was an idea, but 27 e3 would be better of course.

27 ♗c5 ♗f6 28 ♖a3 ♗g5 29 e3 a4 30 ♗c5?!

This gives Black good control over the a-file. White was forced into the ugly 30 b4 ♗f6, when Black has the advantage and nothing more.

30...axb3 31 axb3 ♗f6

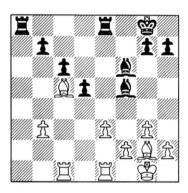

32 e4?

This move just loses a pawn for absolutely nothing. After 32 ♖e2 ♖a6 33 h3 White has some chances to save the game with a tough defence, even though it will be difficult.

32...dxe4 33 ♗f1 g5 34 ♗e3 ♔g7 35 b4 ♗e6 36 b5 ♗d5 37 bxc6 bxc6 38 ♖b1 h5 39 ♖b7+ ♔g6 40 ♖eb1 ♖a1 41 ♖xa1 ♗xa1 42 h3 ♗e5 43 ♗a6 ♖a8 44 ♖a7 ♖xa7 45 ♗xa7 ♗d6 46 ♗b7 ♔f6 47 ♗e3 ♗e7 48 ♔f1 ♔e5 49 ♗a6 ♗e6 50 ♔g2 c5 51 ♗e2 ♗f7 52 f3 c4 53 ♔f2 ♔d5 54 ♔e1 c3 55 ♔d1 exf3 56 ♗xf3+ ♔c4 57 ♗e4 ♗e6 58 ♔c2 ♗f6 59 h4 gxh4 60 gxh4 ♗xh4 61 ♗g6 ♗g4 62 ♗d3+ ♔b4 63 ♗d4 ♗e1 64 ♗f6 ♗e6 65 ♗e7+ ♔a4 66 ♔d1 ♗g3 67 ♗c2+ ♔b3 68 ♗xb3+ ♔xb3 69 ♗g5 h4 70 ♔e2 h3 71 ♔f1 ♗e1 72 ♗f6 c2 73 ♗g5 ♔c3 74 ♗f6+ ♔d3 75 ♗b2 ♗c3 76 ♗c1 ♗d4 77 ♗a3 ♔e4 0-1

Summary

This treatment of the white side of the Classical Dutch does not impress. If Black uses his chance to make a quick advance in the centre with ...e6-e5 at the right moment, he should be fine. Only Game 51 holds any real danger for Black, but with an energetic pawn sacrifice he can take over the initiative and secure a good game.

1 d4 f5 2 c4 ♘f6 3 g3 e6 4 ♗g2 ♗e7 5 ♘f3 0-0 6 0-0 d6 7 b3 a5

7...♕e8 8 ♗b2 (D)
8...♕h5 9 ♘bd2 ♘c6 – *Game 53*
8...♗d8 9 ♘bd2 – *Game 54*

8 ♗b2 ♕e8 (D) 9 ♘bd2
9 a3 ♘bd7 10 ♘bd2 ♕h5 – *Game 52*

9...♘c6 (D) 10 a3
10 ♖e1 – *Game 50*
10 ♘e1 – *Game 51*

10...♗d8 11 ♘e1 – *Game 49*

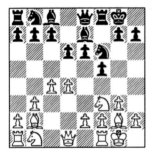 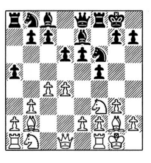 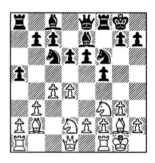

  8 ♗b2   *8...♕e8*   *9...♘c6*

CHAPTER SIX

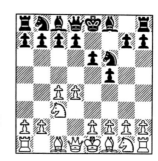

Systems with ♕c2 and/or e3

1 d4 f5 2 c4 ♘f6 3 ♘c3 e6

In this chapter we will look further into more unusual ways of meeting the Classical Dutch. In most of the games White develops his kingside with e2-e3, ♗d3 and ♘ge2 (or ♘f3) or tries to gain control over the centre with f3 and e4. It is my general belief that all these systems should prove to be completely harmless for Black if he has just a little clue to what he is doing.

One idea for White is to play ♗f4 and h2-h3, and sometimes even g2-g4 (Game 61). This should not worry Black at all. A well-timed response in the centre will in most cases give Black a good game.

Against the more modest set-ups, Black can do more or less whatever he likes. A nice way to develop is with ...b7-b6 and ...♗b7 to take control over the light squares in the centre. Black should not have any problems if he develops normally.

Game 55
Titorenko-Stepovaia
Russian Women's Championship 1994

1 d4 f5 2 c4 ♘f6 3 ♘c3 e6 4 ♕c2

White has tried all kinds of other fourth moves. These lines don't need to be memorised as they are not forcing. It is more im-

portant to know the standard system of development for Black.

a) 4 b3!? ♗e7 5 ♗b2 0-0 6 e3 d6 7 ♘f3 ♗d7 8 ♗e2 and now:

a1) 8...♗e8 9 d5!? e5 10 0-0 ♘bd7 11 ♘g5 ♗f7 12 ♘xf7 ♖xf7 13 ♗d3 e4?! (13...g6!? with an unclear game was much better) 14 ♗c2 ♘g4 15 h3 ♘ge5 16 ♘e2 ♗f6 17 ♖b1 a6 18 ♘d4 and White had some advantage in Anderson-Karim, Novi Sad Women's Olympiad 1990.

a2) 8...♘e4 9 ♕d3 ♘xc3 10 ♗xc3 ♗f6 11 e4 c5! equalises.

b) 4 a3 cannot really be dangerous. A logical way to continue is 4...♗e7 5 e3 0-0 6 ♗d3 d6 7 ♕c2 g6!? (preparing ...e6-e5) 8 ♘ge2 e5 9 f3 c5 10 d5 a6 11 ♗d2 ♘bd7 12 a4 ♖b8 with an even struggle in Bönsch-Knaak, Dresden 1988.

4...♗e7

This is the natural move for someone determined to play the Classical Dutch. Also possible is 4...b6!? 5 e3 ♗b7 6 f3 ♗e7 7 ♗d3 0-0 8 ♘ge2 and now:

a) 8...♘h5?! (this does not make a lot of sense) 9 0-0 g6 10 ♗d2 d6 11 ♖ae1 e5 12 ♘d5 (12 e4! would have offered White the possibility for an advantage) 12...♘d7 13 ♘xe7+ ♕xe7 14 ♘c3 ♕g7 15 ♘d5 ♖ac8 16 dxe5 ♘xe5 with equality in Sowray-

D.Ledger, British League 2002.

b) It is better to play in the centre with 8...c5 9 0-0 ♘c6 10 a3 ♖c8, when Black is fully developed and has equality.

For 4...d6, see Game 58.

5 e3

5 ♘f3 0-0 6 e4 fxe4 7 ♘xe4 ♘c6 8 ♘xf6+ ♗xf6 9 ♗e3 e5 was equal in Pachman-Larsen, Havana Olympiad 1966, but in practice White's position is already more difficult to play. The line 5 e4 fxe4 6 ♘xe4 ♘xe4 7 ♕xe4 ♗b4+ does not need a lot of investigation – Black has at least a decent game.

5...0-0 6 ♗d3 d6

For 6...♘c6 see Game 57.

7 ♘ge2

Or 7 ♗d2 a5 8 0-0-0 ♘a6 9 a3 ♗d7 10 f3 c5 (possibly it was a good idea to play 10...c6!?, with the idea 11 e4 b5 and Black has good counterplay) 11 ♔b1 ♕b6 12 ♘ge2 ♖fc8 13 d5! (13 dxc5? ♘xc5 14 ♖c1 ♘xd3 15 ♕xd3 ♕b3 gave Black a clear advantage in Hansen-Nishimura Novi Sad Olympiad 1990) 13...exd5 14 ♗xf5 ♗xf5 15 ♕xf5 dxc4 16 ♕e6+ ♔f8 17 e4 and White has compensation for the pawn.

7...c6

Black has also tried the following:

a) 7...g6!? 8 e4 ♘c6 9 exf5 ♘b4 10 ♕d1 ♘xd3+ 11 ♕xd3 exf5 12 0-0 ♖e8 13 f3 ♗f8 14 ♗d2 c6 15 ♖fe1 ♗e6 16 b3 ♕d7 17 ♗g5 ♗g7 18 ♕d2 ♗f7 with complete equality in Yuferov-Gavritenkov, Moscow 2000.

b) 7...♕e8 8 0-0 ♘c6 9 a3 a5 10 ♗d2 g6 11 f3 e5 12 ♖ae1 (12 d5 ♘d8 13 e4 f4 14 b4 g5 would give a typical King's Indian-style race on the two flanks, the consequences of which are rather unclear) 12...♗d8 with equality in Emma-Palermo, Buenos Aires 1965.

8 ♗d2 a5 9 h3

Here White missed the chance to obtain an advantage with 9 e4! ♘a6 10 a3 fxe4 11 ♘xe4 ♘e8 12 0-0 d5 13 cxd5 cxd5 14 ♘4c3 ♘f6.

9...♕e8 10 0-0-0 ♘a6 11 a3 ♗d7 12 g4

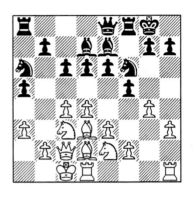

12...b5!

After this move one cannot speak of a white advantage anymore.

13 gxf5

13 g5? ♘e4 14 ♘xe4 bxc4 15 ♗xc4 fxe4 would give Black the advantage – all the open lines are in Black's possession.

13...b4?

Here Black is too optimistic. It was better to play 13...exf5 14 ♖dg1 (14 cxb5 cxb5 15 ♘xb5 ♖c8 16 ♘bc3 ♘b4! would give Black good play; so would 14 ♘g3 d5 15 ♘xf5 bxc4 16 ♘xe7+ ♕xe7) 14...b4 15 ♘d1 bxa3 16 bxa3 d5 17 c5 ♘e4 and the chances are more or less level.

14 ♘b1?!

White returns the favour. Here she could have tried 14 ♘a4! bxa3 (14...♖b8 15 fxe6 ♗xe6 16 ♘f4 ♗f7 17 e4 gives White a little edge and 14...e5 15 c5 ♘c7 16 ♘b6 ♖d8 17 dxe5 dxe5 18 e4 gives her more) 15 bxa3 exf5 16 ♘b6! (the point) 16...♖b8 17 ♘xd7 ♘xd7 18 ♗xf5 d5 19 c5 and White has the advantage. Note that 19...♘axc5?! 20 dxc5 ♗xc5 21 ♗xh7+ ♔h8 is not likely to break through for Black after 22 ♖df1.

14...e5

It might have been better to play 14...bxa3 15 bxa3 c5 16 ♖dg1 cxd4 17 exd4 e5 with a complete mess.

15 ♘g3

An alternative worth considering is 15 c5!? e4! 16 ♗xa6 d5 17 ♗c4 (17 ♗b7 ♖a7 18

♗xc6 ♗xc6 would give Black good compensation on the light squares) 17...dxc4 18 ♕xc4+ ♘d5 and Black has some play for the pawn, but is it enough?

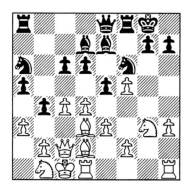

15...bxa3 16 bxa3 exd4 17 exd4 c5 18 ♖de1

18 ♖he1 was logical as the action is in the centre. The main point is, of course, 18...♗a4 19 ♖xe7! ♗xc2 20 ♖xe8 ♗xd3 21 ♖xa8 ♖xa8 22 ♗g5 ♗xc4 23 ♗xf6 gxf6 24 ♘e4 d5 25 ♘xf6+ ♔f7 26 ♘d7 with a small advantage for White.

18...cxd4 19 ♗xa5

White is greedy and this will be her downfall. Also dangerous was 19 ♘e4 ♘c5! (activating the pieces – the key concept in attacking) 20 ♘xd6 ♕d8 21 ♘b5 ♖c8 with a strong position for Black.

19...♕f7

Also possible was 19...♘c5 20 ♗b4 ♕f7 21 ♗xc5 dxc5 with some black advantage.

20 ♗b6

White is in some trouble. Her king is airy while Black's is perfectly safe. One line to illustrate White's problems is 20 ♘e4 ♘xe4 21 ♗xe4 ♗xf5 22 ♗xf5 (22 ♖xa8 ♗g5+ 23 ♗d2 ♖xa8! with a winning attack) 22...♗g5+ 23 ♗d2 ♕xf5 24 ♕xf5 ♗xd2+ 25 ♘xd2 ♖xf5 and White has nothing but a collection of weaknesses.

20...♘c5 21 ♗xc5 dxc5

Black has a clear advantage.

22 ♖e5?!

This exchange sacrifice does not work out as White is not fit to fight for the dark squares. Better was 22 ♖e2 ♗d6 23 ♕d2 ♗c6 24 ♖he1 ♕c7 with a clear edge for Black

22...♗d6 23 f4 ♘h5!

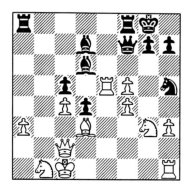

24 ♗e4

Or 24 ♘xh5 ♕xh5 25 f6 ♗xe5 26 fxe5 gxf6 27 exf6 ♔h8 and White has absolutely no compensation.

24...♘xf4 25 ♗xa8 ♗xe5

Black has a winning position. There is little White can do to resist a direct attack.

26 ♖e1

Or 26 ♗e4 d3! 27 ♗xd3 (27 ♕b3 ♖b8 and Black wins) 27...♗a4! 28 ♕xa4 ♘xd3+ 29 ♔c2 ♗xg3 and Black is winning.

26...d3

Also possible is the prosaic 26...♖xa8 27 ♖xe5 ♗a4 28 ♕e4 ♕xc4+ 29 ♔d2 ♖b8 and White will soon be mated.

27 ♕a2 ♗d4 28 ♗h1 ♖e8

28...♖b8 makes more sense. Why exchange pieces when you are the one attacking?

29 ♖f1 ♘e2+ 30 ♘xe2 dxe2 31 ♖e1 ♕xf5 32 ♗d5+ ♔h8 33 ♘d2 ♕d3?!

The alternative 33...♕f2 was more to the point.

34 ♕b3 ♗c3 35 ♕c2 ♗xd2+

35...♕g3 wins on the spot.

36 ♕xd2 ♕xa3+ 37 ♕b2 ♕xb2+ 38 ♔xb2 ♗xh3 0-1

Game 56
Seirawan-Short
Tilburg 1990

1 d4 e6 2 c4 f5 3 ♘c3 ♘f6 4 e3 ♗e7 5 ♗d3 0-0 6 ♘ge2 d6 7 ♕c2 ♘c6 8 a3 ♗d7 9 ♗d2 ♕c8 10 f3 e5

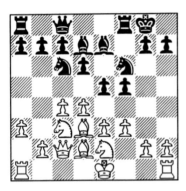

11 0-0-0?!

Seirawan is a great fighter and a player of great originality. But here he should have taken the safer road with 11 d5! ♘d8 12 0-0, when White has more space and generally good play. Now the position is wild, fierce and not at all clear.

11...a6 12 h3 b5 13 cxb5

White is more or less forced to accept the pawn sacrifice, as after 13 g4?! b4! 14 ♘d5 bxa3 15 bxa3 exd4 16 ♘xe7+ ♘xe7 17 ♘xd4 ♖b8 his king looks a bit open.

13...axb5 14 ♗xb5 ♔h8

Short has a good feeling for positional aspects of tactical positions. Here he makes a move that can always come in handy later. Also possible was 14...♘a5!? 15 ♗xd7 ♘xd7 (15...♕xd7?! 16 dxe5 dxe5 17 ♘g3!, with problems for Black, would be wrong) 16 ♘d5 ♗d8 17 dxe5 ♘xe5 and Black has some compensation for the pawn here too.

15 ♗c4 f4 16 d5

White is trying to keep the position closed in the centre, as it is obvious that he will not be able to mobilise an attack himself. The

continuation 16 dxe5 ♘xe5 17 ♗a2 fxe3 18 ♗xe3 ♗f5 would give Black good chances.

16...♘a5 17 ♗a2 fxe3 18 ♗xe3 c6?

This is the beginning of a long variation in which Black wins the exchange but in return gets a lost position. It was better to play 18...♗f5! 19 ♘e4 c6 20 ♘2c3 cxd5 21 ♗xd5 with unclear play.

19 ♘g3 cxd5 20 ♘xd5 ♘xd5 21 ♗xd5 ♗a4 22 ♕xc8 ♖axc8+ 23 ♔b1 ♗xd1 24 ♖xd1 ♘c4 25 ♗c1?

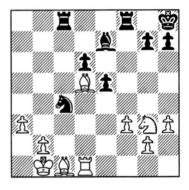

Here the bishop is misplaced. After 25 ♗g1! White remains active. One possible line is 25...♗g5 26 ♘e4 ♘e3 27 ♗xe3 ♗xe3 28 ♘xd6 and White wins. Another is 25...♖c7 26 ♔a2 ♖b8 27 b4 ♘b6 28 ♗xb6 ♖xb6 29 ♔b3 and White has full control over the centre while his passed pawns will sail right down the queenside.

25...♖c7 26 ♘e4 h6 27 b4 ♖d8 28 ♖d3 ♘b6 29 ♗e3 ♘xd5

This exchange is a great relief for Black, as now White's light-squared blockade comes under threat.

30 ♖xd5 ♖b7 31 ♘c3

Here White could have engaged in a race, but after 31 b5 ♔g8 32 b6 ♔f7 33 a4 ♔e6 34 ♖b5 d5 35 a5 dxe4 36 a6 exf3! 37 gxf3 (37 axb7 fxg2! would be good for Black) 37...♖d3 38 axb7 ♗d6 39 ♗c5 ♗b8 40 ♖a5 ♔d5 41 ♗f8+ ♔c6 42 ♗xg7 ♖xb6 43 ♖a4 ♔xb7 the game will be drawn.

31...♔g8 32 ♖d3 ♔f7 33 ♘d5 ♔e6 34

♔b2 ♖a8 35 ♔b3 ♗d8 36 a4 ♗a5 37 ♔a3 ♗d8 38 ♔b3 ♗a5 39 ♔a3 ♗d8

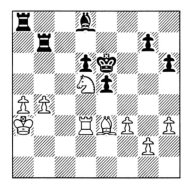

40 ♖d1

40 ♗d2!?, with the idea of a4-a5 and ♔a4, would perhaps still give White some chances to win.

40...♖c8 41 ♔b3 ♗a5 42 b5 ♖bb8 43 ♗a7 ♖b7 44 ♗e3 ♖bb8 45 ♗a7 ♖b7 46 ♗e3 ½-½

Game 57
Ivanov-Glek
Tomsk 2001

---

1 d4 e6 2 c4 f5 3 ♘c3 ♘f6 4 ♕c2 ♗e7 5 e3 0-0 6 ♗d3 ♘c6 7 a3 e5!?

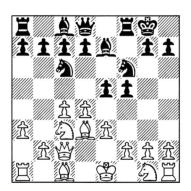

This pawn sacrifice is an attempt to profit from White's rather slow development. White has made four pawn moves and one with the queen, while this is only Black's

third pawn move.

8 dxe5

8 d5 e4 9 ♗xe4?! (9 ♗e2 ♘e5 10 b3 d6 11 ♗b2 ♗d7 12 ♘h3 ♕e8 13 0-0 a6!?, with the idea of ...b7-b5, would give an unclear position) 9...fxe4 10 dxc6 dxc6! gives Black good chances to take over the initiative.

8...♘xe5 9 ♗xf5 d5 10 ♘xd5

Black is opening the position and developing fast, while White is trying to have it all.

10...♘xd5 11 ♗xh7+ ♔h8 12 cxd5 ♕xd5 13 ♗e4

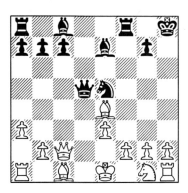

13...♗f5! 14 ♗xd5

14 ♗xf5 should be met with 14...♖xf5! with an ongoing attack, but not 14...♕xg2 15 ♗e4!.

14...♗xc2 15 ♗f3?

15 f4 ♖ad8, with an unclear game, was probably stronger.

15...♗h4 16 ♘e2

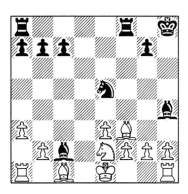

16... ♖xf3??

This is an attempt to be creative, but it is foolish. After 16...♘xf3+ 17 gxf3 ♖xf3 18 ♘g3 ♖af8 19 0-0 c5 Black has the advantage, despite the missing pawn. For example, 20 e4 ♗f6! and Black will regain some material very soon.

17 gxf3 ♘xf3+ 18 ♔f1 ♗d3 19 b4 ♖f8

19...♗f6 20 ♖a2 ♗b1, winning back some material, was better but one feels that Black was still creating his masterpiece.

20 ♖a2 ♘e5 21 f4 ♘c4 22 ♖g1 ♗f6 23 ♔f2 ♖e8 24 ♗d2

White has successfully untangled and is now simply a pawn and an exchange up.

24...♘d6 25 ♘g3 ♗h4 26 ♔f3 ♔h7 27 ♗c3 g6 28 a4 ♗c4 29 ♖d2 ♗b3 30 ♗e5 ♘c4 31 ♖d7+ ♔g8 32 ♘f5 ♖xe5 33 fxe5 ♘xe5+ 34 ♔f4 ♘xd7 35 ♘xh4 ♗xa4 36 ♘xg6 ♘b6 37 e4 ♔f7 38 ♘e5+ ♔f8 39 ♔f5 ♘c8 40 ♔f6 ♗b3 41 ♖g3 ♗a2 42 ♘g6+ ♔e8 43 e5 ♘b6 44 e6 ♘d5+ 45 ♔e5 ♘xb4 46 ♖h3 ♘c6+ 47 ♔f6 ♗xe6 48 ♔xe6 ♘d4+ 49 ♔d5 ♘f5 50 ♖h7 1-0

Game 58
Hulse-Oliveira
New York 1993

---

1 d4 f5 2 c4 e6 3 ♘c3 ♘f6 4 ♕c2 d6 5 ♘f3

Also possible was the immediate attack in the centre with 5 e4 fxe4 6 ♘xe4 and now:

a) The exchange on e4 generally benefits White, as the queen likes to be in front of the bishop when attacking h7: 6...♘xe4 7 ♕xe4 d5 8 ♕e3 c5 9 dxc5 ♕a5+ (9...d4!? 10 ♕a3 e5 11 b4 e4 12 ♗b2 d3 13 ♕c3 also looks somewhat better for White) 10 ♗d2 ♕xc5 11 ♘f3 ♘c6 12 ♖d1! (12 ♕xc5 ♗xc5 13 cxd5 exd5 14 ♖c1 ♗b6 15 ♗b5 ♗d7 is just equal; the same goes for 12 ♗c3 ♕xe3+ 13 fxe3 ♘b4) 12...d4 13 ♕e4 g6 14 a3 ♗g7 15 ♗d3 0-0 16 h4 and White seems to be better. Certainly 16...e5 17 ♕d5+ ♕xd5 18 cxd5 ♘e7 19 h5! would give him the initiative.

b) 6...♗e7 7 ♘f3 0-0 8 ♗d3 h6 9 0-0 ♘c6 10 ♘xf6+ ♗xf6 11 ♗e3 d5 and Black has no problems. The e6-pawn might look a little weak, but the d4-pawn is under just as much pressure.

5...♗e7 6 e4

This is what White is playing for. Not so impressive is 6 h3?!, with the plan of a later g2-g4. These things never work out in practice. After 6...♘c6 7 ♗g5 0-0 8 e3 a5 9 a3 e5 10 d5?! (10 dxe5 dxe5 11 ♖d1 ♗d7 12 ♗e2 h6 13 ♗h4 e4 would have been equal) 10...♘b8 11 ♗e2 ♘a6 12 0-0 ♘c5 13 ♘d2 a4 Black has a more pleasant position, Uimonen-Pessi, Finnish League 1997.

6...0-0 7 ♗d3 ♘c6 8 a3 e5!?

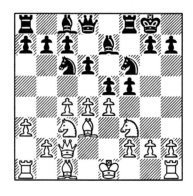

This is a very interesting pawn sacrifice. While White is busy finishing his development, Black takes over in the centre!

9 dxe5 dxe5 10 exf5

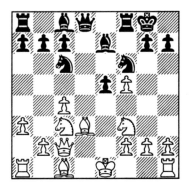

10...♔h8

To avoid any tricks. After 10...♘d4 11 ♘xd4 exd4 12 ♘e4 ♘g4 13 f6 gxf6 14 ♘g3 White would come out with a better position.

11 ♗e3 ♘d4! 12 ♗xd4 exd4 13 ♘e2 c5

Black has some compensation for the pawn. White will have to castle kingside and then the two bishops will prove to be powerful artillery on the long diagonals towards the white king.

14 0-0 ♗d6 15 ♘g3 b6 16 ♖fe1 ♗b7

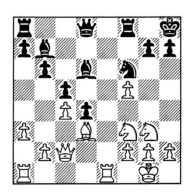

17 ♘g5!

This is stronger than 17 ♘e4, after which the position would remain unclear.

17...♘g4 18 ♘h3?

18 ♕d2! would have given White the advantage. Now Black takes over.

18...h5 19 ♘f1 ♕c7 20 ♗e4 ♗xh2+ 21 ♔h1 ♗xe4 22 ♖xe4 ♗d6 23 ♖ae1 ♕f7

24 f3 ♕xf5 25 ♕e2 ♘f6 26 ♖e6 ♖ae8 27 ♘f2 ♗f4 28 ♕d3 ♖xe6 29 ♕xf5 ♖xe1 30 ♔g1 ♗e3 0-1

> ## Game 59
> ### Filip-Estrada
> *Varna Olympiad 1962*

1 d4 f5 2 c4 ♘f6 3 ♘c3 e6 4 e3

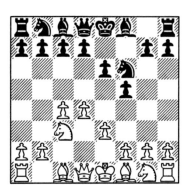

4...d6

This decision could wait. Black can play 4...♗e7 and now:

a) 5 ♘h3?! looks strange: 5...0-0 6 ♗d3 d6 7 f4 e5! (7...c6 8 0-0 d5 9 ♘f2 ♘e4 was equal in Kuhn-Elis Germany 1991, but this is a stonewall set-up, and not everybody wants to play this type of position – it can be rather boring at times...) 8 0-0 e4 9 ♗c2 ♘a6 10 a3 c6 11 b3 d5 with equality.

b) 5 ♗d3 0-0 6 ♘ge2 ♘c6 7 a3 d6 8 0-0 (for 8 ♕c2 see Game 56) 8...a6 and now:

b1) 9 b3 ♕e8 10 ♗b2 e5 11 d5 ♘d8 12 f3 g5 13 ♕c2 ♕g6 14 g4!? (14 b4 ♗d7 is equal) 14...e4 15 fxe4 ♘xg4 16 ♕d2 ♘xh2 17 ♔xh2 ♕h5+ 18 ♔g1 ♕g4+ gives a perpetual check.

b2) 9 ♘g3 ♕e8 10 d5 ♘e5 11 dxe6 ♗xe6 12 ♘xf5 ♘xc4 13 ♘xe7+ (13 ♘d4 ♗f7 14 ♗f5 ♗d8 15 b3 ♘b6 is equal) 13...♕xe7 14 ♘e4 with an even game, Roehl-Von Zweydorf Germany 2000.

For 4...b6 see Game 60.

5 ♘f3 ♗e7 6 ♗d3 0-0 7 0-0 ♘c6 8 d5

exd5

8...♞e5 9 ♝e2 (9 ♞d4 exd5 10 cxd5 ♞xd3 11 ♛xd3 ♞g4 gives Black sufficient counterplay) 9...exd5 10 cxd5 gives White a small structural advantage.

9 cxd5 ♞e5 10 ♝e2 c5

Another path to equality is 10...♛e8 11 ♛b3 ♞xf3+ 12 ♝xf3 ♞d7 13 ♞b5 ♝d8 14 ♝d2 ♞e5 15 ♝e2 a6.

11 dxc6

White also has no advantage after 11 ♞xe5 dxe5 12 ♛a4 (12 ♛c2 a6 13 ♜d1 ♝d6 14 b3 e4 gives good scope to Black's pieces) 12...a6 13 ♜d1 ♝d6 14 b3 ♞d7 15 ♛a3 b6. Black has a strong blockade of the passed pawn and good squares for his pieces.

11...bxc6 12 b3

12 ♞xe5 dxe5 13 ♛b3+ ♚h8 14 ♜d1 ♛b6 15 ♛c4 ♜b8 16 b3 ♛c7 also gives Black a good game.

12...♞xf3+ 13 ♝xf3 d5 14 ♛c2 ♝d7

This move looks a bit awkward. It would have been better to improve the other bishop with 14...♝d6 15 ♜d1 ♞g4 16 h3 ♞e5 17 ♝e2 ♛f6, when Black's pieces are very well placed. The chances are probably even.

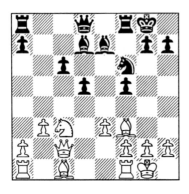

15 ♝b2 ♞e4 16 g3

16 ♜ad1 ♜b8 17 ♛d3 ♝f6 also gives White no advantage.

16...♝f6 17 ♜ac1 ♝xc3?!

This is a very strange decision when one considers the colour of the squares on which the black pawns are placed. It was better to

play 17...♜e8 18 ♝g2 ♜b8 19 ♞xe4 ♝xb2 20 ♛xb2 fxe4, when White has made some positional concessions in order to trade two sets of minor pieces. In this case Black has a good position.

18 ♝xc3 ♞xc3 19 ♛xc3

White has a lasting advantage due to his superior pawn structure.

19...♛f6

19...♛b6 20 ♜fd1 ♜fe8 21 ♛c5 ♜ab8 22 ♝g2 shows that Black can only defend.

20 ♛xf6 ♜xf6 21 ♜fd1 ♚f8 22 ♜c5 ♝e8 23 ♜d4 ♜b8 24 ♚f1 ♜f7 25 ♚e1 ♚e7 26 ♜a5 ♚d6 27 b4!

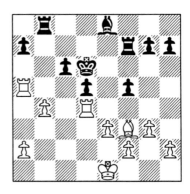

White keeps control over the dark squares in the centre, and thereby emphasises the difference between the two bishops. Also one should notice that the white rooks are far more active than their counterparts.

27...♜e7

27...g5 28 h4 h6 29 a3 ♜e7, to at least try to gain some influence on the dark squares, was probably a better set-up.

28 a3

28 h4, to first prevent ...g7-g5, was more logical.

28...♝f7 29 ♝e2 ♜c7 30 ♜c5 g5 31 ♝d3 ♝e6 32 ♚d2 ♜f8

32...g4? 33 ♝f1 ♜e7 34 h4 ♝c8 35 ♝d3 h6 36 ♜f4 ♜e5 37 ♚c3 gives White a clear advantage.

33 h4 h6 34 ♝e2 g4?

This is an amazing positional mistake.

Black hopes to be able to block the position permanently, but he loses all his flexibility, and now White has a lot of freedom to manoeuvre. Black should play 34...♖e7 35 ♗d3 (35 ♔c3 f4! would gain enough counterplay for a draw, as White cannot keep the pawn: 36 exf4 gxh4 37 gxh4 ♖ef7 38 ♖cc4 ♔c7 39 ♖c5 ♖xf4) 35...♖ef7 36 h5 f4 37 gxf4 gxf4 38 e4 and White retains some advantage.

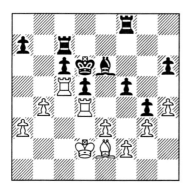

35 ♖d3 ♖b8 36 ♖dc3 ♖b6 37 ♔d3 ♗c8 38 ♔d4 ♖e7 39 ♗d3 a6 40 ♖c1 ♖e8 41 ♔c3 ♗d7 42 ♖a5 ♗c8 43 ♔d4 h5 44 ♖f1 ♖g8 45 f3?!

This gives Black the chance to gain some counterplay. Better was 45 ♖c5 ♖g7 46 ♖fc1 ♖g8 (or 46...♖e7 47 ♖xd5+! cxd5 48 ♖xc8 and the black rooks cannot hold the position together) 47 ♗f1 ♖e8 48 ♗g2 ♗e6 49 ♖1c2, which would keep Black completely passive.

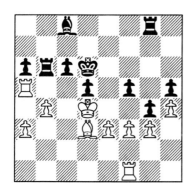

45...♖g7

Black does not see his chance first time around. After 45...gxf3! 46 ♖xf3 ♖g4+ 47 ♔c3 (47 ♖f4 ♖xg3 would make Black's day) 47...♔e5 Black has regained a lot of activity.

46 ♗e2?!

Here White has the chance to prove his advantage with 46 e4! gxf3 47 e5+ ♔c7 48 ♖xf3 ♖g4+ 49 ♔e3, when the f-pawn is in trouble.

46...gxf3 47 ♖xf3 ♖g4+ 48 ♔c3 ♔e5 49 ♔d2 ♖g7 50 ♔e1 ♖g6 51 ♔f2 ♖h6 52 ♖f4 ♖h8 53 ♖c5 ♗d7 54 ♖d4 ♗e6 55 ♖a5 ♗c8 56 a4 ♖h6 57 ♖c5 ♔d6 58 ♖c2 ♖h7 59 ♔f3 ♖hb7??

The tiresome waiting game induces Black to commit a serious blunder. After 59...♖e7 60 a5 ♖b8 61 ♔f4 ♖e4+ 62 ♖xe4 fxe4 63 ♖b2 ♗d7 (63...♗g4 64 ♗xg4 hxg4 65 ♔xg4 ♔e5 66 ♖c2 is similar) 64 ♗xh5 ♖f8+ 65 ♔g5 ♔e5 66 g4 White has serious winning chances, but still nothing is decided.

60 a5!

Oops!

60...♖xb4 61 ♗xa6 ♖b3

Or 61...♖xd4 62 ♗xb7! and White wins.

62 ♗xb7 ♖xb7 63 ♖a4 ♗a6 64 ♔f4 c5 65 ♖aa2 ♖b4+ 66 ♔g5 ♖g4+ 67 ♔xh5 ♖xg3 68 ♖cb2 ♔e5 69 ♖b6 ♗c4 70 a6! ♗xa6

If 70...♗xa2 71 a7 ♖g8 72 ♖b8 and White wins.

71 ♖axa6 ♖xe3 72 ♖e6+ ♔f4 73 ♖xe3 ♔xe3 74 ♔g5 1-0

Game 60
Holst-Jørgensen
Copenhagen 1991

1 d4 f5 2 c4 ♘f6 3 ♘c3 e6 4 e3 b6

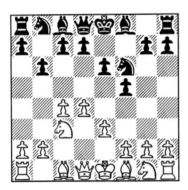

This looks like it should be the strongest move. Black transposes to positions similar to those reached from the Queen's Indian defence.

5 ♗d3 ♗b7 6 f3

6...d6

There is no reason for playing this yet. Actually, it only weakens the light squares in the centre and on the kingside.

It was more precise simply to play 6...♗e7 7 ♘ge2 0-0 8 ♕c2 c5!? 9 d5 ♘a6 10 a3 ♘c7 11 ♗d2 a6 12 e4 fxe4 (not 12...b5? 13 e5 ♘fe8 14 d6 with a clear advantage to White in Holst-Olesen, Copenhagen 1991) 13 ♘xe4

(13 fxe4 ♘g4 looks good for Black) 13...exd5 14 ♘xf6+ ♗xf6 15 ♗xh7+ ♔h8 16 cxd5 ♘xd5 17 ♗e4 ♕c7, with at least equality for Black.

7 ♘ge2 ♕d7 8 ♕c2 g6!?

An alternative way to develop. Still, this puts some demands on Black. He must avoid carelessness later.

9 0-0 ♘c6 10 a3 ♗g7

11 d5

11 e4 fxe4 12 fxe4 0-0 13 ♕a4 ♖f7 would be equal.

11...♘d8

Black also has the possibility of 11...♘e5 12 e4 (12 dxe6?! ♕xe6 13 ♘d4 ♕e7 looks good for Black) 12...♘xd3 (12...fxe4 13 fxe4 exd5 14 exd5 0-0 15 ♘d4 ♘xd3 16 ♕xd3 ♘g4 17 ♗f4 would give White a slight edge) 13 ♕xd3 e5 with equality.

12 e4 fxe4 13 fxe4 0-0 14 ♗g5

Here the position should be equal, but now Black goes astray.

14...h6?

14...e5 15 ♕d2 ♕e7, followed by ...♘f7, would have more or less kept the balance.

15 ♗xf6 ♖xf6 16 ♖xf6 ♗xf6 17 e5!

Now all White's pieces invade on those weakened light squares.

17...dxe5 18 ♗xg6 exd5 19 cxd5 c6?

There is no time for this. For some reason Black does not care about defence.

20 ♖f1 ♗g7 21 ♗h7+ ♔h8 22 ♕g6 ♕e7 23 ♘e4 cxd5

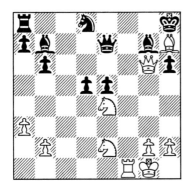

24 ♗g8! dxe4

Or 24...♔xg8 25 ♘f6+ ♔f8 26 ♘xd5+ and White wins.

25 ♕h7 mate

Game 61
Granados Gomez-Vega Holm
Barcelona 2000

---

1 d4 f5 2 c4 ♘f6 3 ♘c3 e6 4 ♘f3

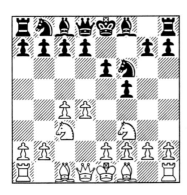

Quieter tries by White include the following:

a) 4 ♗g5 will be studied in Game 62.

b) 4 ♗f4 d6 and now:

b1) Harmless is 5 ♘f3 ♗e7 6 ♕c2 0-0 7 h3 c6 8 e3 ♘a6 9 a3 ♘c7 10 ♗d3 ♗d7 11 ♗h2 b5 (completely wrong is 11...d5? 12 ♘e5 ♗e8 13 g4! g6 14 ♗f4 ♔h8 15 0-0-0 ♘e4 16 ♗h6, with a clear advantage for White in Moutousis-Panagiotopoulos, Ateny

1999) 12 0-0 bxc4 13 ♗xc4 ♘cd5 14 ♖fc1 ♕e8 and Black has complete equality.

b2) 5 e3 (this way of development is more flexible) 5...♗e7 6 ♗d3 0-0 7 ♘ge2 ♘c6 8 ♕b3 a5 9 a3 ♔h8 10 0-0-0 ♕e8 11 h3 e5 12 ♗h2 e4 13 ♗c2 ♗d7 14 ♗f4 (14 ♕xb7 ♖b8 15 ♕xc7 ♖c8 16 ♕b7 ♖b8 would be an immediate draw) 14...a4 15 ♕a2 ♘a5 and Black has a good game, Paasikangas-Pessi, Finland 1995.

4...♗e7 5 ♗f4

Alternatively:

a) 5 h3 0-0 6 ♗f4 ♘e4 7 e3 ♘xc3 8 bxc3 d6 9 c5!? dxc5 10 ♗c4 ♘c6 11 0-0 ♗d6 (also possible is 11...♗f6 12 ♕c2 ♕e7 13 ♖ad1, when White has compensation for the pawn, but no more) 12 dxc5 ♗xf4 (12...♗xc5 13 ♕xd8 ♖xd8 14 ♗xc7 ♖e8 15 ♖fd1 gave White a pleasant game in M.Piket-Den Broeder, Netherlands 1994) 13 exf4 (or 13 ♕xd8 ♖xd8 14 exf4 ♘a5 with equality) 13...♕e7 and Black has no problems.

b) Black should not fear 5 d5 0-0 6 g3 and now:

b1) 6...d6?! 7 dxe6 ♗xe6 8 ♘d4 ♗xc4 9 ♘xf5 ♘c6 10 ♗g2 ♗e6 11 ♘xe7+ ♕xe7 12 0-0 ♕d7 13 ♗g5 ♔h8 14 ♗xf6 ♖xf6 15 ♘d5 gave White the advantage in Uhlmann-Schneider, Havana Olympiad 1996.

b2) 6...♘e4 7 ♘xe4 fxe4 8 ♘d2 e3!? 9 fxe3 exd5 10 cxd5 ♗b4 11 ♗g2 d6 12 ♖f1 ♗f5 13 e4 ♗g6 14 ♖xf8+ ♕xf8 gives Black good compensation for the pawn.

b3) 6...c5! 7 ♗g2 (7 ♗g5 h6 8 ♗xf6 ♕xf6 allows Black to dominate on the dark squares) 7...♘e4 8 0-0 ♘xc3 9 bxc3 ♕f6 and Black has a better structure and control over the dark squares. Even though he suffers somewhat in development, Black is slightly better.

5...d6 6 h3 0-0 7 e3 ♕e8

Equally good was 7...♘e4!? 8 ♘xe4 fxe4 9 ♘d2 d5 10 ♗e2 ♘c6 11 ♗h2 ♗d6 12 ♗xd6 ♕xd6 13 ♖c1 ♘e7 14 ♕b3 c6 15 0-0 ♘f5 with equality in Piket-Nikolic, Wijk aan Zee 1992.

8 ♕c2 ♘c6

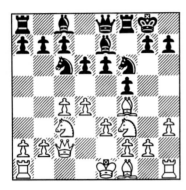

16 ♘h4

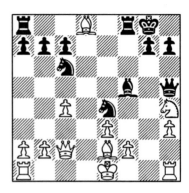

9 g4!

This is the right timing as Black has problems achieving ...e6-e5 quickly. Another aggressive path was 9 0-0-0 ♗d8! 10 a3 e5 11 ♗h2 a6 12 d5 ♘e7 13 ♘g5 ♘g6 14 g4 ♘xg4 15 hxg4 ♗xg5 16 gxf5 ♗xf5 17 ♘e4 with compensation for the pawn in Gurevich-Short, Rotterdam 1990.

9...♗d8 10 gxf5 e5!?

Black decides to play ...e6-e5 anyway. The alternatives were:

a) 10...exf5?! 11 ♖g1 ♘e4 12 ♘d5! ♘e7 13 ♘xe7+ ♗xe7 14 ♗g2 with a small advantage for White.

b) 10...♘h5 11 ♗h2 ♖xf5 12 ♗g2 e5 13 dxe5 dxe5 14 ♖d1 ♕f8 with chances for both players.

11 dxe5 dxe5 12 ♗g5 ♕h5

This looks quite strong, but also possible was 12...e4 13 ♘h4 (13 ♗xf6?! exf3 14 ♗xd8 ♗xf5! 15 ♕a4 ♖xd8 would give Black good chances, while 13 ♘d4 ♘xd4 14 exd4 ♗xf5 would just be equal) 13...h6 14 ♗f4 (14 ♗xf6 ♗xf6 15 ♘g6 ♖f7 would not give Black problems proving compensation for the pawn) 14...♘h5 15 ♘g2 ♗xf5 with equality.

13 ♗e2

Forced, as 13 ♗g2 e4 14 ♘xe4 ♘xe4 15 ♗xd8 ♗xf5 16 ♗xc7 ♘g3 would give Black the better chances.

13...e4 14 ♘xe4 ♘xe4 15 ♗xd8 ♗xf5!

The same trick! Black wins a lot of time.

16...♕f7?!

Black loses momentum with this move. After 16...♘xf2! 17 ♗xh5 (17 ♘xf5 ♕xf5 18 ♕xf5 ♖xf5 19 ♖f1 ♘b4! secures Black a large advantage) 17...♗xc2 18 ♖f1 ♖axd8 19 ♖xf2 ♖xf2 20 ♔xf2 ♖d2+ (20...♘e5 also gives Black a better position) 21 ♔g3 ♗d3 22 b3 ♘b4 23 ♗f3 b6 24 a3 ♘c2 25 ♖a2 White has some defending to do.

17 ♘xf5 ♕xf5 18 ♗h4 ♘b4

Also possible was the continuation 18...♖ae8!? 19 c5 ♘h8 (19...♘xc5 20 ♕xf5 ♖xf5 21 ♖d1 ♘e5 would be equal) 20 ♖d1 ♘b4, when Black has good compensation for the pawn.

19 ♕b1 ♖ae8 20 a3 ♘c6 21 ♕c2?

This just loses. Necessary was 21 f4 and now Black has the following choices:

a) 21...♘d4 22 ♗g4 (but not 22 exd4? ♕xf4 and Black wins) 22...♘c5 23 ♕d3 ♘d6 24 0-0-0 ♘4f5 with an even struggle ahead.

b) 21...♘g6 22 ♕d3 ♕g2 23 0-0-0 ♘c5 24 ♕d5+ ♕xd5 25 cxd5 (25 ♖xd5 ♖xe3 26 ♗g4 ♘a4 would be better for Black, the main idea being 27 f5 ♘b6 28 ♖c5 ♖e4 and Black is doing well) 25...♖xe3 26 dxc6 ♖xe2 27 cxb7 ♘xb7 28 ♖hf1 with level chances in the endgame.

21...♕a5+ 22 ♔f1 g5

Now White loses material because of the pressure against f2.

23 ♖g1 ♕f5! 24 ♔e1 ♔h8

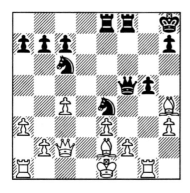

25 ♗g4

There was no salvation: 25 ♗h5 ♖e7 26 ♗xg5 ♘xg5 27 ♕xf5 ♖xf5 and 25 f3 gxh4 26 fxe4 ♕f2+ 27 ♔d2 ♖d8+ 28 ♔c3 ♕xe3+ 29 ♗d3 ♕d4+ are both winning for Black.

25...♕a5+ 26 b4 ♕e5 27 ♖a2 gxh4 28 f4 ♕f6

More precise was 28...♕c3+! 29 ♕xc3+ ♘xc3 30 ♖ag2 ♖xe3+ 31 ♔d2 ♖g3! and White has no counterplay at all.

29 ♕d3 ♘g3 30 ♔f2 ♘e5 31 ♕b3 ♖d8 32 ♖d1 ♘xg4+ 33 hxg4 ♖xd1 34 ♕xd1 ♖d8

34...♘e4+ 35 ♔g1 ♘c3 was also possible.

35 ♕a1 ♘e4+ 36 ♔f3 ♕xa1 37 ♖xa1 ♘d2+ 38 ♔e2 ♘xc4 39 ♖c1 b5 40 a4 a6 41 axb5 axb5 42 e4 ♖d2+ 43 ♔f3 h3 44 e5 ♔g7 45 g5 ♔f7 46 ♖e1 ♖d3+ 47 ♔g4 ♘e3+ 48 ♔h5 h2 49 ♖h1 ♖d2 50 ♔h6 ♖d1 51 ♖xh2 ♘g4+ 52 ♔xh7 ♘xh2 53 g6+ ♔e7 54 g7 ♖h1 0-1

Game 62
Sostaric-Volcansek
Maribor 1997

---

1 d4 f5 2 c4 e6 3 ♘c3 ♘f6 4 ♗g5 ♗e7

This is the natural move, but Black can also obtain a good position with 4...b6!? 5 e3 ♗b7 6 ♘f3 ♗e7 7 ♗e2 0-0 8 0-0 d6 9 ♕c2 ♘bd7 10 ♖fe1 h6 11 ♗h4 and now:

a) 11...g5? (this is careless) 12 ♗xg5! ♔g7 (12...hxg5 13 ♘xg5 ♕e8 14 ♘xe6 ♕g6 15

♘f4 would have given White a very clear advantage) 13 ♗xf6+ ♖xf6 14 ♘h4 gave White an extra pawn without any real compensation in Fernando-Hussein, New Delhi 1995.

b) 11...♘e4 logically untangles the black pieces: 12 ♗xe7 ♕xe7 13 ♖ad1 a6 14 b4 c5 and Black has equalised.

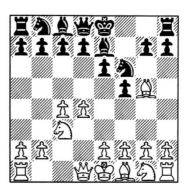

5 e3

Here White has some additional options:

a) 5 f3!? 0-0 6 e3 (6 e4? loses to a well known combination: 6...fxe4 7 fxe4 ♘xe4! 8 ♗xe7 ♘xc3 9 ♗xd8 ♘xd1 10 ♖xd1 ♖xd8 and Black has won a pawn) 6...d6 7 ♗d3 ♕e8 8 ♘ge2 c6 (8...e5 9 0-0 ♕g6 10 ♗h4 ♘a6 was another easy way to equalise) 9 ♕d2 ♘a6 10 0-0-0 ♗d7 11 h4 b5 with unclear play in Epure-Sajter, Romania 1999.

b) 5 ♗xf6 (this idea should never be dangerous) 5...♗xf6 and now:

b1) 6 ♘f3 (this is not ideal) 6...d6 7 ♕c2 (7 e4 fxe4 8 ♘xe4 0-0 9 ♘xf6+ ♕xf6 10 ♗e2 b6 11 0-0 ♗b7 12 ♖b1 ♘d7 and Black was already better in Caldaroni-Jabbusch, Cattolica 1993) 7...0-0 8 e4 fxe4 9 ♘xe4 ♘c6 10 ♘xf6+ ♕xf6 11 ♕d2 e5 12 d5 ♘e7 (even stronger was 12...♘d4 13 ♘xd4 exd4 14 ♗d3 ♖e8+ 15 ♔f1 c5 with a better game for Black) 13 ♗d3 ♗f5 14 ♗xf5 ♘xf5 and Black had equalised in Yakimova-Portnjagina, Moscow 2000.

b2) 6 e4 (this is the logical follow up) 6...fxe4 7 ♘xe4 b6 8 ♕h5+? (8 ♘xf6+ ♕xf6 9 ♘f3 ♗b7 10 ♗e2 0-0 11 0-0 is about equal, even if Black's pieces seem to be more actively placed) 8...g6 9 ♘xf6+ ♕xf6 10 ♕f3 (10 ♕d1 was necessary) 10...♕xd4! 11 ♕xa8 0-0! 12 ♘f3 ♕xb2 13 ♖d1 ♘c6 14 ♖d2 ♕a1+ 15 ♖d1 ♕c3+ 16 ♖d2 ♗a6 and Black went on to win in Penttinen-Kosonen, Finland 1998.

5...0-0

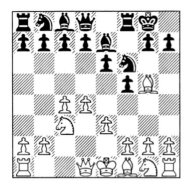

6 ♘f3

White has also tried 6 ♗d3 and now:

a) 6...b6 7 ♘ge2 (7 ♕f3 ♘c6 8 ♘ge2 ♗b7 9 ♕h3 ♘b4 10 ♗b1 ♘e4 11 ♗xe7 ♕xe7 12 a3 ♘a6 13 ♘xe4 ♗xe4 14 ♗xe4 fxe4 15 ♘c3 ♕f7 16 0-0 ♕f5 17 ♕xf5 exf5 was completely level in Tosic-Notaros, Yugoslavia 1994) 7...♗b7 8 f3 ♘c6 9 ♖c1 ♘h5 10 ♗xe7 ♕xe7 11 0-0 ♕g5 12 ♕d2 a6 13 ♖f2 ♖f6 14 ♖d1 ♖h6 15 g3 ♖f8 with equality in Szilagyi-Hapala Balatonbereny 1993.

b) 6...d6 7 ♘f3 ♕e8 8 ♕c2 and now Black has two equally good options:

b1) 8...♘a6 9 a3 ♗d7 (9...♕g6?! would run into 10 g4! ♕f7 11 gxf5 exf5 12 ♖g1 and White is better) 10 0-0-0 h6 11 ♗f4 ♕f7 12 h3 ♗c6 13 ♖he1 ♖ad8 with an equal game.

b2) 8...♘bd7 9 0-0-0 a6 10 ♖he1 (Komljenovic-Crespo, Olot 1992) and now 10...b5!? 11 cxb5 ♗b7 would give Black good play for the sacrificed pawn.

6...d6

Just as good is 6...b6 7 ♗d3 ♗b7 8 0-0 ♕e8 9 ♕e2 ♘e4 10 ♗xe7 ♘xc3 11 bxc3 ♕xe7 with equality in Capablanca-Tartako-

wer, New York 1924.

7 ♗e2 ♘c6

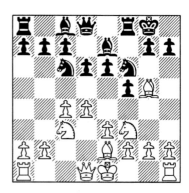

Black can also equalise with 7...♘bd7 8 0-0 and now:

a) 8...♘e4!? seems very safe. 9 ♗xe7 ♕xe7 and now:

a1) 10 ♘xe4 fxe4 11 ♘d2 ♘f6 12 ♕c2 e5! 13 ♘xe4 (13 d5 ♗f5 is fine for Black as 14 f3 fails to 14...exf3!) 13...exd4 14 ♘xf6+ ♕xf6 and Black equalises.

a2) 10 ♕c2 ♘xc3 11 ♕xc3 e5 and apparently Black has a decent game. However, White should probably try to start his queenside action immediately with 12 c5!, when he looks slightly better.

b) 8...h6 9 ♗xf6 ♘xf6 10 ♕c2 ♕e8 (10...♗d7!? would keep the balance; now Black plays some strange-looking moves) 11 ♘b5 ♕c6 12 ♖ac1 (12 d5!, with the idea of 12...exd5 13 ♘fd4, is probably more dangerous) 12...a6 13 ♘c3 ♕e8 14 ♘d2 g5 15 f4 g4 (15...gxf4 16 exf4 e5 17 fxe5 dxe5 18 dxe5 ♗c5+ 19 ♔h1 ♕xe5 20 ♖cd1 gives an interesting game, where Black appears to be slightly worse, while 15...♕g6!?, reaching an unclear position, is another possibility) 16 g3?! (16 e4 ♕g6 17 e5 ♘d7, with great complications, was more testing) 16...h5 17 e4 h4 with equality in Kiviharju-Leukkunen, Lappeenranta 2000.

7...♘e4?! is too soon. 8 ♗xe7 ♕xe7 9 ♘xe4 fxe4 10 ♘d2 d5 (10...e5 11 ♘xe4 exd4 12 ♕xd4 ♘c6 13 ♕d5+ ♗e6 14 ♕g5 does not give Black sufficient compensation for the pawn) 11 0-0 ♕g5 12 ♖c1 and now:

a) 12...e5 13 ♔h1 exd4 (13...c6 14 cxd5 cxd5 15 ♕b3 exd4 16 ♘xe4 ♕e5 17 ♘c5 would give Black and his undeveloped army a lot of problems) 14 exd4 c6 15 cxd5 cxd5 16 ♖c5 ♗e6 17 ♘xe4 ♕h4 18 ♘d6 ♘c6 19 ♗f3 and White is better.

b) 12...c6 13 ♕b3! (13 b4? allows 13...e5! and Black has the initiative, Wagner-Leschorn, Velden 1995) 13...♕g6 14 f3 exf3 15 ♗xf3 with a small plus for White.

8 d5!?

White is trying to create complications. After 8 0-0 e5 9 ♕b3 (9 d5 ♘b8 gives no advantage for White) 9...e4 10 ♘d2 h6 11 c5+ ♔h8 12 cxd6 ♗xd6 13 ♗xf6 ♖xf6 14 ♘c4 b6 Black has no problems. Black also equalises easily after 8 ♕c2 e5 9 dxe5 dxe5 10 ♖d1 ♗d7 11 0-0 e4.

8...♘e5

Here Black misses the easiest way to obtain a good game. He should play 8...♘e4! and now:

a) 9 ♗f4?! ♘xc3 10 bxc3 ♘b8 11 ♗g3 (totally careless would be 11 dxe6?! g5! 12 ♗g3 f4 13 ♕d3 ♘a6 14 ♘xg5 ♗xg5 15 exf4 ♘c5 16 ♕e3 ♗e7 and the black pieces are so well placed, and the White pawns so shattered, that Black has the advantage) 11...e5 and Black has the most promising position.

b) 9 ♗xe7 ♘xe7 10 ♖c1 ♘xc3 11 ♖xc3 e5 with equality.

9 dxe6 ♗xe6 10 ♘d2?!

Too passive. Better was 10 ♘d4!? ♗d7 11 ♕b3 c5 12 ♘f3 ♗c6 with an even game.

10...♘fg4

Also possible was 10...♘e4 11 ♘dxe4 (11 ♗xe7?! ♕xe7 12 ♘cxe4 fxe4 13 0-0 ♗f5 gives Black the better chances because of White's cramped kingside) 11...♗xg5 12 ♘xg5 ♕xg5 13 g3 and White will have some problems keeping the balance.

11 ♗xe7 ♕xe7 12 0-0

12 ♘d5 ♗xd5 13 cxd5 ♘f6 14 ♕b3 ♕f7 would also give White some problems.

12...f4 13 exf4 ♖xf4 14 h3 ♘h6

Objectively the position might be equal here, but in practice Black has a more pleasant position with attacking prospects. In this game between two young players, Black manages to win a pawn and go into the 4th phase with a winning position, until a terrible accident finishes him off.

15 ♘d5 ♗xd5 16 cxd5 ♖d4 17 ♕c2 ♖xd5 18 ♕b3 c6 19 ♖fe1 ♕f7 20 ♘f3 ♘xf3+ 21 ♗xf3 ♖g5 22 ♕e3 ♖e5 23 ♕d3 ♖xe1+ 24 ♖xe1 d5 25 ♕e3 a6 26 a4 ♖f8 27 b4 ♘f5 28 ♕c5 ♕g6 29 ♗g4 h5 30 ♗xf5 ♕xf5 31 ♖e7 ♖f7 32 ♖e8+ ♔h7 33 ♖d8 ♕b1+ 34 ♔h2 ♕f5 35 ♔g1 ♕b1+ 36 ♔h2 ♕d1 37 ♕e3 ♕c2 38 ♕e8 ♕xf2 39 ♕g8+ ♔h6 40 ♖d6+ ♔g5 41 ♕d8+ ♖f6 42 ♖d7 g6 43 ♖xb7 ♕f4+ 44 ♔h1 ♕d6 45 ♖d7 ♕xb4 46 ♖f7 ♕f4 47 ♔g1 ♕d6??

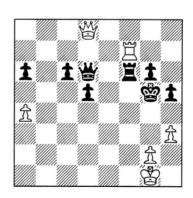

A great blunder. 47...♛e5 gives Black a clearly better game. But still, these are young players.

48 h4+! ♚f5 49 ♛xd6!

Now the rook is pinned!

49...♖xf7 50 ♛xc6 ♚e4 51 ♛e6+ 1-0

Game 63
Kempinski-Gleizerov
Stockholm 2000

---

1 d4 f5 2 c4 ♘f6 3 ♘c3 e6 4 f3!? ♗b4

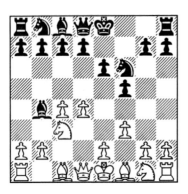

This move is the strongest. Black does not concede the fight for the e4-square. Still, the alternatives are worth a look:

a) 4...♗e7 5 e4 d6 6 ♗d3 0-0 7 ♘ge2 fxe4 8 ♘xe4 ♘xe4 9 ♗xe4 d5 10 ♗d3 dxc4 (the safest; 10...c5!? 11 ♕c2 cxd4 12 ♗xh7+ ♚h8 13 ♗d3 ♘c6 14 a3 ♗h4+ 15 ♘g3 dxc4 16 ♕xc4 ♕d6 reached a more or less level position in Karl-Schmidt, Bad Ragaz 1988) 11 ♗xc4 c5 12 0-0 ♘c6 and Black has equalised.

b) 4...♘c6!? 5 a3 (this cannot be the right way for White to play) 5...d6 6 e3 g6 7 b4 ♗g7 8 ♗d3 e5 9 ♘ge2 exd4 10 exd4 ♘h5 11 ♗e3 f4! and Black has taken over the initiative in Kempinski-Gleizerov, Bydgoszcz 2000, although White could have played the opening a lot better. Still, it is noteworthy that 4...♘c6 is the choice of one of the greatest advocates of the Dutch Defence (even though Gleizerov normally prefers the Stonewall set-up to

the Classical). The game concluded 12 ♗f2 ♕g5 13 ♘d5 ♕xg2 14 ♖g1 ♕xf3 15 ♘xc7+ ♚d8 16 ♘xa8 ♖e8 17 ♗h4+ ♚d7 18 ♕c2 ♘xd4 19 ♕a4+ ♘c6 20 0-0-0 ♖xe2 21 ♗xe2 ♕c3+ 22 ♕c2 ♕xa3+ 23 ♚d2 ♕xb4+ 0-1.

5 ♗d2 0-0 6 a3 ♗xc3 7 ♗xc3 d6 8 e3 ♕e8 9 ♕d2 ♘c6 10 ♗d3 e5 11 ♘e2 e4 12 ♗c2 b5!

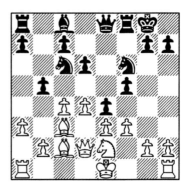

A great positional sacrifice.

13 cxb5 ♘e7 14 fxe4

14 ♘g3 ♗b7 15 fxe4 ♘xe4 16 ♘xe4 ♗xe4 17 ♗xe4 fxe4, followed by ...♘d5, would ensure Black more than sufficient compensation for the sacrificed pawn. Actually, White should probably return the pawn (for the sake of the bishop) straight away with 18 d5!?, although he will still be worse.

14...♘xe4

14...fxe4! is a more reliable idea. The knight on f6 is in no way inferior to the bishop on c2. And in some lines the c3-g7 diagonal can seem infected with danger.

15 ♗xe4 fxe4 16 d5 ♕xb5 17 ♘f4 ♘g6 18 ♕d4 ♖f7 19 ♘xg6

19 ♘e6 ♗xe6 20 dxe6 ♖e7 21 ♕xe4 ♖ae8 would give Black a strong attacking position.

19...hxg6 20 0-0-0 ♗g4

Black is close to equality now. The big mistake he commits in this game is to let White enter the f-file and then he completely overlooks a combination.

21 ♖d2 ♖af8

21...♖e8!?, with the idea of ...♖e5, was also possible.

22 ♖e1 ♕b3 23 ♖f2 ♕a2?

What exactly the queen is doing down there is hard to tell.

24 ♖f4! ♗d7 25 ♖ef1

Now all of a sudden this is possible and Black no longer has any defence.

25...c5

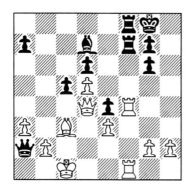

26 ♕xg7+!!

Winning by force.

26...♖xg7 27 ♖xf8+ ♔h7 28 ♖1f7 ♗a4 29 ♖xg7+ ♔h6 30 ♔d2 ♗b5 31 ♖h8+ ♔g5 32 h4+ ♔f5 33 ♖h5+ ♔g4 34 ♖g5+ ♔xh4 35 ♗f6 1-0

Game 64
Botvinnik-Bronstein
Moscow 1951

Many of the lines in this game originate from the annotations of Mikhail Botvinnik.

1 d4 e6 2 c4 f5 3 g3 ♘f6 4 ♗g2 ♗e7 5 ♘c3 0-0 6 e3 d6! 7 ♘ge2

I have decided to put this game into this chapter as it really does not belong in the traditional g3 chapters. White can also transpose to this position via 1 d4 f5 2 c4 ♘f6 3 ♘c3 e6 4 e3 ♗e7 5 g3. It should be said that this line is not dangerous for Black at all and should not be feared.

7...c6 8 0-0 e5

Black has already equalised. White now

decides to close the centre, but this takes time and Black will be ready for it.

9 d5 ♕e8! 10 e4 ♕h5

Black is fighting for the advantage!

After 10...♘a6 the position should be equal, unless White becomes greedy and falls for 11 dxc6 bxc6 12 exf5 ♗xf5 13 ♕a4 ♘c5 14 ♕xc6 ♕h5, when Black has good compensation for the sacrificed pawn, Golombek-Nikolac, Opatija 1953.

11 exf5 ♗xf5

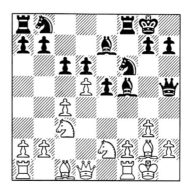

12 f3

Just how dangerous this attack is for White is illustrated by the following analysis. 12 c5 ♗h3! and now White can try a lot of different lines:

a) 13 dxc6 ♘xc6 14 ♕b3+ ♔h8 15 ♕xb7 ♖ac8 16 ♗xc6 ♗xf1 17 ♔xf1 ♘g4 18 h4 ♗xh4 19 ♔e1 ♘xf2 and Black has a very dangerous attack.

b) 13 ♕b3? ♘g4 14 dxc6+ ♔h8 15 cxb7 ♗xg2 16 h4 ♗f3! (16...♗xh4? 17 ♔xg2 ♗xg3 18 ♖h1 ♖xf2+ 19 ♔xg3 ♕xh1 20 bxa8♕ ♕xa8 21 ♘d5 is not clear at all) 17 bxa8♕ (17 ♘d5 ♗xh4 18 ♕xf3 ♖xf3 19 bxa8♕ ♗d8! 20 ♔g2 e4 21 ♖h1 ♖xf2+ 22 ♔g1 ♖h2 would be the end for White) 17...♗xa8 18 ♘d5 ♘h2 and Black retains a menacing attack.

c) 13 cxd6 ♗xd6 14 dxc6 ♘xc6 15 ♕xd6 ♖ad8 16 ♕c5 ♘g4 17 f3 ♗xg2 18 fxg4 (18 ♕c4+ ♔h8 19 fxg4 ♕h3 20 ♖xf8+ ♖xf8 21 ♘f4 exf4 22 ♗xf4 ♗f3 23 ♕f1 ♕xg4 would give Black a very large advantage) 18...♖xf1+ 19 ♔xg2 ♕f7 20 ♘f4 ♖xc1 (20...♖e1? 21 ♕f2! and White defends) 21 ♖xc1 exf4 22 ♖f1 ♖d2+ 23 ♔g1 f3 and Black has a rather obvious advantage.

d) 13 f3! ♗xg2 14 ♔xg2 dxc5 15 ♕b3 b5 16 dxc6+ ♕f7 17 c7 ♘a6 with equality.

12...♕g6 13 ♗e3 ♘bd7 14 ♕d2 cxd5 15 cxd5

15 ♘xd5 ♘xd5 16 cxd5 was stronger. As it is Black who is considering an attack, exchanges might favour White. Also, the e2-knight now has somewhere useful to go.

15...♗d8! 16 ♖ac1?!

This runs into an ugly pin. Better was 16 ♘b5 ♗d3 (16...♘e8 17 f4 would give White counterplay) 17 ♘xd6 ♘xd5 18 ♗f2! ♗g5 19 f4 ♘xf4 20 gxf4 ♗xf4 21 ♘xf4 exf4 22 ♖fe1! f3 23 ♗g3 fxg2 24 ♕xg2 ♘f6 and now 25 ♖e7 would keep things going. Here White is quite active and will probably regain his pawn. Still, his inferior king position might give problems if he does not play exactly.

16...♗a5!

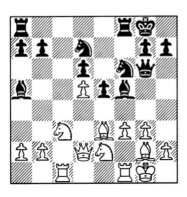

This move really exposes the problems in the white camp. His only hope for active play was connected to a ♘b5 sortie, but now this is out of the question. And ...♘b6-c4 is a serious threat.

17 g4

White is forced to do something, otherwise he ends up in trouble beyond his imagination: 17 ♖fd1?! ♘b6! 18 g4 (after 18 ♗xb6

♗xb6+ 19 ♔h1 Black also has a strong initiative) 18...♘c4 19 gxf5 ♕xf5 20 ♕d3 ♕xd3 21 ♖xd3 ♘xe3 22 ♖xe3 ♗b6 23 ♘d1 (23 ♔f2 ♘g4+) 23...♘xd5 and White is suffering badly.

17...♗d3 18 ♖fd1 ♗c4 19 ♕c2?

Here it was better to play 19 b3 ♗xe2! (or 19...♘b6 20 ♘g3 ♗xd5 21 g5 ♘fd7 22 b4 ♗xb4 23 ♕xd5+! ♘xd5 24 ♘xd5 ♖f7 25 ♘xb4 ♘c5 and Black might be a little bit better, but White has created counterchances) 20 ♕xe2 ♗b6 21 ♘b5 ♘e8 22 ♕f2 ♕f7 and White is structurally worse, but still fighting.

19...♕xc2 20 ♖xc2 ♘b6! 21 ♖cd2 ♗a6

21...♖ac8 was a natural move, giving Black a good game too.

22 ♗f2 ♘c4?

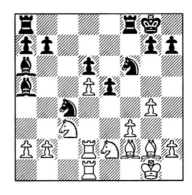

This is simply a matter of tactics. After 22...♗xe2! 23 ♖xe2 ♗xc3 24 ♗xb6 axb6 25 bxc3 ♘d7, followed by ...♖f4!, ...♔f7-e7 and ...♘c5, Black will have a winning endgame.

23 ♖c2 ♗b6

Or 23...♖ac8 24 g5! and g2-bishop comes to life; the game is level.

24 ♗xb6 axb6 25 ♖e1 ♘e3

25...♖ac8 26 ♘g3 ♘xb2 27 ♖xb2 ♖xc3 28 ♖xb6 ♘xd5 29 ♖xd6 ♘e3 is also a draw.

26 ♖d2 ♘c4 27 ♖c2 ♘e3 28 ♖d2 ♘c4 ½-½

The advantage has gone and g4-g5 is perhaps on the way, so Black takes a draw by repetition.

Summary

White has tried many kinds of fourth moves in the e3 systems. The only one I would recommend to be studied a little bit closer is the system with 4 f3!?, which can prove rather poisonous. Otherwise, playing through these games and making note of the main ideas and concepts should be adequate for success.

1 d4 f5 2 c4 ♘f6 3 ♘c3

> 3 g3 e6 4 ♗g2 ♗e7 5 ♘c3 0-0 6 e3 – *Game 64*

3...e6 4 ♕c2

> 4 ♘f3 ♗e7 5 ♗f4 d6 6 h3 0-0 7 e3 – *Game 61*

> 4 ♗g5 ♗e7 5 e3 – *Game 62*

> 4 f3 – *Game 63*

> 4 e3 (D)

>> 4...d6 5 ♘f3 – *Game 59*

>> 4...b6 – *Game 60*

4...♗e7

> 4...d6 5 ♘f3 ♗e7 6 e4 – *Game 58*

5 e3 0-0 6 ♗d3 (D) **d6**

> 6...♘c6 – *Game 57*

7 ♘ge2 (D) **c6**

> 7...♘c6 – *Game 56*

8 ♗d2 – *Game 55*

4 e3

6 ♗d3

7 ♘ge2

CHAPTER SEVEN

Systems with ♞h3

1 d4 f5 2 g3 ♞f6 3 ♗g2 e6 4 ♞h3

In this chapter we will look at three games in which White develops in typical fashion with g2-g3 and ♗g2, but then chooses to put the knight on h3 instead of f3. This presents some advantages and some disadvantages. On the positive side, it can be said that the knight is quite actively placed on f4 (when it gets there), and in some cases it finds a good resting point at d5. In this way the knight can have a more active role than in the usual lines with ♞f3. Finally, White has some options with e2-e4 he might not have in other situations, as the knight no longer impedes the g2-bishop.

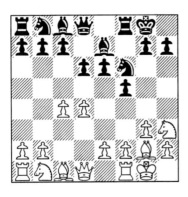

The problems with ♞h3 are just as obvious. First of all, there is the matter of time. It takes another move before the knight joins the fight for the central squares. Secondly, Black's main dream in this system is often to find the right time to play ...e6-e5. Not only is the white knight not involved in preventing this, but it also might allow Black to gain time by being kicked away from f4 to a less convenient square. Finally, the knight might actually get stuck out there on h3 as in Game 67!

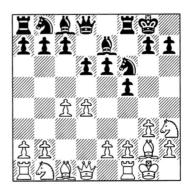

Game 65
Karpov-Short
Linares 1992

1 d4 f5 2 g3 ♞f6 3 ♗g2 e6 4 ♞h3
This idea belongs to Joseph Blackburne.

According to the famous Grandmaster Paul Keres, this move is good only if Black plays the Stonewall system. In that case it is actually the most critical continuation. Here it is less dangerous.

4...♗e7 5 0-0 0-0 6 c4 d6 7 ♘c3 ♕e8

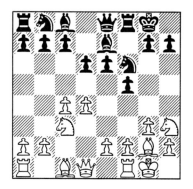

This is the main move here, although some alternatives have been tested.

a) 7...c6 8 e4 e5 9 dxe5 dxe5 10 ♕e2 ♕c7 11 f4 ♘xe4 12 ♘xe4 fxe4 13 ♗xe4 h6 14 ♔g2 ♘d7 15 ♗c2 gave White a better position in Koch-Enigk, Germany 1961 – Black's development is not easy.

b) The immediate 7...e5!? makes more sense: 8 dxe5 dxe5 9 ♕xd8 ♗xd8 (9...♖xd8 10 e4 fxe4 11 ♘g5 is better for White according to Keres, but of course Black doesn't play that way) 10 b3 (after 10 e4?! ♘c6! White is experiencing serious problems with the knight on h3) 10...♘a6 11 ♗a3 ♖e8 12 ♘b5 ♗e7 13 ♗xe7 ♖xe7 14 ♖ad1 (or 14 ♘g5 e4 15 ♖ad1 ♗d7 and Black has equalised) 14...c6 15 ♘d6 h6! 16 f3 ♗e6 17 ♘f2 ♘e8! 18 ♗h3 ♘xd6 19 ♖xd6 ♘c5 with equality in Vladimirov-Psakhis, USSR 1985.

8 ♘f4 g5?

This surprisingly proves to be a big positional mistake. Both alternatives are stronger.

a) 8...c6!? 9 e4?! (this is not fully sound; better is 9 ♘d3 ♘bd7 with equality, or 9 d5 e5 10 dxc6 bxc6 11 ♘fd5 ♘xd5 12 ♘xd5 ♗d8 13 b3 ♗b7 14 ♘c3 with a level position in Taulbut-Rumens, London 1977) 9...fxe4

10 ♘xe4 ♘xe4 11 ♗xe4 e5 12 dxe5 dxe5 13 ♘d3 ♗h3 14 ♖e1 ♘d7 15 ♗g2 ♗xg2 16 ♔xg2 ♕f7 with a plus for Black in Goncharov-Malysev, Russia 1996. Note that due to the easy development of the Black pieces, the weak e-pawn is not really important. Black has a lot of pressure on the f-file and an attack against the weakened position of White's king.

b) 8...♗d8!? is an alternative way to protect c7 and prepare ...e6-e5: 9 ♘d3 e5 10 d5 ♘bd7 11 f3! (fitting the circumstances; the d3-knight controls c5, so the d7-knight has really made a fool of himself) 11...a5 12 e4 fxe4 (12...f4? 13 gxf4 exf4 14 ♘xf4 ♘e5 15 b3 ♘h5 16 ♘e6 ♗xe6 17 dxe6 ♕xe6 18 f4 ♘g4 19 e5 would give White a positionally and tactically winning position) 13 fxe4 ♕g6 and White was a little better in Poliak-Kan, Moscow 1949.

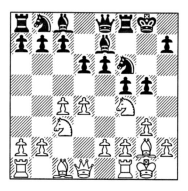

9 ♘d3 ♕g6

This position is unclear according to Paul Keres.

10 f4!

But this position gives White a clear advantage according to Anatoly Karpov!

10...h6 11 d5 ♘a6 12 b4!

White has a strong initiative on the queenside, while Black has got more or less nothing going on the kingside.

12...exd5

How bad a state Black is really in can be seen from these lines:

a) 12...♘e4 13 ♘xe4 fxe4 14 ♘f2 exd5 15 cxd5 ♗f5 16 g4 and White wins.

b) 12...e5 13 b5 ♘b8 (13...♘c5 14 ♘xc5 dxc5 15 fxe5 ♘g4 16 e6 ♗f6 17 ♕e1 and White is just a protected passed pawn up for nothing) 14 fxe5 dxe5 15 ♘xe5 ♕g7 16 ♗b2 and White has a winning position.

13 ♘xd5 ♘xd5 14 ♗xd5+ ♔h7 15 b5 ♘c5 16 ♘xc5 dxc5

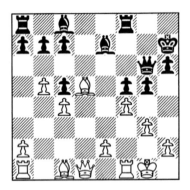

17 ♕c2!

Typical of Karpov's style – a move of real prophylaxis. The idea is to prevent Black from freeing his queenside. After 17 ♖b1?! ♗e6 18 ♗xb7 ♖ad8 Black would gain some unnecessary counterplay.

17...a6

17...c6 18 bxc6 bxc6 19 ♗g2 gives White a lasting structural advantage.

18 a4!

This is more precise than 18 ♗b2?! gxf4 19 ♖xf4 ♗g5, when it's obvious that the bishop has abandoned the squares nearest to his own king – the position is unclear.

18...♖b8

18...axb5 19 cxb5 c6 20 bxc6 bxc6 21 ♗c4 would give White a clear advantage due to his outside passed pawn.

19 fxg5!

Time for action!

19...hxg5 20 ♖a3 c6

Black still cannot free his queenside. One example is 20...♗e6 21 ♗xe6 ♕xe6 22 ♖e3 ♕f6 23 g4 and White wins.

21 ♗g2 ♗f6

This move is forced. After 21...cxb5 22 g4 (with the idea of ♖h3) and 21...♗e6 22 ♖e3! Black is facing too many problems.

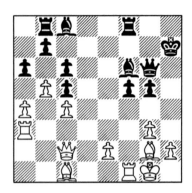

22 ♗e3!

This again prevents the opponent's plan. After 22 g4 ♗d4+ (22...♗e5!? is another possibility, protecting f5 and the king at the same time) 23 e3 ♗e5 24 ♗e4 ♔g7 25 gxf5 White is doing very well, but his rook on a3 is shut out of the game unnecessarily.

22...♗d4 23 ♗xd4 cxd4 24 e3 dxe3 25 ♖xe3 ♗e6

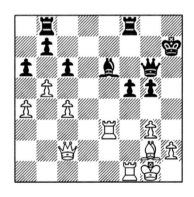

26 g4!

Finally this comes, and now with deadly effect.

26...♖be8 27 bxc6 bxc6 28 c5!

Precise to the end. After the automatic and greedy 28 ♗xc6? ♖c8 29 gxf5 ♖xf5 30 ♖xf5 ♗xf5 31 ♖e7+ ♔h6 32 ♗e4 ♗xe4 33

♕xe4 ♕xe4 34 ♖xe4 Black has real chances of saving this endgame.

28...♕f6 29 ♗xc6 ♖b8

White wins after 29...♕d4 30 ♕c3 ♕xg4+ 31 ♖g3 ♕c4 32 ♗xe8 ♕xc3 33 ♖xc3 ♖xe8 34 c6, when the exchange and passed pawn decide matters.

30 gxf5 ♗f7 31 ♗g2 ♖b2 32 ♕c3 ♕xc3 33 ♖xc3 ♖d8 34 c6 ♖dd2 35 ♗e4 ♖e2 36 c7 ♖xe4 37 c8♕ 1-0

Game 66
Reshevsky-Botvinnik
The Hague 1948

I have in some part based my annotations on those by Keres from the tournament book.

1 d4 e6 2 c4 f5 3 g3 ♘f6 4 ♗g2 ♗e7 5 ♘h3 0-0 6 0-0 d6 7 ♘c3 ♕e8 8 e4

8 ♘f4 was considered in the previous game.

8...fxe4

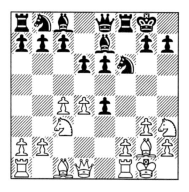

9 ♘f4

Also possible is 9 ♘xe4. In *Encyclopaedia of Chess Openings* by Chess Informant this position is regarded as much better for White. This is, of course, not true. After 9...e5 10 dxe5 (or 10 ♘hg5 ♘c6 with an unclear position) 10...dxe5 11 ♘hg5 ♘c6 12 ♘xf6+ ♗xf6 13 ♖e1 ♗f5 Black seems to have equalised without any problems. White has the e4-square, but Black is active and can

make good use of the d4-square.

9...c6

9...e5 would be too soon due to 10 dxe5 dxe5 11 ♘fd5 and White is better.

10 ♘xe4 ♘xe4 11 ♗xe4 e5 12 ♘g2?!

12 dxe5 dxe5 13 ♘d3 with an unclear game was more prudent.

12...♘d7 13 ♘e3 exd4!

13...♘f6 14 ♗g2 e4 15 d5!, with the plan ♗d2-c3, would give White the advantage as the e4-pawn is in trouble.

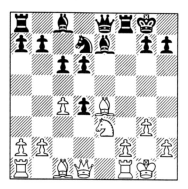

14 ♕xd4 ♘e5 15 f4 ♘g4 16 ♘xg4 ♗xg4 17 ♖e1

17 ♕d3 ♕h5 18 ♗f3, to play for a draw, was also possible.

17...♗f6 18 ♕d3

18 ♕xd6 ♖d8 19 ♕a3 (19 ♗xh7+? ♔xh7 20 ♖xe8 ♖fxe8 is a nice tactic as the black rooks go in for the kill) 19...♕h5 would leave White in trouble. Black has serious attacking chances.

18...♕h5 19 ♗d2 ♖fe8 20 ♖ab1?

Both 20 ♗c3 ♗xc3 21 ♕xc3 ♖e6 22 ♖e3 ♖ae8 23 ♖ae1, with a defensible position, and maybe even 20 ♖e3!? were better.

20...♖e7?

This is careless play. Black leaves the d6-pawn en prise unnecessarily. 20...♖e6! 21 b4 (21 ♖e3? ♖ae8 22 ♖be1 can simply be meet with 22...♗xb2 23 ♖b1 ♖xe4! 24 ♖xe4 ♖xe4 25 ♕xe4 ♗f5 26 ♕e1 ♗d4+ with a winning position) 21...♖ae8 22 ♖bc1 ♔h8 would give Black a large advantage. If you think it is not so apparent, then try to look at what threats the black pieces create, and then turn to the white pieces and see what they can do!

21 ♗b4!

Reshevsky does not miss this chance to win a pawn with tempo.

21...♖ae8 22 ♗xd6 ♖e6

Maybe Botvinnik had miscalculated the following line: 22...♖xe4? 23 ♖xe4 ♖xe4 24 ♕xe4 ♗f5 and it looks good for Black. Yet after 25 ♕e3 ♗xb1 26 ♕e6+ ♔h8 27 ♕c8+ it is White who wins.

23 ♖e3?

Much better was 23 c5! ♗f5 24 ♗e5 ♗xe5 25 ♗xf5 ♗d4+ 26 ♔f1 and White liquidates into a highly advantageous endgame.

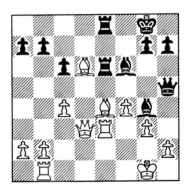

23...♖xd6!?

Also possible was 23...♗f5 24 ♗e5 ♗xe4 (24...♗xe5?! 25 ♗xf5 ♖d6 26 ♗xh7+ ♔h8 27 ♖xe5 ♖xe5 28 ♕xd6 ♖e2 29 ♕d8+ ♔xh7 30 ♕h4 ♕xh4 31 gxh4 would give White some chances in the endgame, even though it does not look like many) 25 ♖xe4 ♗xe5 26 ♖be1 ♕f5 27 fxe5 ♖xe5 28 ♖xe5 ♕xd3 29 ♖xe8+ ♔f7 and, because the position of the white king is so open, Black will not have any problems drawing this position.

24 ♕xd6 ♖d8

24...♗e7 25 ♗d5+! and White wins.

25 ♕c7

25 ♕b4? ♗d4 26 ♖be1 ♖e8 would turn the tables. Also not good is 25 ♕a3 ♖d2 and Black is penetrating into White's position.

One possible line is 26 ♗g2 ♗d4 27 ♖be1 (otherwise ...♖e2) 27...♗h3! and White has no defence. But not 27...♗f3? after which White has the miracle save with 28 ♕e7 ♗xe3+ 29 ♖xe3 ♖xg2+ 30 ♔f1 h6 31 ♕d8+ ♔h7 32 ♕d3+.

25...♕c5?!

This is probably an attempt to win the game, which is rather foolish. 25...♖d2?? 26 ♗d5+ also does not work, but 25...♖d7 26 ♕c8+ ♖d8 would draw. Black even wins after 27 ♕xb7? ♗d4 28 ♖be1 ♗xe3+ 29 ♖xe3 ♖d1+ with mate to follow in just a few moves.

26 ♖be1 ♖c8 27 ♕xb7 ♗d4 28 ♔f2?!

Now it is White's turn to miss his golden chance. After 28 ♕b3 ♖d8 29 ♔g2 ♗xe3 30 ♕xe3 ♕xe3 31 ♖xe3 ♖d2+ 32 ♔f1 ♖xb2 33 ♗xc6 White has some chances to win the endgame.

28...♗xe3+

The alternatives were:

a) 28...♕a5? 29 ♗f3 ♕d2+ (29...♖e8 30 ♗xg4 ♖xe3 31 ♖xe3 ♕d2+ 32 ♔f1! ♕xe3 33 ♕c8+ ♔f7 34 ♕d7+ ♔f8 35 ♕d6+ ♔f7 36 ♔g2 would give White very good chances to win the game) 30 ♖1e2 ♗xe3+ 31 ♔g2 and White has won a pawn.

b) 28...♖d8?! 29 ♕b3 ♗xe3+ 30 ♕xe3 ♖d2+ 31 ♔g1 ♕xe3+ 32 ♖xe3 ♖d1+ 33 ♔f2 ♖d2+ 34 ♔f1 ♖xb2 35 ♗xc6 transposes to the line above.

29 ♖xe3 ♕d4?!

Here Black misses the chance to draw directly with 29...♖d8 30 ♕b3 ♖d2+ 31 ♔g1 ♖d1+ 32 ♔f2 and the natural continuation leads to a perpetual check.

30 ♕b3?

30 ♗f3! ♖e8 31 ♕b3 ♖xe3 32 ♕xe3 ♕xb2+ 33 ♕e2 ♕d4+ 34 ♔g2 ♗xf3+ 35 ♔xf3 would give White an extra pawn in the queen ending. Sure, it is still very hard to win, but in practice it is just as hard to draw, so if White just continues to play normal moves, then he will most likely obtain some reasonable chances.

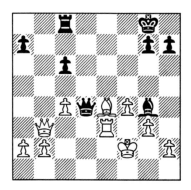

30...♕d2+ 31 ♔g1 ♕c1+ 32 ♔f2 ♕d2+ 33 ♔g1 ♕c1+ ½-½

Black chooses to take the perpetual check. This is probably a good decision, as after 33...♗e2 34 h4 ♕e1+ 35 ♔h2 ♕f2+ 36 ♔h3 White has good chances to prove an advantage.

Game 67
Sliwa-Tolush
Riga 1959

---

1 c4 f5 2 d4 ♘f6 3 g3 e6 4 ♗g2 ♗e7 5 ♘h3 0-0 6 0-0 d6 7 b3

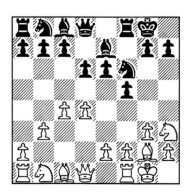

There are some alternatives here:

a) 7 ♕b3 c6 and now:

a1) 8 ♘d2 e5! 9 c5+ d5 10 e3 (10 dxe5 ♘g4 and Black regains his pawn without any problems) 10...♕c7 and Black probably already has the better position.

a2) 8 ♘c3 ♘a6 9 ♘g5 e5 10 ♖d1 ♕e8 11 d5 h6 12 ♘f3 ♘c5?! (12...cxd5 with unclear play is better according to Karpov) 13 ♕a3 cxd5 14 ♘xd5 ♘xd5 15 cxd5 with a slight advantage to White, Karpov-Nikolic, Reykjavik 1991.

b) 7 ♘f4 c6 8 ♘c3 e5 9 dxe5 dxe5 10 ♘d3 ♕c7 11 b3 ♘a6 12 a3 ♘c5 gives Black a good game.

7...♕e8 8 ♘d2?!

This move does not do anything to prevent Black from his main advance ...e6-e5. It was better to play 8 ♗b2 ♗d8 9 ♘f4 ♘a6 (9...e5?! 10 dxe5 dxe5 11 ♘d5 would give White a small advantage and – what is worse – would completely justify his play, Ulybin-Poluljahov, Budapest 1992) 10 ♘c3 c6! and now, fully prepared for ...e6-e5, Black has equalised.

8...e5 9 dxe5 dxe5 10 ♗b2 ♘g4!

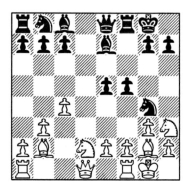

A main difference from the variations with the knight in f3. In those lines White would have h2-h3, but now he has nothing of the sort, only a misplaced knight out there.

11 e3 a5 12 ♕e2?

12 ♖e1!, with the idea of 13 ♘f1 and 14 f3 followed by ♘f2, would still give White some chances for equality.

12...♘a6 13 ♘f3

13 f3? ♘xe3 would just drop a pawn.

13...♗d6 14 ♔h1 ♘c5 15 ♖ad1 ♗d7

Black has a clear advantage. The white position might not look so bad at first glance, but really, all of his pieces are beautifully controlled by their black counterparts. The knights, especially, have no future at all.

16 ♘e1

So White tries to do something to change the course of the game and untangle himself from all this mess.

16...e4!

Preventing f2-f3.

17 ♗d4 b6 18 ♕b2 ♘e6

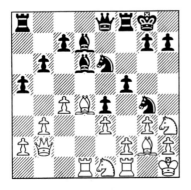

Black has a clear advantage and so he takes it easy. The sacrificial line with 18...♕h5!? 19 ♗xg7 ♖f7 20 ♗d4 ♘xe3 21 fxe3 ♕xd1 apparently wins material, but after 22 ♘f3! ♕xf1+! (or 22...♕d3? 23 ♘fg5 ♖ff8?! – not the best defence, but the position is falling apart – 24 ♗h8! and White wins) 23 ♗xf1 exf3 24 ♘g5 ♗c6 25 ♔g1 the position is deeply unclear.

19 ♖d2?!

White needed to change the course of the game, as if everything continues down the same lane, Black will just win. Better was 19 ♗xb6!?, when Black has a lot of pleasant options, as the loss of this pawn wasn't critical. Probably he should go for the direct kill with 19...♕h5!? 20 ♗xc7 (White's main idea) 20...♗xc7 21 ♖xd7 ♖ad8!, with ideas of ...♘g5 and ...♖f6-h6 with a very dangerous attack.

19...♕h5!?

Played with the idea of 20...g5 and 21...f4. Also possible was 19...♘xd4 with a solid positional advantage.

20 f4

The only move, otherwise ...♘g5 was disturbing.

20...exf3

This is not the most logical move as the knight is rather inactive on e1, but now it protects h2. 20...♘xd4 21 ♕xd4 ♗e6 would give a winning position.

21 ♘xf3 ♘xd4 22 ♕xd4

Or 22 exd4 ♘e3! (22...f4?!, with threat of ...♘e3, would give White time to defend a little with 23 ♘e5! f3 24 ♖xf3 ♗xe5 25 dxe5 ♗c6 26 ♖xf8+ ♖xf8 27 ♖d5 and White is still hanging in there, though only by a fine thread) 23 ♖ff2 ♘xg2 24 ♔xg2 f4 25 ♘xf4 ♗xf4 26 gxf4 ♖xf4 and Black has an easily winning attack

22...♖ae8 23 ♘f4 ♕h6 24 ♖e2?!

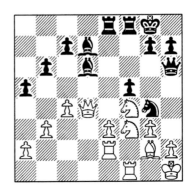

24 ♘h4!? was stronger, the idea being that after 24...♘xe3 25 ♖e1 White only loses a pawn. Now it is the king that is in danger.

24...♗c6 25 ♕d2 ♗b4 26 ♕c1 ♗c5 27 ♘h4 g5 28 ♗xc6 ♕xc6+ 29 ♘d5 gxh4 30 e4 fxe4 31 ♖xf8+ ♖xf8 32 h3 ♘f2+ 33 ♔g2 ♕g6 34 g4 ♘xg4 35 ♔h1 ♘f2+ 36 ♖xf2 ♖xf2 0-1

Summary

White probably cannot hope for an opening advantage at all after playing the knight to h3. The simplest way to equalise seems to be a quick ...e6-e5. Black should be careful about playing ...g6-g5 as Short did against Karpov. The structure arising after 10 f4! in that game is surely much better for White. The right way for Black to play is to play in the centre.

1 d4 f5 2 c4 ♘f6 3 g3 e6 4 ♗g2 ♗e7 5 ♘h3 0-0 6 0-0 d6 (D) 7 ♘c3

      7 b3 ♕e8 (D) – *Game 67*

7...♕e8 8 ♘f4

      8 e4 – *Game 66*

8...g5 9 ♘d3 (D) – *Game 65*

 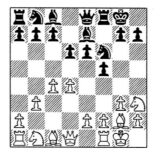 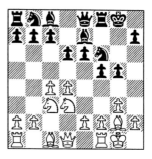

   6...d6   *7...♕e8*   *9 ♘d3*

CHAPTER EIGHT

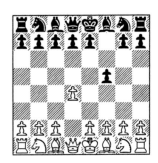

Second Move Alternatives

1 d4 f5

In this chapter we will look at more unusual second move options for White. The Staunton Gambit with 2 e4 (Game 68) is perhaps the most violent try against the Dutch. White immediately sacrifices a pawn in order to speed up development while trying to exploit the slight weakness on Black's kingside. However, Black's resources in this line seem to be more than adequate. Another, more subtle, approach from White is early piece play with either 2 ♘c3 or 2 ♗g5 (Games 69-72). These lines are tricky but the well-versed Dutch player should have nothing to fear.

Game 68
Gulko-Gurevich
USSR 1985

---

1 d4 f5 2 e4 fxe4

This is the only serious move. Here are the passive alternatives:

a) 2...e6?! gives White a better structure right from the start. A good illustration of what this can lead to is given in the following game: 3 exf5 exf5 4 ♗d3 g6 (4...d5!? 5 ♗f4 gives White only a slight advantage) 5 ♘f3 ♕e7+ 6 ♔f1! ♘f6 7 ♘c3 ♗g7 8 ♗g5 c6 9 ♕d2 0-0 10 ♖e1 ♕d8 11 h4 (White has an

overwhelming attack) 11...d6 12 h5 ♖e8 13 hxg6 hxg6 14 ♘e2 ♘bd7 15 ♘h4 ♘f8 16 g4 ♘8h7 17 ♘xg6 ♘e4 18 ♗xd8 ♘xd2+ 19 ♔g2 ♘f8?! (or 19...♖xd8 20 ♘e7+ ♔f7 21 ♖xh7) 20 ♗a5 ♘e4 21 ♘xf8 ♗xf8 22 f3 b6 23 gxf5 ♘f6 24 ♗d2 ♘d5 25 ♖eg1 ♗g7 26 ♔f2 ♔f8 27 ♖h7 1-0 Sveshnikov-Trajkovic, Pula 1990.

b) 2...d6?! 3 ♘c3 ♘f6 4 ♗d3 fxe4 5 ♘xe4 g6 6 ♘f3 ♗g4 7 h3 ♗xf3 8 ♕xf3 ♘xe4 9 ♗xe4 c6 10 h4 with a clear advantage for White in Grosar-Blatnik, Sentjur 1996. Two bishops, a clear attacking point and a lead in development – Black is more or less busted if you think about it.

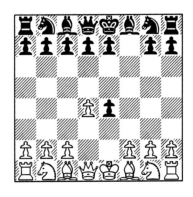

3 ♘c3

On 3 f3!? I recommend 3...♘f6! 4 ♘c3 or

3...d5 4 ♘c3 d5, both of which transpose to the main text. In the latter case Black shouldn't continue with 4...exf3 5 ♘xf3 ♗g4 6 h3 ♗xf3 7 ♕xf3 e6 8 ♗d3 as this gives White a lead in development and a possible attack on the light squares.

3...♘f6

On 3...g6!? White has the logical 4 h4!, using his lead in development to attack, not to regain a ridiculous pawn (4 ♘xe4 d5 5 ♘g3 ♗g7 6 h4 ♘c6 7 ♗b5 ♕d6 8 ♗xc6+ bxc6 9 ♘1e2 ♗a6 10 c3 e5 was preferable for Black in Fuderer-Alexander, Belgrade 1952). After 4...d5 5 h5 ♗g7 6 f3 ♘c6 7 ♗b5 ♕d6 the position is a mess.

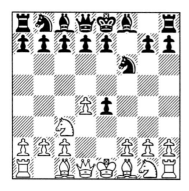

4 f3

The most aggressive line here is 4 ♗g5

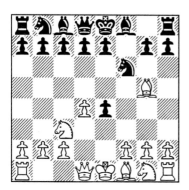

after which Black can play:

a) 4...g6 5 h4! (5 f3!? exf3 6 ♘xf3 d5 7 ♗d3 ♗g7 8 ♕e2 ♘c6 9 0-0-0 ♗g4 10 ♕e3

0-0 11 h3 ♗xf3 12 gxf3 ♘h5 and the position is unclear according to Cabrilo) 5...d5 6 h5 ♗g7 7 h6 ♗f8 8 f3 ♕d6 9 ♘ge2 exf3 10 gxf3 c6 11 ♕d2 ♘bd7 12 0-0-0 ♘b6 13 ♘f4 with a strong attacking position in Rabar-Kluzinski, Yugoslavia 1949.

b) 4...e6 5 ♘xe4 ♗e7 6 ♗xf6 ♗xf6 7 ♘f3 transposes to Game 72.

c) 4...c6 looks awkward. 5 f3! exf3 6 ♘xf3 d6 7 ♗d3 ♗g4 8 0-0 ♕a5 9 ♕d2 ♘bd7 10 b4 ♕c7 11 ♖ae1 0-0-0 12 b5 c5 13 b6! ♕xb6 14 ♖b1 with a strong white attack in Serebrinsky-Makarov, USSR 1950.

d) The most popular choice is 4...♘c6!. Time has shown that this aggressive-looking move is also the strongest. One of the key ideas is that after 5 ♗xf6 exf6 6 ♘xe4 d5! Black is developing fast and has a pleasant position to look forward to. Instead White can choose:

d1) 5 f3!? d5 (5...e5 6 d5 ♘d4 7 ♘xe4 ♗e7 8 ♗xf6 ♗xf6 9 ♕d2 0-0 10 0-0-0 d6 11 c3 ♘f5 leads to equality, Hørberg-Larsen, Stockholm 1966/67) 6 fxe4 ♘xe4 7 ♘xe4 dxe4 8 d5 ♘e5 9 ♕d4 ♘f7 10 ♗h4 c6 with an unclear game according to Mark Taimanov.

d2) 5 ♗b5?! does not make a lot of sense. After 5...g6! 6 ♗xf6 exf6 7 ♘xe4 ♕e7! 8 ♗xc6 dxc6 9 ♕e2 f5 10 ♘c3 ♗g7 11 ♕xe7+ ♔xe7 Black has the comfortable advantage of having the two bishops in an ending, Zelic-Palac, Pula 2000.

d3) 5 d5 ♘e5 6 ♕d4 ♘f7 7 ♗xf6 (7 h4 c6 8 0-0-0 ♕b6 9 ♕d2 ♘xg5 10 hxg5 ♘xd5 11 ♘xd5 cxd5 12 ♕xd5 ♕c6 13 ♕b3 ♕c5 was unclear in Schuster-Calaviere, Ezeiza 2000, but more logical is 13...a6!? 14 ♗e2 g6 15 ♗c4 e6 16 ♕c3 ♖g8 17 ♖xh7 ♗e7 18 ♕d4 d5, when the powerful centre guarantees Black the advantage) 7 ♗xf6 and now:

d31) 7...gxf6!? 8 ♘xe4 (8 ♕xe4!?) 8...c6 9 ♗c4?! (9 0-0-0 is more logical) 9...♕b6! 10 ♘f3 ♕xd4 11 ♘xd4 cxd5 12 ♗xd5 e6 13 ♗b3 f5 14 ♘f6+ ♔e7 15 ♘h5 ♖g8 16 g3 ♖g4 and Black's strong centre gives him the advantage, Osman-Sebe, Bucharest 2001.

d32) 7...exf6 (the normal move) 8 ♘xe4 ♗e7 (equally good is 8...f5!? 9 ♘g3 g6 10 0-0-0 ♗h6+ 11 f4 0-0 12 ♘f3 ♗g7 13 ♕d2 b5 14 ♘d4 ♘d6 and Black has no problems, Shumitsev-Shaposnikov, correspondence 1969; actually this is the line I would recommend) 9 0-0-0 0-0 10 ♘g3 d6 11 f4 (logical is 11 ♘h3 c5 12 ♕c3 g6 13 ♘f4 ♘e5, when Black has a strong knight on e5, but White perhaps can use the e6-square for something) 11...c5 12 ♕c3 ♘h6 13 ♗d3 with an unclear game in Krvatsov-Vyzmanavin, Novgorod 1997.

4 g4 has been played quite a few times, but the annoyance of the knight on f6 is not nearly as important as the weaknesses created in the white camp. One game continued 4...h6 5 g5 hxg5 6 ♗xg5 d5 7 h4 ♘c6 8 f3 ♗f5 9 ♗h3 ♕d7 10 ♗xf5 ♕xf5 11 a3 0-0-0 and Black was fine in Dalkiran-Onischuk, Heraklio 1997. But here Konikowski suggests that Black could play even better with 11...exf3! 12 ♘xf3 (12 ♕xf3 ♕xc2 [12...♘xd4!?] 13 ♗xf6 gxf6 14 ♖d1 ♕xb2 15 ♘xd5 0-0-0 and Black wins) 12...0-0-0 and White has no compensation for the sacrificed pawn.

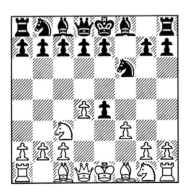

4...d5

Black's alternatives are risky:

a) 4...♘c6 5 fxe4 e5 6 dxe5! (never mind structure – time is the important aspect right here) 6...♘xe5 7 ♘f3 ♗d6 8 ♗g5 h6 9 ♗h4 ♘g6 10 ♗g3 ♗xg3+ 11 hxg3 ♕e7 12 ♕d4 with an advantage to White in Grigorian-Tal, USSR 1972.

b) 4...exf3 5 ♘xf3 g6 6 ♗f4 ♗g7 7 ♕d2 0-0 8 ♗h6 d5 gives White good compensation for the pawn, but Black also has his resources, Bronstein-Alexander, Hastings 1953/54. Most players would probably like to avoid playing like this with Black, as this was clearly the type of game White was hoping for.

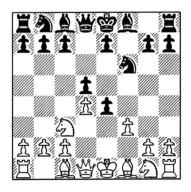

5 fxe4 dxe4 6 ♗g5 ♗f5 7 ♘ge2

7 ♗c4 ♘c6 8 ♘ge2 ♕d7 9 0-0 e6 10 ♕e1 0-0-0 11 ♖d1 ♘a5 was equal in Schultz-Wille, correspondence 1956/57.

7...e6

7...♘c6? 8 d5 ♘e5 9 ♕d4 ♘f7 10 ♗xf6 exf6 11 ♘g3 would give White time to develop an attack, so Black should be a little careful.

8 ♘g3 ♗e7

Also possible is 8...♗b4!? 9 ♗b5+ c6 10 ♗e2 (10 ♗c4 ♕a5 11 0-0 ♗xc3 12 bxc3 ♕xc3 and the compensation is not really apparent) 10...0-0 11 0-0 ♗xc3 12 bxc3 ♕a5 and Black has a better game.

9 ♕d2

Or 9 ♗c4 ♘c6! (attacking the weak spot in the White position) 10 ♗xf6 ♗xf6 11 d5 ♘e5 12 ♗b3 ♗g4 13 ♕d2 c6! 14 d6?! (14 dxc6 ♕xd2+ 15 ♔xd2 0-0-0+ 16 ♔e1 ♘xc6 17 ♘gxe4 ♘d4 is only slightly better for Black) 14...♗g5 15 ♕d4 ♕f6 16 ♕xe4 0-0 with a very promising Black position.

9...h6 10 ♗e3

After 10 ♗xf6 ♗xf6 11 ♘cxe4 ♗xe4 12 ♘xe4 ♕xd4 Black is just a pawn up.

10...♘bd7

Also possible is 10...♘c6 11 d5?! (11 ♗b5 0-0 12 0-0 ♘g4 is only slightly better for Black) 11...♘b4 12 ♗b5+ (12 ♗c4 ♘g4! 13 ♗b3 c6! and White is in trouble) 12...c6 13 dxc6 ♕xd2+ 14 ♔xd2 bxc6 15 ♗c4 ♘g4 and Black has an overwhelming advantage.

11 ♗e2 ♘b6 12 0-0

White could also try 12 ♘h5!?, with the trap 12...0-0? 13 ♘xg7! ♔xg7 14 ♗xh6+ ♔h8 15 ♗xf8 ♗xf8 16 0-0-0 and the position is less clear. But Black can beat White off with 12...♗g6! 13 ♘xg7+? (13 ♘f4 ♗f7 14 0-0 0-0 and Black is better) 13...♔f7 14 ♗xh6 ♗f8 15 ♘xe6 ♔xe6 16 ♗xf8 ♕xf8 and Black wins.

12...♕d7!

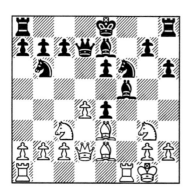

Black is preparing to castle queenside as White's king seems a bit open. Also possible is 12...♗g6 13 ♖ae1 and White is only slightly worse.

13 ♘h5

If White does nothing he is in trouble as the following line illustrates: 13 a4 0-0-0 14 a5 ♘bd5 15 a6 b6 16 ♖ad1 ♖hf8 and Black has a clear advantage.

13...♖g8 14 ♘xf6+ ♗xf6 15 ♗h5+ g6 16 ♗e2 ♕g7!

16...0-0-0? is not good due to 17 g4! (17

♖ad1? would return the favour after 17...♕g7! with a clear advantage) 17...♗xd4 18 ♕xd4 ♕xd4 19 ♗xd4 ♖xd4 20 gxf5 exf5 and, though Black has lost a piece, the position remains unclear.

17 ♗xh6?

After this the game is just lost. Better was 17 g4 0-0-0 18 ♔h1 (18 ♖ad1 h5 would provide Black with a terrifying attack) 18...♗xd4 19 gxf5 gxf5 20 ♖g1 ♗xc3 and Black is better, but it is still a game.

17...♗xd4+ 18 ♔h1 ♕h8 19 ♗f4

There is no longer time for 19 g4; Black plays 19...0-0-0 20 gxf5 e3 21 ♗xe3 ♗e5 22 ♗d3 ♘c4 and wins.

19...0-0-0!

Finishing development.

20 ♘b5

Or 20 ♕e1 ♘d5 21 ♘xd5 exd5 and the game is more or less over.

20...e5 21 ♗e3

Another long line looks like this: 21 ♗g5 ♗xb2! 22 ♗xd8 ♖xd8 23 ♕b4 ♗xa1 24 ♖xa1 ♘d7! 25 ♘xa7+ ♔b8 26 ♕a5 ♖h7 27 h3 ♗xh3 and White should resign.

21...a6 22 ♘c3 ♖g7 23 ♖f2 ♖h7 24 g3 ♕e8 25 ♗f1 ♕c6 26 ♕e2 ♘d7

Clearer was 26...♗xc3! 27 bxc3 ♕xc3 28 ♖b1 ♘d5.

27 ♘d1 ♘f6 28 c3 ♗g4?!

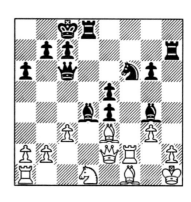

Here Black is not playing his best. After 28...♘g4! 29 cxd4 exd4 30 ♖c1 ♘xf2+ 31 ♘xf2 ♕f6 Black wins everything.

29 ♖xf6?!

29 ♕c4! ♕xc4 30 ♗xc4 ♗xe3 31 ♘xe3 ♗f3+ 32 ♔g1 ♖d6, with the idea of ...♖hd7, still gives Black a large advantage, but the blockade of the central pawns provides White with some hope.

29...♗xe2 30 ♖xc6 ♗f3+

Over and out.

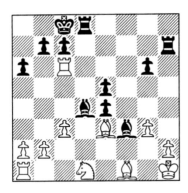

31 ♔g1

Or 31 ♗g2 ♗xg2+ 32 ♔xg2 ♗xe3 33 ♖f6 ♖d2+ and White probably resigns.

31...♗xe3+ 32 ♘xe3 bxc6 33 ♗xa6+ ♔b8 34 ♖f1 ♖d2 35 ♖f2 ♖xf2 36 ♔xf2 ♖xh2+ 0-1

Game 69
Kasparov-Illescas Cordoba
Dos Hermanas 1996

The annotations to this game are based on those by Illescas Cordoba in *Chess Informant 66*.

1 d4 f5 2 ♗g5

This move should not be dangerous for Black, though he will have to be careful.

2...h6

In my opinion this is the best choice for Black. Of the alternatives only 2...g6 has a good reputation:

a) 2...d5?! 3 c4 ♘f6 4 ♘c3 dxc4 5 e4 ♘xe4 6 ♘xe4 fxe4 7 ♗xc4 gave White good compensation for the material in Agdestein-Yilmaz, Yerevan 1996.

b) 2...♘f6 is very popular. White should obtain a slight edge due to Black's weak pawn structure. 3 ♗xf6 exf6 4 e3 (White is better after the simple 4 c4!, or 4 g3!? d5 5 ♕d3 ♗d6 6 ♘c3 c6 7 ♘f3 0-0 8 0-0-0, as in Chistakov-Antoshin, Moscow 1948) and now:

b1) 4...d5 5 c4 c6 6 cxd5 ♕xd5 7 ♘c3 ♕f7 8 ♗d3 ♗d6 9 h4 f4 10 exf4 ♗xf4 11 ♕c2 g6 12 ♘ge2 ♗c7 13 0-0-0 with a crushing attack on the way, Cebalo-Wiley Basle 1999.

b2) 4...c6 5 c4 ♗b4+ 6 ♘c3 ♗xc3+ 7 bxc3 0-0 8 ♗d3 ♕a5 9 ♕c2 d6 10 ♘e2 is somewhat better for White, Radzhabov-Yueferov, Moscow 1996.

b3) 4...♗e7 5 ♗d3 d5 6 ♘e2 0-0 7 c3 ♗d6 8 ♘d2 c6 9 ♕c2 g6 10 0-0-0 b6 11 h3 ♗a6 12 g4 ♗xd3 13 ♕xd3 fxg4 14 hxg4 ♘d7 15 ♖h6 with a strong position for White in Mchedeishvili-Froeyman, Rotterdam 1998.

b4) 4...♕e7! 5 ♘c3 c6 6 ♕f3 d5 7 ♗d3 g6 8 h3 ♗e6 with equality. In the game Moiseenko-Moroz, Ordzhonikidze 2000, Black played the weak 8...♘a6 and after 9 ♗xa6 bxa6 10 ♘ge2 ♖b8 11 ♘a4 ♕b4 12 ♘ec3 a5 13 0-0 White obtained a much better position.

c) 2...g6 and now:

c1) 3 ♘d2 ♗g7 4 c3 h6 5 ♗f4 d6 6 e3 e5 7 ♗g3 ♕e7 gave Black an easy game, Kunter-Mering, East Germany 1969.

c2) 3 c3 ♘h6! (this is Grandmaster Vlastmil Jansa's idea) 4 ♘f3 ♘f7 5 h4 ♗g7 6 e3 h6 7 ♗f4 d6 8 ♗c4 e6 9 ♕c2 ♕e7 with equality in Staiger-Glek, Bern 1994. Black is finally ready to play ...e6-e5.

c3) 3 h4!? ♗g7 4 h5 h6 5 ♗c1 g5 6 ♕d3 e6 7 e4 d6 8 ♘f3 f4 9 e5 ♘e7 10 exd6 cxd6 11 ♘bd2 0-0 12 c3 ♘f5 with an even game in Gipslis-Reize, Leningrad 1960.

c4) 3 ♘c3 ♗g7 (3...d5!? 4 e3 ♗g7 5 h4 c6 6 ♗d3 ♕b6 7 ♖b1 ♘d7 8 ♘f3 ♘gf6 9 h5 ♘e4 10 hxg6 hxg6 11 ♖xh8+ ♗xh8 [Zsu.Polgar-Beliavsky, Munich 1991] and now according to Polgar White is slightly better after 12 ♗f4) 4 e4 fxe4 5 ♘xe4 d5! (an essential move; Black is stalling slightly with his development and wins time this way) 6 ♘c5 b6 (6...♕d6?! 7 ♘f3 e5 does not work out due to 8 ♘xe5 ♗xe5 9 ♕e2 ♘c6 10 ♘b3 ♘xd4 11 ♘xd4 ♔f7 12 ♘b5 ♕e6 13 f4 ♗d6 14 0-0-0 h6 15 ♕xe6+ ♔xe6 16 ♘xd6 ♔xd6 17 ♗h4 ♖h7 18 ♗e2 ♗e6 19 g4 c6 20 h3 with a clear advantage for White, Hodgson-Lim, Manila 1992 – the idea is simply ♗d3xg6) 7 ♘b3 ♘f6 8 ♘f3 0-0 9 ♗e2 ♕d6! (this is an important move; after 9...c5?! 10 c3 ♘e4 11 ♗e3 cxd4 12 cxd4 ♘d7 13 0-0 ♘d6 14 ♖c1 ♘c4 15 ♖xc4! dxc4 16 ♗xc4+ ♔h8 17 ♘g5 White has a good attacking position) 10 0-0 ♘bd7 11 ♗h4 (11 ♕c1 e5! is unclear according to Grandmaster Mikhail Tseitlin; 11 c4 ♗b7 also looks like just another game of chess) 11...♘h5 12 ♖e1 ♘f4 13 ♗b5 ♘f6 with unclear play in Fominyh-Dubinsky, Nizhny Novgorod 1998.

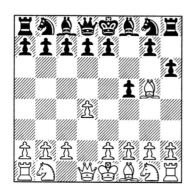

3 ♗h4

Also possible is 3 ♗f4 ♘f6 4 ♘c3 (4 e4!? fxe4 5 ♘c3 d5 6 f3 ♗f5 7 fxe4 dxe4 8 ♗c4 g5 9 ♗e5 ♘bd7 10 ♘b5 ♘xe5 11 dxe5 ♘g4 12 ♗e2 [Finegold-Tukmakov, Reykjavik 1990] and now after 12...♕xd1+ 13 ♖xd1 ♖c8 14 ♘d4 e6 15 ♘xf5 exf5 16 ♗xg4 fxg4 17 ♖d4! is unclear) 4...d5 5 e3 e6 6 ♗d3 ♗d6 7 ♘f3 0-0 8 ♘e5 ♘c6! (fighting for the e5-square) 9 ♘xc6 bxc6 10 ♘a4 ♕e7 11 0-0 e5! with equality in Soffer-Rechlis, Bern 1990.

3...g5

3...c5?! is too optimistic. A good illustration of how White should fight for the initiative can be seen in the following game: 4 e3 ♕b6 (this does not look good, but that is Black's idea...) 5 ♘c3! cxd4 6 exd4 ♕e6+ 7 ♗e2 g5 8 ♘f3! gxh4 9 ♘e5 ♘f6 10 0-0 h5 11 ♖e1 ♕b6 12 ♘d5! ♘xd5 13 ♗xh5+ ♔d8 14 ♘f7+ ♔c7 15 ♘xh8 ♗g7 16 ♘g6 e6 17 c4 ♘f6 18 d5 ♘e4 19 c5 ♕xb2 20 d6+ ♔d8 21 ♖c1 ♕xf2+ 22 ♔h1 ♕b2 23 ♖xe4 fxe4 24 ♕e1 ♘a6 25 ♕xh4+ ♗f6 26 ♖f1! 1-0, Gormally-Zeidler, Dyfed 1999.

4 e3

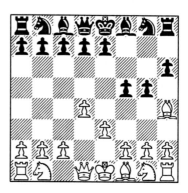

The alternatives pose no dangers for Black if he knows what he is doing.

a) 4 ♗g3 and now:

a1) 4...f4? 5 e3! and White wins a pawn. An old classic is meant to run 5...h5 6 ♗d3 ♖h6 7 ♕xh5+! ♖xh5 8 ♗g6 mate, but which one? It is not in my database...

a2) 4...♘f6! 5 e4 (5 e3 transposes to the main game) 5...fxe4 6 ♘c3 ♗g7 7 f3 d5 8 fxe4 dxe4 9 ♗c4 ♗g4 10 ♘ge2 ♘c6 11 h3?! (11 0-0 was better, but White has still not really justified the pawn sacrifice) 11...♘a5 12 ♗b5+ ♗d7 13 b4 c6 14 bxa5 cxb5 15 ♗e5 ♕xa5 16 0-0 0-0 with a clear advantage for Black, Machulsky-Sarwinsky, Poznan 1986.

b) 4 e4 was the big trick the English came up with in the 1990s. But the antidote has been found. Black should be fine:

b1) 4...♖h7?! 5 ♕h5+ ♖f7 6 ♘f3! ♘c6 7

♗c4 (7 ♗xg5 fxe4 8 ♘c3! is also interesting; the main idea is 8...exf3 9 ♗c4! and White wins) 7...e6 8 ♗xg5 hxg5 9 ♘xg5 gives White a strong attack.

b2) 4...♗g7 5 ♗g3 f4? (5...fxe4 6 ♘c3 ♘f6 is probably okay – see variation 'a2') 6 ♗xf4! gxf4 7 ♕h5+ ♔f8 8 ♕f5+ ♘f6 (or 8...♔e8 9 ♗e2 ♘f6 10 e5 d6 11 ♕xf4 e6 12 exf6 ♕xf6 13 ♕xf6 and White has a clear advantage) 9 e5 d6 10 ♕xf4 dxe5 11 dxe5 ♘c6 12 ♘f3 ♕d5 13 exf6 ♕e6+ 14 ♗e2 ♗xf6 15 ♘c3 gave White a clear advantage in Ward-Rasmussen, Copenhagen 2000.

b3) 4...♘f6! (this is by far the best move)

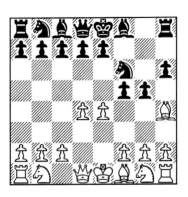

5 e5 e6 and now:

b31) Trying to win material with 6 ♗g3 f4 7 ♗xf4 gxf4 8 exf6 ♕xf6 9 ♕h5+ ♕f7 10 ♕e5 ♗g7 11 ♕xc7 leads nowhere after 11...♘c6 12 c3 (12 ♘a3 ♘xd4 13 c3 ♘c6 14 ♘c4 0-0 15 ♘d6 ♕g6 16 0-0-0 ♗f6 looks good for Black) 12...e5 with an initiative. After 13 dxe5 ♗xe5 the white queen is trapped, so White has serious problems.

b32) 6 exf6 ♕xf6 7 ♗g3 f4 8 ♗d3 (8 ♘f3 ♘c6 9 c3 b6 10 ♗b5 ♗b7 11 ♗xc6 dxc6 12 ♘bd2 0-0-0 13 ♕e2 c5 14 dxc5 ♗xc5 15 0-0-0 ♖he8 was slightly better for Black in Prie-Santo Roman, Narbonne 1997) 8...♘c6 9 ♕h5+ ♔d8 10 c3 d5 11 ♘f3 ♗d7 12 0-0 ♗d6 13 ♘bd2 ♕e7 14 ♖ae1 ♖ag8 and Black has a good position in Moiseenko-Jakubiec, Poland 1999. The key point to this set-up for Black is that he will not capture on g3 until

he absolutely has to. If White captures on f4 he will open a highway down to his own king and if he plays h2-h3 he will lose a pawn. So for now the situation is most annoying for White.

4...♘f6 5 ♗g3 d6 6 h4 ♖g8?!

This leaves White the h-file. Better was 6...g4 7 h5 ♗e6! 8 ♘e2 (or 8 ♗d3 ♕d7 9 ♘e2 ♗f7 10 ♘f4 ♖g8, with the idea of ...♘c6, ...0-0-0 and ...e7-e5 with an excellent position for Black) 8...♗f7 9 ♘f4 ♘c6 10 ♗b5 a6 11 ♗a4 ♗g7 12 ♗b3 d5 with unclear play in Seirawan-D.Gurevich, Durango 1992.

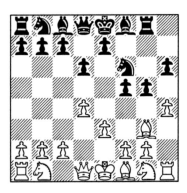

7 hxg5 hxg5 8 ♘c3! e6 9 f3 ♕e7 10 ♕d2

Development, development!

10...♘c6 11 0-0-0 ♗d7 12 e4!

12 ♔b1 0-0-0 13 ♘ge2 ♗g7 would give Black a chance to develop in peace and then equalise later.

12...fxe4

Time is important here. 12...f4 13 ♗f2 ♗g7 (or 13...a6 14 e5! dxe5 15 dxe5 ♘xe5 16 ♗d4 and White wins) 14 ♘b5 would expose the black king to danger as d4-d5 is coming.

13 fxe4 0-0-0 14 d5?!

This gives Black a good game. Better was 14 ♗c4 ♗g7 (14...♘xe4 15 ♘xe4 d5 16 ♗d3 dxe4 17 ♗xe4 leaves e6 as a weakness) 15 ♘f3 (15 ♕xg5?! ♗h8 16 ♕f4 ♖df8 gives good play) 15...♘g4 16 ♗e2 and White retains a slight advantage. Also possible were

14 ♗b5!? and 14 ♔b1.

14...exd5 15 exd5

15 ♘xd5 ♘xd5 16 exd5 ♘e5 is equal according to Illescas Cordoba's annotations, and he is probably right. White has no way to exploit the weakening of the king's position after 17 ♕d4 ♔b8 18 ♖e1 ♗g7 19 ♗f2 b6!.

15...♘e5 16 ♖e1?!

White has some alternatives to this:

a) 16 ♘f3 ♘xf3 17 gxf3 g4 looks okay for Black after 18 ♖e1 ♕g7 19 ♕e3 ♔b8 20 ♗f2 b6 as White has no apparent way to improve his position.

b) But 16 ♕d4! ♔b8 17 ♘b5! would perhaps give Black some problems after 17...b6 18 ♕c3 ♖c8 19 ♕a3 a5 20 ♘f3 and the king seems to be somewhat exposed now. Note that 17 ♗f2 b6 18 ♗b5 ♗g7 is okay for Black.

16...♔b8 17 ♔b1 ♗g7

18 a3

Alternatively:

a) 18 ♕xg5?! ♘xd5 is good for Black.

b) 18 ♘f3 ♘xf3 19 gxf3 ♕f7 20 ♗f2 (20 ♕xg5? ♗h8 21 ♕f4 ♕g7! would leave White in trouble as ...♘xd5 is threatened and probably White is forced to play 22 ♖xh8) 20...g4 with equality.

c) 18 ♗b5 ♖h8! 19 ♖xh8 ♖xh8 20 ♗xe5 dxe5 21 ♗xd7 (21 ♘f3?! ♗xb5 22 ♘xb5 g4! 23 ♖xe5 [not 23 ♘xe5 ♘e4!! 24 ♖xe4 ♖h1+ 25 ♖e1 ♕xe5 and Black wins] 23...♘e4 24 ♖xe7 ♘xd2+ 25 ♔c1 gxf3 and Black has

good winning chances) 21...♘xd7 22 ♘e4 ♘f6 with equality.

18...♖h8!?

18...g4 19 ♗b5 ♗xb5 20 ♘xb5 a6! would also equalise as 21 ♘d4 is met by 21...♘xd5!.

19 ♖xh8 ♖xh8 20 ♗xe5!?

Trying to create an imbalance. After 20 ♘f3 ♘xf3 21 gxf3 ♕f7 22 ♕xg5 ♗h6 23 ♕h4 ♘xd5 24 ♘xd5 ♕xd5 White has no advantage, nor a chance to get any.

20...dxe5 21 ♘f3 e4!

Opening things up for the g7-bishop.

22 ♕xg5

After 22 ♘xg5? ♗h6 White is in trouble. 22 ♗d3 g4 23 ♘d4 ♗h6 also looks good for Black.

22...♖h5! 23 ♕d2

23 ♕f4 ♖h1 24 ♕e5 (24 ♘e5?! ♘xd5 25 ♘xd7+ ♕xd7 26 ♘xd5 ♕xd5 gives Black the advantage) 24...♕xe5 25 ♘xe5 ♗f5 is better for Black.

23...♕d6?!

Correct was 23...♖h1 24 ♗d3 e3! 25 ♕e2 ♖xe1+ 26 ♕xe1 ♘g4 with a good position for Black, even though White should not be in real danger.

24 ♘d4?!

Illescas thinks that White is better after 24 ♘xe4 ♘xe4 25 ♖xe4 ♖xd5 26 ♗d3 but something like 26...♕f6 27 ♕c1 ♖h5 seems to me to give Black sufficient compensation for a draw. Still, this is clearly the winning attempt.

24...a6

24...罝h1!?, with the idea of 25 奧c4?
罝xe1+ 26 豐xe1 豐c5, looks strong.

25 奧c4 罝h4 26 奧b3 罝g4?!

Here Black could have given White more
headaches with 26...奧h6! and now:

a) 27 豐e2 e3 28 ⃝f3 奧g4! (not 28...罝g4
29 罝h1 罝g6 30 奧c4! 奧f5 31 奧d3 奧xd3 32
豐xd3 with an advantage for White) 29 ⃝d1!
奧xf3 30 gxf3 (30 豐xf3 ⃝e4 is good for
Black) 30...罝h2 31 豐f1 豐g3! with good play
for Black.

b) 27 豐f2 罝f4 28 豐e2 奧g4 29 豐c4! e3
30 罝xe3 c5 31 ⃝c6+ is unclear.

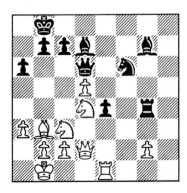

27 罝e2 e3

Or 27...豐h2 28 ⃝e6! 奧h8 29 ⃝d1 and
White keeps control over the situation.

28 豐xe3 ⃝xd5 29 ⃝xd5?!

More dangerous for Black was 29 奧xd5
奧xd4 30 豐e7! 豐xe7 31 罝xe7 奧xc3 32 bxc3
奧c6 33 奧xc6 bxc6 34 罝e2 with a few
chances for some advantage in the rook endgame, even though a player like Illescas Cordoba should be able to draw this.

**29...奧xd4 30 豐e7 豐xe7 31 罝xe7 奧c6
32 ⃝xc7 罝xg2 33 奧d5**

33 ⃝e6 would have kept some pressure
on Black.

**33...罝g1+ 34 曲a2 罝g7! 35 罝xg7
奧xd5+**

35...奧xg7 36 ⃝xa6+ bxa6 37 奧xc6 a5 is
also drawn.

36 ⃝xd5 奧xg7 37 c4 曲c8 38 a4 曲d7

**39 a5 曲d6 40 b4 奧d4 41 曲b3 奧f2 42
⃝f4 奧e3 43 ⃝d3 曲c6 44 曲a4 奧g1 45
b5+ axb5+ 46 cxb5+ 曲c7 47 ⃝b4 奧f2
48 b6+ 曲b8 ½-½**

Game 70
Salov-Malaniuk
USSR 1988

The annotations to this game are partly
based on those by Valery Salov in *Chess Informant 46.*

1 d4 f5 2 ⃝c3

This game illustrates well what it is that
White wishes for in this system.

2...d5

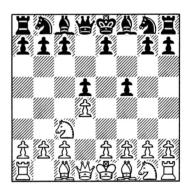

This and 2...⃝f6 are the most logical
moves. After 2...g6?! White can play:

a) 3 e4!? fxe4 4 ⃝xe4 奧g7 5 奧f4 d6
(5...⃝f6 6 ⃝xf6+ exf6?! 7 豐e2+ 曲f8 8 0-0-0
looks very promising for White, Mikhal-
chishin-Grigoriev, Lvov 1986) 6 豐d2 ⃝f6 7
⃝xf6+ exf6 8 0-0-0 0-0 9 h4 with a white attack.

3 h4! (the most logical) 3...⃝f6 (3...奧g7 4
h5 d5 5 hxg6 hxg6 6 罝xh8 奧xh8 7 奧f4 is
just somewhat better for White) 4 h5 奧g7 5
h6 奧f8 6 奧g5 d5 7 豐d2 e6 8 0-0-0 奧b4 9
f3 with a clear advantage in Möhring-
Knezevic, Hradec Kralove 1977/78.

3 奧g5

This is the main attempt. The alternatives
are:

---

a) 3 ♗f4 ♘f6 4 e3 e6 (the odd development with 4...c6?! 5 ♗d3 g6 6 ♘f3 ♗g7 7 0-0 ♗e6 8 ♘e2 ♘bd7 9 ♖c1 0-0 10 c4 ♘b6 11 b3 ♘e4 12 ♘e5 ♘d7 13 f3 gave White some advantage in Dokhoian-Zidkov, Tula 1987) 5 ♘b5 ♗d6! (a very strong idea originating from the talented Polish national master Rafal Przedmojski) 6 ♘xd6+ cxd6 (the control over e5 and e4 compensates fully for the loss of the bishop) 7 ♘f3 0-0 8 ♗e2 b6 9 ♕d3 ♗a6 10 ♕a3 ♗xe2 11 ♔xe2 ♘e4 12 ♘d2 g5! 13 ♘xe4 gxf4 14 ♘xd6 ♘c6 15 ♘b5 a6 16 ♘c3 fxe3 with an attack for Black in Va.Shishkin-Przedmojski, Police 1997.

b) 3 e4!? dxe4 4 ♗f4 (4 f3 is probably best met with 4...e5!? 5 dxe5 ♕xd1+ 6 ♔xd1 ♗e6! 7 ♘b5 ♘a6 8 ♗e3 0-0-0+ 9 ♔c1 ♗c5 10 ♗xc5 ♘xc5, as in Miralles-M.Gurevich, France 1988, when 11 ♘xa7+ ♔b8 12 ♘b5 ♘e7 gives Black compensation for the pawn according to Grandmaster Adrian Mikhalchishin) 4...♘f6 5 f3 exf3 6 ♘xf3 e6 7 ♗c4 ♗d6 8 ♕d2 c6 9 ♗g5 0-0 10 0-0-0 ♘a6 11 ♕e1 ♘c7 12 g4 b5 13 ♗b3 b4 with an unclear position in Gelfand-Nikolic, Munich 1994.

c) 3 g4?! ♘f6! (3...fxg4 4 ♗f4! ♘f6 5 ♕d3 c6 6 h3 gives White compensation) 4 g5 (4 h3!?) 4...♘e4 5 ♘xe4 fxe4 6 f3 ♗f5 and Black stands slightly better, Spielmann-Mieses, Berlin 1920.

d) 3 f3 c5! (3...e6?! 4 e4 ♗b4 5 exf5 exf5 6 ♘h3 and White stands slightly better) 4 e4 e5! 5 de5 (after 5 ♗b5? ♗d7 6 ♗xd7+♘xd7 7 ♘d5 cxd4 8 ♘e2 fxe4 9 fxe4 ♘gf6, Black stands much better, Pomar-Larsen 1975) 5...d4 6 ♗c4 ♘c6 7 ♘d5 ♘e5 8 ♕e2 ♘c4 9 ♕c4 ♗d6 10 ♗f4 ♘e7 11 ♗g5 ♗e6 12 ♘e2 fxe4 13 fxe4 is equal, Rossetto-Pelikan, Argentina 1959.

3...♘f6 4 ♗xf6 exf6 5 e3 c6

5...♗e6! is considered in the next game.

6 ♗d3 ♘a6 7 a3 ♘c7 8 h4 h5 9 ♘h3 g6 10 ♘f4 ♔f7 11 ♘ce2 ♘e6 12 c4!

White has a slight edge. The knights are in no ways inferior to the bishops.

12...♘xf4 13 ♘xf4 dxc4 14 ♗xc4+ ♔g7 15 ♖c1

It is more natural to castle directly. 15 0-0!? ♗d6 16 g3 ♗xf4 17 gxf4 ♕e7 18 ♖c1 ♗e6?! (18...♖d8!, with close to equality, is better) 19 ♗xe6 ♕xe6 20 d5! cxd5 21 ♖c7+ ♔h6 22 ♖xb7 ♖hb8 23 ♕b3 would give White a promising initiative.

15...♗d6 16 ♕f3 ♖e8 17 0-0

17 ♖h3 ♗xf4 18 ♕xf4 ♗e6 would equalise.

17...♗xf4 18 ♕xf4 ♗e6

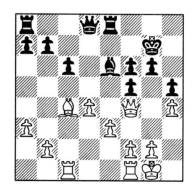

19 ♗d3!

It is to White's advantage to keep pieces on the board when he has the safer king. 19 ♗xe6 ♖xe6 20 d5? does not work this time around (20 ♖c5 is equal): 20...♖e4! 21 ♕h2 ♕xd5 22 ♕c7+ ♕f7 and Black has won a pawn. Also, 19 d5?!, with the idea of 19...cxd5 20 ♗b5 ♖e7 21 ♖c2 ♖c8 22 ♖fc1

♖xc2 23 ♖xc2 with compensation, does not work due to 19...♗xd5! 20 ♗xd5 ♕xd5 21 ♖fd1 ♕f7 and the compensation cannot be found!

19...a5?!

This unnecessarily weakens the queenside. After both 19...♕b8 and 19...♗d5 20 b4 ♕b8 the position is completely level.

20 ♖c2 ♗b3 21 ♖c5 ♕b8 22 ♕xb8 ♖exb8 23 g3 ♖e8

23...a4?! 24 ♖fc1 ♖e8 25 ♗c2 ♗xc2 26 ♖1xc2 would provide White with a better endgame.

24 ♖fc1 ♗d5 25 ♗f1!

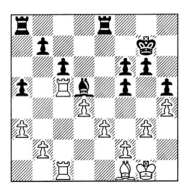

The main defender in the black camp is the bishop on d5. By eliminating this piece, White is improving his chances of winning the endgame.

25 b4 axb4 26 axb4 b6! (26...b5?? 27 ♗xb5) 27 ♖xc6 is unclear, while 27 ♖5c3 b5! gives Black counterplay on the a-file and against the weak b-pawn.

25...♔f7 26 ♗g2 ♗xg2 27 ♔xg2 ♔e6 28 b4

28 b3!?, to keep all doors open, was also interesting.

28...axb4 29 axb4 ♔d6?!

This is the wrong piece to focus on. The main rule of rook endgames is to keep the rooks active. Better moves are 29...♖a2 30 b5 cxb5 31 ♖xb5 ♖e7 and 29...♖ed8 30 b5 cxb5 31 ♖xb5 ♖d7, both with only a slight advantage for White.

30 d5!

The strongest as this provides the rooks with all the freedom in the world. After 30 b5 ♖a5! 31 bxc6 ♖xc5 32 ♖xc5 bxc6 33 ♖a5 ♖c8 34 ♖a7 c5 35 dxc5+ ♖xc5 36 ♖g7 ♔e6 37 ♔f3 ♖a5 38 ♖xg6 ♔f7 39 ♖h6 f4 40 ♖h8 fxe3 41 fxe3 Black has good drawing chances.

30...cxd5 31 ♖b5 ♖ac8 32 ♖xc8 ♖xc8 33 ♖xb7 g5 34 hxg5

34 ♖h7 gxh4 35 gxh4 ♖b8 36 ♖xh5 ♔e6 would allow Black to escape with a draw quite easily.

34...fxg5 35 ♖h7

35...g4?

This is the first real mistake Black commits in this game, and the reason why it comes right now is obvious. After a couple of inaccuracies his task has been more and more difficult, and the necessity to find exact moves has increased. Here he fails.

35...h4! 36 gxh4 gxh4 37 Rxh4 Rc4 was the right way to defend. Now after 38 Rh6+ (or 38 Rxc4 dxc4 39 ✿f3 ✿c6 40 e4 fxe4+ 41 ✿xe4 ✿b5 42 f4 ✿xb4 and the pawn ending is drawn) 38...✿e5 39 b5 f4 40 b6 fxe3 41 fxe3 Rb4 Black should be able to draw as his rook and his king are both very well placed.

36 Rxh5 ✿e5 37 Rh1 Rb8

37...d4 38 exd4+ ✿xd4 39 Rd1+! would cut off the black king from the queenside and give White excellent winning chances.

38 Rb1 d4

The passive 38...Rb5 holds no chances for survival: 39 f3 d4 40 exd4+ ✿xd4 41 fxg4 fxg4 42 Rf1 ✿e3 43 Rf4 Rg5 44 b5 Rxb5 45 Rxg4 with a theoretically winning endgame for White.

39 exd4+ ✿xd4

40 b5?

The right path was to bring the king into the game. After 40 f3! Black is in trouble:

a) 40...✿c4 41 b5! Rb6 (41...✿c5 42 b6 would just continue the march forward) 42 ✿f2 ✿c5 43 fxg4! fxg4 44 ✿e3 and White wins.

b) 40...Ra8 41 b5 Ra2+ 42 ✿f1 gxf3 43 b6 Ra8 44 b7 Rb8 45 ✿f2 and White wins.

c) 40...Rb5 41 ✿f2 ✿d3 42 Rd1+ ✿c3 43 ✿e3 and now:

c1) 43...Rxb4 44 Rd5 is a close-to-winning position for White.

c2) 43...gxf3 44 ✿xf3 Rxb4 45 Rd5 is worse for Black, as the king is cut off. Still, there might be a few practical chances.

40...✿c5 41 f3 ✿b6 42 Rb4

White would also not be able to force a win after 42 fxg4 fxg4 43 Rb4 Rg8 44 ✿f2 ✿c5! (removing the rook from its brilliant place on the fourth rank) 45 Rb3 ✿b6 46 ✿e2 Rg7 47 ✿e3 Rf7! – White cannot make serious progress.

42...✿a5

Simpler was 42...gxf3+! 43 ✿xf3 Rg8! and White cannot win. After 44 Rd4 ✿xb5 45 Rd5+ ✿c6 46 Rxf5 ✿d6 47 ✿f4 ✿e6 48 g4 Ra8 we have a theoretical draw.

43 Rb3

Or 43 Rd4 ✿xb5! 44 Rd5+ (44 fxg4 ✿c5!) 44...✿c6 45 Rxf5 Rb2+ and Black draws.

43...✿b6 44 Rb4 ✿a5 45 Rb3 ✿b6 46 ✿f2 Ra8?

After this Black is in trouble. Better was 46...Rg8! with the idea of 47 ✿e3 gxf3 and White will not be able to make progress. After 48 ✿xf3 Rg4 49 Rb1 Rg8 50 ✿f4 Rg4+ Black has reached a drawing position.

47 fxg4 fxg4 48 Rb4!

Now this comes with a tempo.

48...Rf8+ 49 ✿e2 Re8+ 50 ✿f2 Rf8+ 51 ✿e2 Re8+ 52 ✿d3 ✿c5

52...Rg8 53 ✿e3! ✿c5 54 Rb1 ✿b6 (54...Rf8 55 b6! and White wins) 55 ✿f4 and White will win the g-pawn and the game.

53 Ee4 Ed8+ 54 Φe3 Φxb5 55 Exg4 Φc5

55...Φc6 56 Ec4+! decides.

56 Eg6 Φd5 57 Φf4 Ef8+ 58 Φg4 Φe4 59 Ee6+ Φd5 60 Eh6 Φe4 61 Φh5 Ef5+ 62 Φh4 Φf3 63 g4 Ef8 64 g5 Ef4+ 65 Φh5 Φg3 66 Ea6 Eh4+ 67 Φg6 Eb4 68 Φh7 Φg4 69 Ea5 Eb7+ 70 Φh6 Eb2 71 g6 Eh2+ 72 Φg7 Φf4 73 Φf7 1-0

Game 71
Gavrilov-Yagupov
Moscow 1992

---

1 d4 f5 2 Öc3 d5 3 Åg5 Öf6 4 Åxf6 exf6 5 e3 Åe6!

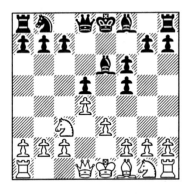

This is a more logical way to develop.
6 Åd3 Öc6

Very similar is 6...Wd7 7 Öge2 Öc6 8 Öf4 Åf7 9 a3 Öe7 10 h3 h5 11 h4 c6, which was equal in Zsu.Polgar-Winants, Wijk aan Zee 1990.

7 a3 Wd7 8 Öge2

8 Wf3 g5 9 Öge2 0-0-0 10 h3?! (10 h4, with unclear play, was clearly better) 10...h5 11 g3 h4 gave Black a small plus in Agrest-Yagupov, Czestochowa 1992.

8...g5 9 Wd2 0-0-0 10 0-0-0 a6 11 h4 h6 12 Öa4 Φb8 13 Φb1

Good careful play. 13 Wc3 would invite 13...Öb4! 14 Wb3 (14 Öc5? Öa2+ 15 Φd2 Åxc5! 16 Wxc5 b6 and the queen is trapped)

14...Öxd3+ 15 cxd3 with an unclear game where it might be more fun to be Black.

13...Φa7 14 Öac3 Åd6 15 g3 b6 16 Öa2 Öb8

16...Öe7!? seems more natural.

17 Ec1 c5 18 c4 Öc6 19 Wc2 f4 20 gxf4

Or 20 hxg5 fxe3! 21 Exh6 Exh6 22 gxh6 exf2 with unclear play.

20...gxf4 21 dxc5 bxc5 22 cxd5

White is dragging Black's pieces to their ideal squares. 22 Öac3 dxc4 23 Åe4, with unclear play, seems better.

22...Åxd5 23 Åe4 Åxe4 24 Wxe4 Ehe8 25 Wd3 fxe3 26 fxe3 Öe5 27 Wd5 Ög4 28 Ec3 Öxe3 29 Wf3 Wf5+ 30 Wxf5 Öxf5 31 Öac1 Åe5 32 Exc5 Ed2 33 Ec2 Exc2 34 Φxc2 Öe3+ 35 Φb1 Öc4?!

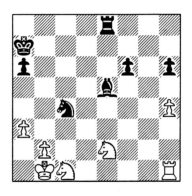

35...Ed8!, with the threat of ...Ed2, would have caused White much more trouble. Instead Black plays a combination that leads to a draw.

36 Öd3 Åxb2 37 Öxb2 Öxb2 38 Φxb2 Exe2+ 39 Φb3 Ee3+ 40 Φb4 Φb6 41 Ef1 a5+ 42 Φc4 Ee4+ 43 Φb3 a4+ 44 Φc3 Exh4 45 Exf6+ Φc5 46 Ef5+ Φc6 47 Ea5

The extra pawn does not matter as the White rook and king are more active than their counterparts.

47...h5 48 Ea6+ Φc5 49 Ea5+ Φc6 50 Ef5 Φd6 51 Ea5 ½-½

Game 72
Høi-Piskov
Copenhagen 1991

1 d4 f5 2 ♘c3

This game can also arise from the move order in variation 'd'. After 2 ♘f3 we have:

a) The position after 2...e6 3 d5 is uncomfortable for Black.

b) 2...g6 3 h4! ♗g7 4 h5 d5 5 hxg6 hxg6 6 ♖xh8 ♗xh8 7 ♗f4 with positional weaknesses and an unsafe king position for Black.

c) 2...d6 3 ♘c3 ♘f6 4 ♗g5 d5 5 e3 e6 6 g4! fxg4?! (it is better simply to ignore this kind of stuff) 7 ♘e5 ♗e7 8 ♗d3 ♘bd7 9 ♖g1 ♘xe5 10 dxe5 ♘d7 11 ♕xg4 ♗xg5 12 ♕h5+ g6 13 ♗xg6+ and White is very close to winning, Kempinski-Jakubiec, Polanica Zdroj 1999.

d) 2...♘f6! (this is the safest) 3 ♗g5 e6 4 ♘bd2 ♗e7 5 ♗xf6 ♗xf6 6 e4 0-0 7 ♗d3 d5!? (7...fxe4 8 ♘xe4 ♘c6 9 c3 would transpose to the main game) 8 exf5 (8 e5!?) 8...exf5 9 0-0 ♘c6 10 c3 ♕d6 11 ♕c2 g6 12 ♖fe1 ♗d7 with equality in Piasetsky-Larsen, St. John 1970.

2...♘f6 3 ♗g5 e6 4 e4

4 d5 is a potential threat to this set-up for Black. Also 4 g4!? seems to be worth a try.

4...fxe4 5 ♘xe4 ♗e7 6 ♗xf6 ♗xf6 7 ♘f3

The alternative is 7 ♕h5+ g6 8 ♕h6 ♕e7 9 ♘xf6+ ♕xf6 10 0-0-0 ♘c6, but so far no advantage has been discovered for White. The following game shows that White cannot do exactly as he pleases: 11 ♘f3 d6 12 d5? exd5 13 ♗b5 ♗d7 14 ♖he1+ ♘e7 15 ♗xd7+ ♔xd7 16 ♘d4 ♖ae8 17 ♕h3+ ♘f5 18 ♖xe8 ♖xe8 19 ♕xh7+ ♖e2 20 ♕h3 ♕g5+ 21 ♔b1 ♕d2 22 ♕f3 ♖e1 0-1 Kouatly-Tseshkovsky, Wijk aan Zee 1988.

7...♘c6 8 c3 0-0 9 ♗d3 d6 10 ♕c2 h6 11 h4

This position is known to be unclear in theory, but Black has a very good score.

11...e5!

Opening up for the c8-bishop, which needs to be developed.

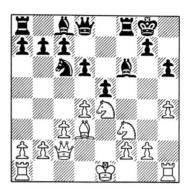

12 ♘eg5

This is an adventure, but after 12 d5 ♘e7 it is not obvious that White has made progress. After 13 c4 ♗g4!, the idea of ...♘f5, ...♗xf3 and ...♘d4 with the advantage is something that will force White to make awkward moves. And the fully-fledged gamble with 13 ♘fg5 ♘f5 14 g4?! ♘xh4 15 ♘xf6+ ♖xf6 16 ♘h7 loses to 16...♘g2+! 17 ♔d1 ♕f3+ and White resigned in Gonsior-Gazik, Stary Smokovec 1979. Black wins material after 18 ♔c1 ♘e3!.

12...d5!

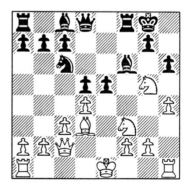

This is the most logical move. White is attacking only on the light squares, and especially on the c2-h7 diagonal. The threat of ...e5-e4 now has to be dealt with.

12...♗xg5 13 hxg5 ♖xf3 14 gxf3 ♕xg5 15 ♕e2 ♗f5 16 ♗c4+ ♔h8 17 ♕e3 was better for White in Wagner-Kerzdoerfer, Bayern 1995, while 12...exd4 13 ♗c4+ forced resignation in Leskiewicz-Quintero, Yerevan 1999.

13 dxe5 ♘xe5

Also possible was 13...♗xe5 14 0-0-0 ♗f4+ 15 ♔b1 ♘e7 16 ♘h3 ♗d6 17 ♖de1 ♗f5 with a good game for Black in Mertanen-Tella, Kuopio 1995.

14 ♘xe5 ♗xe5

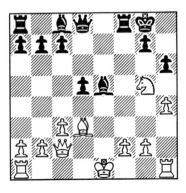

15 ♘h7

Apparently Carsten Høi, now a GM, showed this game to everyone who wanted to see it after it was played, just to show this move. 'Daddy does not take the early train home' he proclaimed, 'Daddy is going to hit the Town!' Unfortunately, the attack is not taking off, and Black already has a better game.

15...♖f4!

The rook is naturally safest on the dark squares.

16 0-0-0 ♕d6 17 g3 ♖f3 18 ♗e4!?

18 ♖he1 ♗g4 19 ♔b1 was stronger, but Black must be better in the long run. Just a move like 19...♖xd3 20 ♕xd3 ♗xd1 21 ♖xd1 should expose the knight's problems.

18...dxe4!

Black has no reason to hesitate with this queen sacrifice as the knight is and will remain lost. The only question is when it will leave the board.

19 ♖xd6 cxd6 20 ♕xe4 ♖xf2 21 ♘g5 hxg5 22 ♕d5+ ♔h7 23 hxg5+ ♔g6 24 ♕g8 ♔xg5 25 ♕e8 ♖c2+ 26 ♔b1 ♗f5!

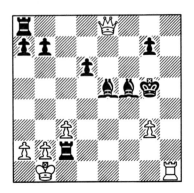

A little finesse to finish the game.

27 ♕e7+ ♔g6 28 g4 ♗e4 29 ♕e6+ ♔g5 30 ♕e7+ ♔f4 0-1

> ### Game 73
> ### Tregubov-Malaniuk
> *Linares 1996*

1 d4 f5 2 g4?!

This line should only hold dangers for White, if Black has any idea of what he should do.

2...fxg4!?

This move is adventurous, but it's better simply to be calm and play for the positional factors with 2...d5!.

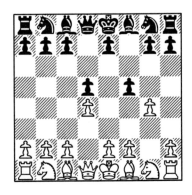

The main problem for White in this line is that the loss of the g-pawn is a greater positional minus than the loss of the f-pawn. Now we have the following possibilities:

a) 3 gxf5 ♗xf5 and Black is slightly better according to Malaniuk.

b) 3 g5 e6 4 ♘f3 c5 5 c3 ♘c6 6 h4 ♕c7 7 ♗g2 ♗d7 8 ♔f1 0-0-0 9 dxc5 ♗xc5 10 b4 ♗d6 was better for Black in Movsziszian-Gracia, Manresa 1997.

c) 3 ♘c3 ♘f6 4 g5 ♘e4 5 ♘xe4 fxe4 6 f3 ♗f5 7 ♗g2 e5! (the typical refutation of such flank gambits is to return the pawn in the centre at the right time in order to secure fluent development) 8 dxe5 ♘c6 9 fxe4 ♗xe4 10 ♗xe4 dxe4 11 ♗f4 ♗c5 12 e3 ♘b4 13 a3 ♘d5 14 ♕h5+ g6 15 ♕e2 ♕e7 and Black had a very large positional advantage in Abdulla-Sulskis, Elista 1998.

d) 3 ♕d3 g6 4 gxf5 ♗xf5 5 ♕b5+?! (5 ♕b3 was better, but the opening strategy is not impressive) 5...♘c6 6 c3 (after 6 ♕xb7 ♘xd4 White is in trouble, while 6 ♘f3 ♗g7 7 ♕xb7 ♘xd4 8 ♘xd4 ♗xd4 9 ♕c6+ ♔f7 10 ♗g2 e6 11 c3 ♗b6 gave Black the advantage in Arnalds-Einarsson Reykjavik 2000) and now:

d1) 6...♕d6! 7 ♗h3 (7 ♕xb7? ♖b8 8 ♕a6 ♘xd4! 9 ♕a4+ ♘c6 and Black has benefited most from the pawn exchange and has a clear advantage) 7...♗xh3 8 ♘xh3 0-0-0 9 ♗f4 ♕d7 10 ♕d3 ♗g7 11 ♘d2 e5!

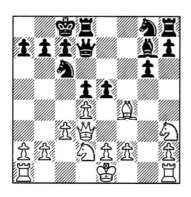

and Black stands much better, Tregubov-

Malaniuk, Moscow 1996.

d2) Also possible is the wild and creative 6...e5!? 7 ♕xb7 (7 dxe5 a6 8 ♕xb7?? ♘a5 would trap the queen. This does not work directly though, as after 6...a6 7 ♕xb7 ♘a5 White has 8 ♕b4.) 7...♘ge7 8 dxe5 ♗g7 and Black has a very speedy development for his material investment.

3 h3

This is the natural way to continue the gambit. Other tries include:

a) 3 e4 d5! (3...e5 4 dxe5 ♘c6 5 ♕xg4 d6 6 ♕g5 ♕xg5 7 ♗xg5 ♘xe5 was only equal in Kozlovskaya-Prudnikowa, Rjazan 1992) 4 e5 ♗f5 5 ♘e2 e6 6 ♘g3 ♘e7 7 ♗g5 ♕d7 8 ♗e2 ♕a4!? 9 ♘c3 ♕b4 10 0-0 c6 11 ♖b1 ♔d7 and Black has the better position, Drogou-Marcelin, France 2000. There must be a million ways for Black to gain an advantage in this line. The main problem for White is not the pawn, but rather that he lost control of some important squares on the kingside.

b) 3 ♗f4?! does not mix well with White's sacrifice: 3...♘f6 4 h3 d5 5 ♘c3 c6 6 ♕d2 b5 7 ♗g2 ♘a6 8 0-0-0? (it seems crazy to castle straight into the attack) 8...♕a5 9 a3 e6 10 ♔b1 b4 11 ♘a2 ♕b6 12 axb4 ♘xb4 13 ♘xb4 ♗xb4 14 c3 e5! and Black had a very powerful attack in Martinovsky-Glek, Spain 1996 (...♗f5+ is coming).

3...g3!

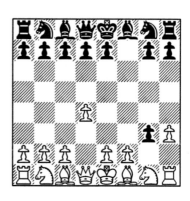

Black refuses to play with pieces other

than this pawn. Actually, this move is very logical. White has earned a little space for development, but after this his structural weaknesses on the kingside are an important factor in the game as well.

Very risky is 3...gxh3?! 4 e4!, when White has more than enough compensation for the pawn. Here the White king is not exposed as in the other line, and the lead in development has increased. Possible, though, is 3...d5!? 4 hxg4 ♗xg4 5 ♕d3 ♘f6 6 ♗h3 ♗xh3 7 ♘xh3 ♘c6 8 ♘g5 ♕d6 9 ♘c3 a6 with a slight edge for Black according to Andrew Martin. Still, it is not so easy for Black to finish his development, as a potential ♘f7 is looking him in the eye at every turn.

4 fxg3 ♘f6 5 ♘c3 d5 6 ♗g2 e6 7 ♘f3

White decides to finish his development before he opens the position, which adheres to the old guidelines. Still, it was possible to try 7 e4 ♗b4 and now:

a) 8 exd5 exd5 9 ♕e2+ seems inferior because of 9...♔f7! (9...♕e7 10 ♕xe7+ ♔xe7 11 ♘ge2 would be slightly better for White) 10 ♘f3 ♖e8 11 ♘e5+ ♔g8 12 0-0 ♘c6 and Black's position looks preferable.

b) 8 e5 ♘e4 9 ♗xe4 dxe4 10 ♘ge2 0-0 11 a3 ♗xc3+ 12 ♘xc3 b6 13 ♗e3 ♖f3! (13...♗b7 14 ♕g4 is very good for White) 14 ♕d2 ♗b7 15 0-0-0 with a very unclear position.

7...♗d6 8 ♘e5?!

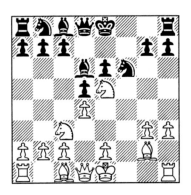

This move seems to be a misconception.

White was ready to sacrifice a pawn earlier for free development, and should still be so. Better was 8 0-0! ♗xg3 (8...0-0!, with equal chances, is a safer and probably better option) 9 e4!? (9 ♕d3 ♘c6 10 e4 dxe4 11 ♘xe4 ♘xe4 12 ♕xe4 0-0 – 12...♕d5? 13 ♕g4 ♗d6 14 ♕xg7 would be a disaster – 13 ♗e3 would give White good compensation for the pawn too) 9...dxe4 10 ♘g5 0-0 11 ♘cxe4 ♘xe4 12 ♖xf8+ ♕xf8 13 ♘xe4 and White has a very active position – Black should be very careful.

8...c5 9 ♗f4 ♘h5!

After 9...0-0?! White would have time for 10 e3!, preventing this sortie.

10 0-0

White is losing control over the dark squares. One line is 10 e3 ♘xf4 11 exf4 0-0 12 ♘e2 cxd4 13 ♕xd4 ♕a5+ 14 ♘c3 ♘c6 15 ♘xc6 bxc6 16 0-0-0 ♖b8 and Black has good attacking prospects against b2, which (lo and behold!) is on a dark square.

10...0-0 11 e3 ♘xf4 12 exf4 ♘c6 13 ♘xc6 bxc6 14 ♔h2 ♗a6 15 ♖e1 ♕f6 16 dxc5 ♗xc5

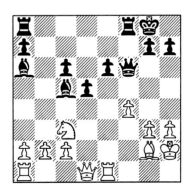

Black has a nice position with two dominating bishops. White has nothing active to do, so he will have to wait.

17 ♕d2 ♖ae8 18 ♖ab1

White takes it easy. He can win a pawn with 18 ♘a4 ♗d6 19 ♕a5 ♗c8 20 ♕xa7, but I doubt that he can save his position after 20...h5!, tearing up the dark squares on the kingside. After 21 h4 e5! White is already lost, but it is not apparent which way Black will wield the knife.

18...h6

18...h5!? also makes sense.

19 b4?!

This is no good. Better was 19 ♖e5! ♗b6 (19...♗d6? 20 ♘e4! would bring White back in business, while 19...g5? 20 ♘e4! would also give some unnecessary counterplay) 20 ♖be1 ♔h8! (20...♗c7? 21 ♘xd5! cxd5 22 ♖xe6 ♖xe6 23 ♖xe6 ♕xe6 24 ♗xd5 and suddenly White has a very strong position) 21 ♘a4 ♗c7 22 ♘c5 ♗c8 23 ♖5e2 e5 and Black has the advantage. 23...h5!? also looks good.

19...♕d4 20 ♕xd4!

20 ♖ed1 ♕xd2 21 ♖xd2 ♗e3 22 ♖dd1 g5 and the white position collapses on the dark squares. A possible line is 23 fxg5 ♖f2! and the second rank belongs to Black, who is also enjoying the two bishops and the passed e-pawn.

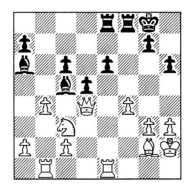

20...♗xd4 21 ♘d1 g5

Black has the initiative, but has some trouble in converting his advantage in the most effective way. Still, the way he does it is good enough.

22 fxg5 hxg5 23 a4! ♗c4 24 c3 ♗g7 25 b5 cxb5

25...c5!? was more double edged.

26 axb5 ♖f7 27 b6 ♖b7 28 ♘e3 ♖xb6

Black should not fall for 28...♗a2? 29 ♖a1

♗xc3 30 ♖xa2 ♗xe1, when White has 31 ♘xd5! ♖xb6 32 ♘f6+ ♔f7 33 ♘xe8 ♔xe8 34 ♖xa7 with a draw.

29 ♖xb6 axb6 30 ♘xd5

30 ♘xc4 dxc4 31 ♖b1 ♗xc3 32 ♖xb6 ♗d2 would give White an eternal headache in the form of an extra passed pawn for Black.

30...b5

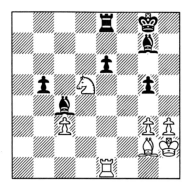

31 ♖e3?!

Better was 31 ♘b6, with the idea of 31...♗xc3? 32 ♖c1 with a draw. 31...♗d3! would keep White under pressure.

31...♖d8 32 ♘b6

Or 32 ♘b4 ♖d2 and Black has control.

32...♗b3 33 ♗f1 ♖d6 34 ♘c8 ♖d2+! 35 ♖e2 ♖d1 36 ♖f2 ♗xc3 37 ♘e7+ ♔g7 38 ♗xb5 ♗d4?

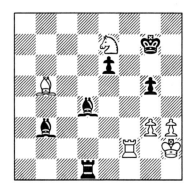

A slip in time trouble. After 38...♗f6! 39 ♘c6 (or 39 ♘c8 ♗d5 40 ♗f1 ♗d4 and

Black wins) 39...♗d5 40 g4 ♖c1 White cannot keep his pieces together. Now Black has to play on for some moves before the game is decided.

39 ♖f3 ♖d2+ 40 ♔h1 ♗a2 41 ♖d3 ♖xd3 42 ♗xd3 ♔f7 43 ♘g6

The knight is also in trouble after 43 ♘c8 ♗d5+ 44 ♔h2 ♗c5 45 ♗a6 e5 46 h4 g4 47 h5 ♗f3 and Black will win.

43...♗d5+ 44 ♔h2 e5! 45 ♗f5 e4 46 h4 e3 47 ♗d3 ♗e4! 0-1

White has had enough.

Game 74
Kmoch-Alekhine
Semmering 1926

---

1 d4 f5

2 ♕d3?!

Other second move alternatives for White include:

a) 2 h3 ♘f6 3 g4 d5! 4 g5 ♘e4 5 ♘f3 e6 6 ♗f4 ♗d6! and now:

a1) 7 ♘e5? h6! and White has a lot of problems, as his position is lost after 8 gxh6 ♕h4!.

a2) 7 ♗xd6 cxd6 and Black has a good position with complete control over the centre.

a3) 7 ♕c1 and 7 e3!? are perhaps better tries and Black should not feel too sure about having an advantage. But afraid? No way!

b) 2 ♗f4 ♘f6 3 e3 e6! (3...g6 4 h4 ♗g7 5

h5 gxh5 6 ♖xh5 ♘xh5 7 ♕xh5+ ♔f8 8 ♕xf5+ ♔g8 9 ♘f3 looked very dangerous for Black in Sapis-Lukasiewicz, Poland 1990) 4 ♗d3 b6 5 c4 ♗b7 6 ♘f3 and the position is equal. One move could be 6...♘h5!?, trying to gain the two bishops.

c) 2 c3 ♘f6 3 ♗g5 g6 (3...e6!? cannot be bad here) 4 ♗xf6 exf6 5 e3 d5 6 h4 h5 7 ♘h3 ♗d6 8 g3 c6 9 ♕f3 ♔f7 10 ♘d2 ♘d7 11 ♗d3 ♘f8 was equal in Bohm-Timman, Wijk aan Zee 1975.

2...d5!

2...d6 3 g4 fxg4 4 h3 g3 5 fxg3 ♘f6 6 e4 is unclear according to Andrew Martin. The text move makes more sense.

3 ♗f4

Or 3 g4 g6! and Black is OK! Look at the line 2 g4 d5 3 ♕d3 g6 from the previous game.

3...e6 4 ♘f3

After 4 ♕g3 ♘a6 5 e3 c6! Black is equal. 6 ♗xa6 is mistake due to 6...♕a5+, when Black stands better.

4...♘f6 5 e3 ♗d6 6 ♗e2

This is rather cautious, but White has no advantage – 6 c4 c6 7 ♘c3 would also have been equal. This kind of Stonewall holds no dangers for Black, despite the exchange of the dark bishops, as the queen is slightly misplaced on d3. Black will always find time to regroup the c8-bishop to a useful square.

6...0-0 7 ♘e5 c5 8 c3 ♘c6 9 ♘d2 ♕c7 10 ♘df3 ♘d7!

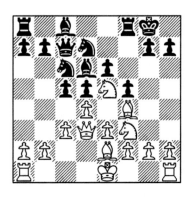

Black has with simple means used his extra space to take control over e5. Now he is simply better.

11 ♘xd7 ♗xd7 12 ♗xd6 ♛xd6 13 0-0 c4

This is the ambitious try. White has no way to create anything on the kingside or in the centre, and now Black starts an advance on the queenside.

After 13...e5?! 14 dxe5 ♘xe5 15 ♘xe5 ♛xe5 16 ♖ad1 ♗c6 17 ♗f3 ♖ad8 18 ♖d2 White is only slightly worse, and seems to have improved his position.

14 ♛d2 b5 15 ♘e1 g5!

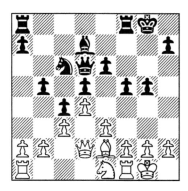

Alekhine is fully prepared for a war on two fronts.

16 f4 g4 17 b3 ♖fb8 18 ♘c2 a5 19 bxc4 bxc4 20 ♖fb1 ♘a7 21 ♛e1 ♗a4 22 ♗d1

White is forced into retreating. After 22

♛h4? Black simply dances out of the checks: 22...♗xc2 23 ♛g5+ ♔f7 24 ♛h5+ ♔f8 25 ♛h6+ ♔e8 and Black wins.

22...♛e7 23 ♛d2 ♘b5 24 ♖b2 ♖b7 25 ♖ab1 ♖ab8 26 ♗e2 h5

Black has strengthened his position to the maximum on the queenside and White has so far kept his pieces together. Now Black exploits his space advantage on the kingside to create further weaknesses.

27 g3 h4 28 e4

Clever, but why should Black care?

28...♘d6 29 ♖xb7 ♖xb7 30 ♖xb7 ♛xb7

31 ♛c1

Now everything falls apart. After 31 exd5 ♛b2 32 ♗d1 ♘e4 33 ♛e2 exd5 34 ♘e3 ♛c1 Black wins material.

31...♘xe4 32 ♘e3 hxg3 33 hxg3 ♘xg3 34 ♔f2 ♘e4+ 0-1

Summary

White does not have any real alternatives to the main lines if he wants to fight for an advantage. In this Chapter a sound strategy has been provided against 2 g4, 2 ♕d3 and all the other strange second move alternatives. The strategy is simple: develop normally and do not go on unnecessary pawn hunts.

2 e4 is not a bad move, but Black has more than one way to reach equality. 2 ♘c3 is best met with 2...d5, when Black will normally obtain the two bishops in and a set of doubled pawns. If Black knows how to place his pieces, this should not be a problem.

2 ♗g5 was hot in the 1990s. Some English professionals won some easy games, but the solution has been found and this should not be considered dangerous for Black at all.

1 d4 f5 2 e4

     2 ♗g5 (D) – *Game 69*
     2 g4 – *Game 73*
     2 ♕d3 – *Game 74*
     2 ♘c3
          2...d5 3 ♗g5 ♘f6 4 ♗xf6 exf6 5 e3
               5...c6 – *Game 70*
               5...♗e6 – *Game 71*
          2...♘f6 3 ♗g5 e6 (D) – *Game 72*

2...fxe4 3 ♘c3 ♘f6 (D) – *Game 68*

    2 ♗g5   3...e6   3...♘f6

INDEX OF COMPLETE GAMES

LaVergne, TN USA
04 December 2009
166020LV00004B/12/P